Modern Kazakhstan

ICEUR Insight Studies

Edited by Hans-Georg Heinrich
and Ludmilla Lobova

Vol. 1

PETER LANG
Frankfurt am Main · Berlin · Bern · Bruxelles · New York · Oxford · Wien

Aydar Amrebaev
Hans-Georg Heinrich
Ludmilla Lobova
Valikhan Tuleshov
(eds.)

Modern Kazakhstan

Image and Realities

PETER LANG
Internationaler Verlag der Wissenschaften

Bibliographic Information published by the Deutsche Nationalbibliothek
The Deutsche Nationalbibliothek lists this publication in the Deutsche Nationalbibliografie; detailed bibliographic data is available in the internet at http://dnb.d-nb.de.

Cover Design:
© Olaf Gloeckler, Atelier Platen, Friedberg

ISSN 2194-797X
ISBN 978-3-631-62605-4

www.peterlang.de

Preface

20 years ago we were largely ignorant about the Soviet republics which today constitute the map of Central Asia. We were familiar with some places from space flights, we had heard about oil wells, but that was basically it. The world has changed in many respects, but here we can see clearly that we live through an era of change. I also believe that our image of Kazakhstan is too primitive. To reduce Kazakhstan to oil would be simplistic; and we have to add that we still know very little.

This is why this volume is important. We need updated and enriched knowledge in order to realize our European responsibility. We should not forget that Ka-zakhstan and the other central Asian states belong to the European regional organization of the UN, are members of the OSCE and are more and more turning into a region where European business is represented as a matter of course. Any contribution aiming at deepening our knowledge and intensifying contacts can only be welcomed. I would like to express my gratitude to all those who joined their efforts to work towards these ends.

Erhard Busek

Vienna, Fall 2012

The editors would like to thank Kerstin Steiner and Lisa Hessenberger for translating and Karin Zambra for formatting this volume.

Contents

Aydar Amrebaev, The Cultural and Civilisational Basis for the Development of Kazakhstan

The Social Model of Interethnic and Interreligious Harmony and Prospects of the Modern Cultural Identity of Kazakhstan's People

The purpose of this paper is to identify the characteristics of cultural and civilisational development of Kazakhstan, which allow us not only to trace the historical path of the formation of the Kazakh nation, but, mainly, to characterize the specific features of the national world view, the value system and social models of development in the past, present and future. Of course, it is impossible to fully reveal the historical, cultural and civilisational path of the Kazakh nation in only one article, so we mention only a few special features and destinies of our present cultural life. This will give the reader some ideas of how the process of Kazakh social, political, economic and cultural planning differs from similar European models. Thus, we hope that the European reader not only understands the history and culture of the Kazakh people better, but also that the reader understands the hopes, victories and defeats of the past and present, which shaped the Kazakh nation to what it is today.

Referring to the historical roots and getting rid of the usual cultural stereotypes regarding the Kazakhs - the people of the centre of Eurasia, will provide an opportunity for a fresh look at the role of the civilisation of our nation, its possibilities and perspectives of the spiritual and practical moderation in different areas and processes, which also take place in the world's history of today. Furthermore, civilisation "spreads", which the Kazakh nation faced and realized in its dramatic in content and "heat of passions" history, clearly demonstrate the existence of such a moderation potential of the Kazakh people. Initially, this potential was presented in a "natural way" as a kind of specific ethnic power, "the steppe passionarity", as a special type of social energy of the nomadic peoples of Eurasia, about which L.N. Gumilev[1] wrote. Though, in the following period, with the processes of industrialization and modernization of the unfolding social, economic and political relations, it presented itself in the form of social capital, as the already functional strength of society in formulating and solving actual problems of development. It should be noted that the inclusion of the "vigorous" and passionate Kazakh ethnicity in the global processes of modernization, the active way in the "area" of forming an independent nation and the formulation of their own priorities and vectors of national development, both in the country itself and beyond its borders, shows not only the presence of potential, but already tangible results of development of human capital in modern Kazakhstan.

In this regard, we believe that it is important to detect the original, purely Kazakh cultural and civilisational identity, values and ethical codes that build the basis of the nation's human capital, which allowed it to first "present" itself as an ethnic "self" and then "survive" in a rather complex "civilisational environment", which did not disappear in the "historical turbulences" of global and regional modernization in the late 19th-20th century.

Formed by the 15th century as a distinct ethno-cultural type, the Kazakh people syncretically embodied a variety of cultural worlds of East and West, nomadism and settled way of life, values of different world-views, philosophical and religious traditions, which, in focused terms, were their bottom line in ethnic "codes" and the codes assessment of the world and the behavior. These "codes" are encrypted in a specific "national image of the world" (G. Gachev) and the "universal categories of culture" (A. Ya. Gurevich) of the people. Culturologist Georgi Gachev defines the content of the national image of the world as follows: "We are not interested in the national character, but in the national conception of the world, not psychology, but, so to speak, gnosiology, the national artistic "logic", the mindset: with which "coordinate net" the given people catch the world and, respectively, which cosmos (in the old sense of the word: as a harmonious system or world order) is built in front of its eyes. This particular "version", by which the existence of this nation is represented, also makes up the national image of the world".[2] And the historian A. Ya. Gurevich noted: "Human society is constantly moving, changing and developing. In different times and in different cultures people perceive and understand the world in their own way, they organize their experience and knowledge in their own way and construct their particular, historically conditioned view of the world. And if we want to know the past how it was "really", we cannot seek to approach it with for it adequate criteria, to explore the inherent things, to reveal its own internal structure, taking care not to impose on it our modern evaluation."[3] Thus, this is not a useless interest in their own history, but rather an attempt to reconstruct the national world view in its historical retrospective, which helps to understand the inner logic of the ethnic development, its socio-cultural connections and relationships which are essential to fully understand and appreciate the significance of the Kazakh cultural history and its current content and appearance, even in the era of post-industrialism. This cultural and historical connotation provides to see the depth of national consciousness and a real transformation processes that occurs in the Kazakh nation beyond the obvious, which today can be seen outside by the inexperienced traveler, who visited Kazakhstan. What we see today in

Kazakhstan is not a ready-made, "newly established social relationship" of the market era, the result of a socio-cultural development, but rather the fruit of a long cultural formation of the nation, expressed in civilised results which formed and still continue to shape social relations. And here, on the one hand, it is very important to not stop and remain fixed on the "position of historicism", but on the other hand, to not get carried away by the "sociologisation of today". It is important to understand that the process of becoming and forming a nation, is prepared by the whole course of the cultural-historical process, the social traditions that have developed historically, and in this sense determined by the specific mental character of the people, developing in the lap of a particular civilisation. At the same time, further development of the people must necessarily be linked, both to trends of modernization, as well as to socio-cultural foundations, in which the same trends are "digested" by society.

The purpose of this paper is to draw the reader's attention to the fundamental set of social categories and links which permeate through Kazakh society and create a certain degree of "mental and moral tension" in order to adapt to external challenges, on the one hand, and, if there is enough passionate energy, to create conditions to form an own national paradigm of social development, on the other.

We agree with the opinion that in a historical retrospective the Kazakh ethnicity and its former ethnic substrates played the role of the original "ringleaders" of world history on the territory of Eurasia[4], "tightening the cultural processes", creating challenges for a civilisation formed in ancient times in this vast territory, from India and China in the east, to Byzantium and Rome in the west. The "axial age", the meaning of which, according to K. Jaspers, is that "the new which arose in this period, is that man becomes aware of his existence as a whole, himself, his limits. The dreadfulness of the world and his own helplessness opens up before him. Standing on the edge of a precipice, he asks radical questions, craves for liberation and salvation. Aware of his limits, he sets himself the highest goals, experiences the absoluteness in the depths of self-awareness and in the lucidity of transcendence. All this took place through reflection. Consciousness became once more conscious of itself, thinking became its own object. Spiritual conflicts arose, accompanied by attempts to convince others through the communication of thoughts, reasons and experiences. The most contradictory possibilities were tested. Discussions, the formation of different parties and the division of the spiritual realm, despite the contradiction of its parts, preserves their interdependence, all this created anxiety and movement to the very brink of spiritual chaos. In this age new fundamental categories were established, within which we still think today which built the basis of the world religions, and which today determine the life of every human being. In all directions the transition to universality took place. This process has caused many to rethink, to question, to analyze all unconsciously adopted earlier beliefs, customs and conditions. Everything entered into a vortex. To the extent to which the substance perceived in the tradition of the past was still alive and effective, its effects became clear, and it is thus transformed".[5] In this case, the formal and substantive "content" of the "axial age" was built with the active participation of nomadic people, including the Dasht-i Kipchak, the territory which is inhabited by the Kazakhs today. Exactly that is why H.J. Mackinder called the land the "heartland", as a kind of "civilised, energetic voltage field of Eurasia".[6] Thus, our ancestors were in the heart of the cultural history of the world, absorbing and recognizing the different spiritual paradigms and, at the same time, realizing their own potential nomadic spirit. And it seems only quite fair to get rid of the stereotype of the nomads in general, and the Kazakh nomads in particular, to be "the eternal barbarians who have stuck to the nipples of the Arabic, Chinese, Persian and Indian civilisations".[7]

For this article, it makes sense, as mentioned above, to pay attention to the "social relations" which developed in this territory, to the projects, which played an important role in shaping the great human potential which developed in a stable form of national statehood under the conditions of the spreading modern model of market relations and relations in modernized societies. Of course, we are far from archaic idealization. For us, the issue of the cultural and civilisational foundations of the modern Kazakh ethnicity in terms of its social component, on the basis of which the modern human resources of Kazakhstan and the possible planning and development of our society in the future formed on their own, is of scientific interest. In all of this, it should be noted that the tribal social ties which had existed for eras did not completely disappear, they transform and adapt to impartial changes in economic processes, political and social models' forms of statehood. The roots of these relations lie deep in the foundations of the nomadic culture and today it is a sample of reconstructing "nomadism" of an already new order, if we use the terminology of Deleuze and Guattari.

This task may be accomplished on the methodological basis of cultural-anthropological approaches and cultural-historical reconstruction. Therefore, we will be forced to turn to a more in-depth analysis of the historical development of the Kazakh nation in terms of social relations, links and institutions for the development of the nation. The clarification and the formulation of values and aims of social development in each historical period is very important, because all stages, in which the aging of the elements and the attributes of a developed society went on, are not just mutually linked to a linear historical scheme, but substantiated as cycles of political, economic and social processes, swirled in a historical spiral.

In this regard, also the whole history of the path of the Kazakh nation to its today's state, in our view, is reminiscent of the historical spiral of cyclic public areas and processes and, in general, is characterized by two defining features. First, the earliest and also all subsequent forms of Kazakh statehood until the early twentieth century, when the Kazakhs got caught in the circle of cultural and civilisation influence of the Western rational world view and the liberal-democratic trends in public life, have been characterized as martial-nomadic, steppe democracy, the most stable form of them were the khanate and the horde.

The martial-democratic forms of statehood which prevailed until the first quarter of the twentieth century when the Kazakh Soviet Socialist Republic was formed within the USSR, also later were postponed to the forms of mass and individual consciousness of stereotypes and archetypes of the respective nomadic (Tengrian) world view. Though, to completely change them was not achieved in the time of the Soviet Union, and, also an independent Kazakhstan will not be achieved in the near future, as natural and historic changes in public (national) consciousness take much more time (for example, in Japan, it took 100 years since the Meiji Restoration until the Japanese nation had acquired cultural and civilisational stability in the 1980s). "The collective unconscious", compressed by the time of five thousand years of predominance of forms of martial-nomadic democracy, to correct for one generation or two is impossible. Moreover, the Asiatic production method was not based on private ownership traditions and democratic institutions.

The martial-nomadic society was a hierarchical society, both in terms of administrating processes of social life, and in terms of the effects of ethical codes (as explained i.e. by V. U. Tuleshov: "The traditional law of the Turkic people (the Kazakhs), originally expressed, established and enshrined in postulates of ethical system Tengri, and subsequently, in the codes - the Code Mode, the "Dzhasake" of Genghis Khan, the "Shining Path of Kasim-Khan", the "Ancient way of Yesim-Khan", the "Zheti-zhargy" of Tauke Khan, etc., was transformed into the institutions of the state's legal system, where a domineering, martial line was added to the "steppe democracy" and "steppe law" which resulted in the creation of a special governance structure, and the appearance of special features of the state system"[8]). Up to this day, the state system resembles a martial and political pyramid, in which all its parts are dedicated to the task of strengthening its top. Furthermore, the family builds the main components of the system or foundations interconnected to each other. In fact, all reflections on the family as a social institution which is characterized by certain social norms, sanctions, patterns of behavior, rights and duties, governing the relationship between spouses and between parents and children, on the family as a joinder of persons connected, from the economic point of view, by a common family budget, on the family as a territorial unit comprising persons on the basis of living together, and on the family as a biological structure, consisting of parents and children, will not endure without further definition of the family as an ethnic community. For Kazakhstan this is everlasting and of utmost importance, since in the family and clan structure of the Kazakh society also the nature of the whole being of the life of Kazakhs is enclosed, including all historical types of martial-nomadic democracy and the whole of their cultural and historical order of life.

F. Fukuyama notes that many cultures, from China to southern Europe and Latin America, encouraged attachment to family life, nepotism, in other words, applying the custom "to place duties to family and relatives above other social obligations" which, in his opinion, is "a source of two-tier morality in which moral obligations towards public authorities of all kinds are inferior to those towards the family".[9]

Just like this, it was the case in the Kazakh steppe, where, on the other hand, the lack of social capital outside of kindred groups was made up for with codes of ethics (as F. Fukuyama noted), but also through a deep metaphysical sense of responsibility and mission of the individual to the family, clan, tribe, horde (union of tribes) and the nation, with birth and childhood which was filled with epic and poetry, with legends, myths, fairy tales and heroic bylinas, and with the continuity of moral and economic strategies, through the rites and rituals. This is a profound philosophical vision, and so it was with this really effective "glue" - a kind of social capital, created not only and not simply on trust, but on the penetration, immersion in the sacred meanings of its own nature as a generic human nature. Cohesion and socialization in the Kazakh society were nothing natural, they were no arbitrary and spontaneous processes, but based on kinship and tribal consciousness. Therefore, as the family and all of its members built the basis of nomadic communities, the relationship between family members was constructed as the relation between interconnected entities, they, per se, were essentially different, dissimilar, but inseparable parts of one family body. All the basic elements of the Kazakhs' mentality came from the family (tribe) as a nomadic community. Z. Sarsenbaeva notes that "the core of the social relations of nomads and the basic pivot of the world view was a kindred tribal beginning which advocated a fundamental principle of self-identification of the individual with the community, and with the natural habitat, especially with the territory as a continuation of his natural life. Accordingly, the central place in the hierarchy of the traditional values held the concepts of "Atameken" (Homeland) and "Ata Konys" (Territories of generic nomades). Although every nomad as to his way of life was self-sufficient, he saw the meaning of his life in the service to the Sacred, and therefore in the voluntary service to the clan. Expulsion from the clan was regarded as a separation from the cosmos, from God and was considered a disgrace".[10] The specification of the social structure of generic nomadic people, in addition to the hierarchy and strict subordination, also implied a mutual cohesion and responsibility of each subject, not only for his/her own fate, but also the fate of the nearest clansman or -woman, and in general for social harmony within the clan. Such relationships are held together by a kind of social code of ethics, as expressed in the covenants of the ancestors, the "ата-сөзі" (the words of the fathers) and the "atalardan қalғan osiet" (the edification of the ancestors) which are expected to remain united under any circumstances. For example, the famous covenant: "Бірлік бар жерде, тірлік бар" (translated as to its meaning: "In the unity there is strength and ability to act") is quite revealing, and perceived by any Kazakh community.

The stability of tribal social relations is maintained by the singularity of economic relations of nomads and the method of military self-organization, like of the type of Genghis Khan's troops, and even earlier, in the triad of more ancient martial tribes like the Saka or Turkic speaking tribes. The Kazakhs adopted this threefold form of tribal military organization also in their own social structure and hierarchy. Traditionally, the Kazakh were divided into three tribal unions: the Great Horde (tribal alliance, literally zhuz meaning "hundreds"), the Middle Horde and the Little Horde. Moreover, the area of settlement and nomadic economic management was strictly assigned to each alliance: the Great Horde inhabited the territory of the South and South-East of modern Kazakhstan, the Middle Horde settled in Central and Eastern Kazakhstan, and the Little

Horde in Western Kazakhstan. The mutual relationships between a tribal alliance and within clans were defined and regulated by the steppe traditional law and traditions ("ədet-ғұryp"). As the cultural tradition of the steppe was basically passed on orally, only fragments of written laws and codes of ethics have survived in history, and very often as described by various travelers from other countries and civilisations. From this emerged the rather firm stereotype of their nonconformity with civilisation, the cultural backwardness of the nomads and the need for change in their social, economic, political and cultural way of life. However, the nomads themselves live in harmony with each other and the world. Their consciousness is distinguished by extreme environmental compatibility and universalism. For example, during seasonal nomadic migrations, they always left the territory in the same condition as they discovered it, without trying to change or "master" nature in accordance with their cultural beliefs, because they, according to nomadic views, are transient, and the world of nature is eternal and irreversible.

It is possible that the origins of the Kazakh tolerance and capacity for integrating social communication and solidarity lie in this perception. Individualism and originality, in the nomadic perception of categories, have rather negative than positive connotations. What is interesting in this context is that even in the conditions of market competition it is supposed to not only support the individual potential, but also the strength of the rod tribe, social connections or the "roof of the patron". The cultural history of the nomads is rich in examples of nomadic, especially in the epic tradition, when a man in the name of higher values, for example, love, has contravened the generic principles and well-established attitudes and finds himself an outcast and a renegade, who deserves only blame and to be condemned to loneliness. By the way, condemnation to loneliness means misfortune and punishment, sent down to man from above, or on behalf of the society. Childlessness and doom to live in a foreign country (outside of your social environment) is a curse. "Bөten elde Sultan bolғansha, өz eliңde үltan bol" (translated as to its meaning: "It is better to be a slave at home, than to be the ruler in a foreign country"), this more exactly demonstrates the generic attachment and social solidarity of the nomadic society.

Kazakhstan's President N. Nazarbaev, noting this feature of nomadic families, wrote that "the true family of several people, at the same time, was one body, one organism. The different parts of it lived and pulsated in total physical, psychological, and moral mutual relationships. This classical model of the family is the natural basis of the historical composition and of bigger organic communities - families, clans, kins, tribes, tribal population, hordes (union of tribes), and finally, the Kazakh people itself".[11] In a traditional nomadic society which represented Kazakhstan until the early twentieth century, each family member was never perceived as a separate, isolated identity, but has always been one of the parts of united community at all levels - families, kins (tribes), horde (national roots) and the people. For this purpose, as the President of Kazakhstan N. Nazarbaev writes, "the Kazakh people have established within itself a unique body for their sustainable self-assertion in the specific conditions of a nomadic society that allowed it to preserve itself ... as a whole. Its whole historical body is preserved regardless of the presence or absence of the state membrane. It's about the indispensable knowledge of every Kazakh about the "Zheti ata жеті ата" - seven fathers, seven generations. For the Kazakhs in the steppe genealogy was like a compass for the sailor at sea. It was this which was solely appropriate to the historical, geographical, commercial, political, economic and cultural circumstances in which, by will of the historical destiny, the Kazakh people are." [12]

It is particularly important to emphasize that in contrast to F. Fukuyama, who considers the mutual relationship of the family and social capital in a completely abstract way and far from social reality and the historical context, the President of Kazakhstan N. Nazarbaev very precisely points to the importance of a cultural-anthropological approach concerning the investigation of the given problem. In this regard, he writes: "A unique kin-tribal, clan-hordal united body of the Kazakh people was spreading naturally over the centuries on the basis of the following principle: all Kazakhs are fledglings of one "nests", the branches of one tree, of one root. This is why the awareness of people's unity which according to European canons isolated nomads would have lacked, is divided into three basic parts, namely the hordes (alliances of tribes), furthermore, separated from each other at large distances. And this unity is perceived exactly through genealogy. In this the genetic unity of Kazakhs becomes apparent, the origin from one common family tree. For Kazakh nomads it was always obligatory to know about their roots and kinship ties. This was built to a single moral and ethical criterion for the entire nation. It was always like this in our history. Therefore, the principle of "жеті ата" (knowledge of the seven generations of the ancestors) naturally ensures ethno-biological, ethno-cultural and, generally, spiritual integrity of the whole of the Kazakh people. Knowledge about your seven ancestors allows everyone to trace his/her neighboring branches of the family tree of Kazakhs to an adequate depth and make out the closeness of all Kazakhs in general. Thereby, their inseparable integrity is maintained".[13]

The family-kin capital is therefore expressed by supporting individuals in everyday life, which, in turn, is reflected in codes of conduct which all tribesmen and –women (tribe, ethnic group) are trained to know from childhood on. We are talking about the principle of "жеті ата" known by every Kazakh – seven ancestors, seven generations –, for the whole Kazakh people an inherent internal craving for the better, for the ideals of their ancestors, for the eternal, for something inexpressible and common for all Kazakhs, that is – for the spiritual difference, for the faith of the people. That is no cold and exalted faith, but the self-sensation of every ordinary nomad generally based on concrete facts of history.

Remembering the feats and defeats, triumphs and troubles of all my ancestors of seven generations gave hope that also I can overcome any difficulties on my path. It is this ideology which lives in the heart of every Kazakh.

Moreover, the spirits of the ancestors, the "aruahi", help me with this every day. Religious feelings and my faith in the ancestors - this is my mission in life. I know that the aruahi helped them, and I believe they will help you, and also me. This was the way, from our point of view, how the Kazakhs of the classic traditional Kazakh nomadic society lived.

Thus, various phenomena and occurrences of social life, showing their human capital, not only in the family, but also collectively and in the state which were based on the Kazakh principle of genealogy – "жеті ата", built the most important, in this context, cultural and civilisational basis for the development of the Kazakh society. Such phenomena and occurrences of social life were faith and religious feelings which, through the institution "жеті ата", were passed on from generation to generation.

Firstly, such "a belief, specified by the whole chain of direct ancestors, was the inner essence of man, and greatly expanded the space where he could seek and find a way out when life conflicts occur."

Second, such "a faith allows man and the people in hard times not to restrict their options under external pressure, but to keep a clear mind, a pure heart, clear conscience, and, based on them, to find brilliant ways out of difficult historical situations". [14] Along with this, the singularity of religious beliefs of Kazakh nomads is their syncretic-pragmatic character focusing on their social and ethical connotations and the search for freedom as the inner and outer harmony. The perception of freedom also has certain characteristics, as freedom is knowledge and adherence to the path specified by the ancestors, by previous social experience, by public practice, i.e. a kind of "recognition of necessity" (Hegel) in the steppe. Hence, a hierarchy is not merely formal, but also meaningful and practical. "Kөp zhasaғannan, kөp kөrgennen sүra" (translated by meaning "Ask more from those who have seen a lot, than from someone who has lived long") or "Moldanyң zhasaғanyn zhasama, aytқanyn Zhasan" (translated by meaning "Do not do what a Mullah does, but do what he says"). So, a nomad acts on social practice, as a kind of criterion of truth and righteousness of the chosen path. In this case, even the perception of religious canons, i.e. Islam, is realized in the light of everyday life experience. Steppe religious tradition took shape in the form of a special kind of syncretic worldview, capable to revise a variety of religious systems and adapt them to the needs of the moral and ethical nomadic spiritual tradition.

On the other hand, the principle of "жеті ата" allowed not only to survive, when after the Holodomor of the 20s and 30s only one third of the Kazakh population stayed alive, but, while preserving the primary genetic material (a total of 2 million people from 6 million until the Holodomor), literally "to be reborn from the ashes", having recreated the level of cultural and historical development which, after a long colonial dependence from the Russian Empire and the modernization project of the Bolsheviks (Soviet Union), allowed the Kazakh nation to tackle the task of restoring self-esteem, describing an objective history, with its positive and negative sides, its victories and defeats. The principle of "жеті ата", as the President of Kazakhstan writes, when the "Kazakh society in terms of socio-economic and general cultural development was to lag behind the surrounding nations, and to suffer defeat against external enemies, when being torn by internal contradictions," played "the role of a storage of defeatist mood which suppressed the will of the people and created over the centuries an apparent consciousness of its backwardness, a national complex which is at least 300 years old. In addition, a conscious humiliation by eurocentrists, also largely used by Soviet propaganda and science, of the history of the nomads, its interpretation as a history of careless and lazy people lacking of initiative, leading a semi-animal life, had a destructive and disastrous influence on the Kazakh national consciousness."[15] In this era of colonial dependence the institution "жеті ата" has become this accumulator of human capital which did not allow to fall attack an ethnic group, and also did not allow it to neither die physically nor spiritually. Action based on precedent which continued on a large scale for many centuries and millennia, if we remember the five millennial rule of the Tengrian nomadic world view in Eurasia, then, in the course of time, formed a powerful layer of various ritual actions, regulatory behavior models and practices of responsibility to the ancestors' spirits for their actions and behaviors. "'Малым - жанымнын садагасы, жаным - арымнын садагасы'(All my wealth is nothing against my life, my life is nothing when it comes to my honour.). This unique psychological basis of the life of nomads has been proven well for centuries and perfected to its limits. The behavior, rituals, moral motivation, standards and assessment of human communication in the desert are concentrated in it. All the material and spiritual aspects of a Kazakh's life, the whole life was regulated by a strict sophisticated etiquette of intergeneric relations, supported by the principle of "жеті ата". This principle also included a strict moral code of life of the Kazakhs, forming the basis of traditions, rituals, customs and taboos."[16]

Tolganay Umbetalieva notes that "in the nomadic Kazakh society the system of authoritative domination is based on the principle of genealogical kinship which derived from the traditional views of nomads concerning the law of primogeniture and seniority. The genealogical kinship system which fulfills an ideological function in a nomadic society, served as the primary tool for regulating social relations. Furthermore, an important role in the socio-legal ranking of nomads played the historically established terms "senior" and "junior" tribes. Based on these criteria of status, the structure of the political organization of the Kazakhs was built as a genealogical hierarchy of clans and tribes. The strong (senior) clans and tribes in this case built the core of the Kazakh martial-potestary alliances. Around them less powerful (junior) tribes and clans were integrated and on this basis state foundations took shape. The system of status ranking of various subjects of power relations also resulted from the genealogical criterion of social statuses concerning various potestary-political groups of Kazakhs. Therefore, the degree of influence of the hierarchy of clans and tribes in the decision-making processes of the government depends on the heritage of the institutions of the past and present political calculations."[17] Political decisions in a nomadic community are not only legitimized by the power of the Khan or Khagan, but also by the approval of the society or political elite – "ел ағасы" - those who have led the clan or by virtue of own qualities (military valour, wisdom, or wealth) were granted the public authority. For a nomadic Kazakh society with a rational not-institutionalized, formal-legal, political system, moral and ethical criteria were the main grounds of political socialization. And if the Western political tradition has survived breach of morality and law in favour of the law and objective norms, standards of behavior, then the nomadic political tradition maintained for a long time a loyalty to their established moral principles. The "boisterous freemen and outlaws" of the steppe, representing themselves from outside as a kind of "bandit monastery", actually had a fairly strict structural-functional hierarchy, as discussed above, and a high degree of compliance with ethical norms and taboos, included in political behavior. The destruction of this heroic ethic of the steppe in Russian and then Soviet colonialism, led to the leveling of the traditional moral and ethical origin in the political consciousness by replacing them with ideological and class clichés, and then with the Machiavellian principles of the political market. In this respect, very important in the era of the formation of an own independent statehood of Kazakhstan with an independent political culture appears the question of the revival of the moral and ethical models of political behavior, already adapted to the new conditions. The presence of high, cultural well-founded trust of the people to the "wealthy powers" and the social responsibility of the authorities in relation to the common people is an important guarantee of social and political stability and harmony in the country. Though, in fact, the beginnings of a collective or associative social communication of the Kazakh nomads established with the solution of intergeneric or inter-tribal disputes and, to a greater extent, under external aggression, when a collective solidarity in defending family, nation and homeland was developed. During such periods, the ability of people to internal consolidation and mobilization on the basis of shared values, moral and ethical attitudes, became apparent to its full extent, which, in our opinion, is an indicator of the presence of a high moral status concerning the human capital of the steppe, as well as, of positive, high ethical values uniting this human resource.

The transition from martial-nomadic forms of democracy to a form of Western state and public organization in terms of independence took and take place under the influence of democratic liberal trends (private property, rights and freedom, republican government, etc.). However, the movement in this direction supposes an active search for new forms of national identity, reminiscent of a two-way street. On the one hand, today the Kazakh cultural tradition discovers for it the values of the West, new cultural horizons and social standards, rational economic and political models, and on the other hand, we hope that the West finds new traditional and modernist energy in the Kazakh culture, not only unusual aesthetic forms, substantial deep nomadic ethics, capable of universalizing the meanings of social behavior in any part of the modern world. And here, Kazakhstan, from our point of view, plays a unique cultural and integrative role, "mixing" the tradition of cold rationalism and pragmatism of the West with sophisticated forms of intuition and the deep sense of ethics of the East, meeting with questioning, surprising by its communicative openness, and seeing off with the new content of adherents of the East and West, envoys from the North and South.

Strictly speaking, this process of modernization as an “update” of the quality of social resource began long before the era of independence and became apparent in the universal transfer of Kazakh nomads to settlement, development of new areas of economy, professions and specializations and the national processes of urbanization. In the Russian Empire the “economic niches” in Kazakhstan were rather strictly divided between the settlers and the local population who preferred “free nomads' camps” and, accordingly, the development of social capital was carried out mainly on an established “social-professional ethnic track”. However, as Western travelers pointed out, the nomads of the Eurasian steppes treated the settled and urban residents with a touch of supremacy, thinking about farming as a sign of “poverty and decline. A Kyrghyz is born as nomad. When a Kyrgyz became settled farmer, he changed and become a Sart.”[18]

The transition of a nomad to a settled life, i.e. to the category of traders, farmers or craftsmen, automatically turns off the whole system of tribal relations. In the opinion of N. Masanov, it is the nomadic way of life served as the main integrating factor of a nomadic society. Nomadism was a “core system quality, differentiating Kazakhs from other ethnocultural formations of Central Asia, Western Siberia, Altai and South-Eastern Europe. In case of loss of characteristics of nomadism and failure of nomadism processes, also a loss of specific nomadic self-awareness, and, accordingly, of the ethnonymic “Kazakh” occured.”[19] But this is true mainly for those Kazakhs who settled and created mixed ethnocultural formations. This “ethnic self-awareness is replaced by economic-cultural and becomes a self-sufficient value.” The process of “settling” the nomadic population in Kazakhstan was carried out under the pressure of the empire's centre, and not as a result of the natural and historical course of socio-economic development of the Eurasian steppe zone. A particularly active sedentarisation of nomads was carried out in the 1930s during the large-scale violent state policy of “Small October”. As a result of the totalitarian policy, in fact, not only the natural course of history was disturbed and the traditional domestic economic way of life, but most importantly, there was a marginalization of the social structure of the Kazakh society, which resulted in a splitting of the national consciousness accompanied by a decline in social and ethical norms and principles. In general, there was a reduction in the quality of human resources. The repressive state apparatus leveled ethical standards by reducing them to the level of blind subordination to the ideological attitudes of the party.

Under these circumstances one could not speak about the development of social capital. The problem was the simple regeneration of an ethnic group after the tragedies of the 30s, the Holodomor and the elimination of the nation's elite - the national intelligentsia. The spirit of the nation was undermined. Fear, conformism and distrust for a long time settled in the minds and souls of people in the area of the Great Steppe, defining a vector and priorities of social and political life until the collapse of the Soviet empire and acquisition of sovereignty. Under these conditions, the emergence of innovative, individual and collective, social breakthrough projects arising from the Kazakh ethnic milieu was rather the exception than the rule. For example, the emergence of a national engineering science, associated with the enthusiasm and the activity of individual outstanding representatives of the national intelligentsia which have received an excellent education at Russian universities or independently developed new areas of knowledge, such as M. Tynyshpaev, S. Sadvakasov, A. Bukeykhanov, K. Satpaev and other.

By and large, the emergence of various sciences and technological fields in Kazakhstan together with the increment of knowledge, intellectual capacity, adaptation of new social and ethical paradigms and "worked" on the accumulation of eventually building a potential of national social capital in the country, albeit in a very "truncated" form of the Soviet empire. According to the law on dialectic of the transition of quantitative changes into qualitative changes in the republic within the USSR there were large-scale quantitative changes in the social structure of Kazakh society. An increasing number of people who migrated to the city and mastered the industrial profession, receiving vocational and higher education, actively develop and build up the science, education and culture. According to the law of the dialectic of the transition of quantitative changes into qualitative changes in the republic within the USSR, there were large-scale quantitative changes in the social structure of the Kazakh society. Moreover, even the existence of an authoritarian-commanding, repressive system which destroyed the elite of the national intelligentsia in the 1930s and a third of the population due to Holodomor, failed to stop the growth of the national human resource which was to become the basis for future quality of social capital. Of course, the path of history is not linear, and on this path there were various conflicts and national tragedies (described above), but they were the "challenges" that "hardened" the nation. As Alma Sultangalieva pointed out: "After the destruction of the traditional economic structure of Kazakh nomads, also the for centuries polished structure of their social ties collapsed, of which the basis is built by kindred relations on the family, community, kins and tribal unions (horde, жуза).

Despite the fact that the material basis of these relationships disappeared, it does not mean that it is not preserved in the memory of them."[20] Further, the active modernization of the social structure leads to its transformation in all spheres, including also that of the "ancestral memory". In the new post-Soviet market conditions "it is no longer required to expand the circle of ancestral ties to confirm the identity of the Kazakhs". Rather, they are more and more "commercialized", and, thus, gaining market value. "Therefore, for the wealthy Kazakh class, these relations become an additional competitive advantage (the more ancient the kin, horde, or family, the more legitimate is the right of their representatives to certain resources, such as power, money, and status). For the majority of the impoverished Kazakhs, the dependence on the tradition is turning into their social capital, for want of tangible capital. Moreover, the relationship between rich and poor kinsmen assume a "patron – client"-relation. Thus, once again a readjustment of "tradition" takes place, but this time to the terms of a capitalist society."[21]

The process of gaining independence and designing a new national identity is not only based on historical social resources, but is to a great extent linked to the reality of new public relations and social ties which assert the formation of a new community based on an independent, national modernization project of Kazakhstan. In this context, looking at the experience of realizing a model of the modernist model project, it should be mentioned that it is important for the Kazakhs, for example, as the Germans, despite the fact that they once were divided into 300 different principalities and monarchies, have acquired spiritual unity through philosophy, poetry and music. It was an intellectual breakthrough of global significance.

By creating a fantastic holistic spiritual universe in which, on the one hand, in abstract form all the real contradictions of the time were expressed, but on the other hand, certain mechanisms for their solution in the form of an active, action-creating subject were proposed, the German philosophy prepared the spiritual ground for the French Revolution. This purely German method of history work could only be invented by a "grim German genius". In contrast, the French changed the world with "arms and legs". If Martin Luther imparted the high ideals of Christianity through reformatory activity of each individual believer, then the baptism of the Rus was realized to a large extent by coercive methods.

Individual spiritual future is impossible without the reformation of the national consciousness and identity, it uncovers in the process of reformation of one's personal spiritual self-sentiment and self-identification, based on the correlation of the individual "I" with the reference group which would have a long historical evolution. In this respect, it becomes clear why you can never just train, teach or compel a Kazakh feel himself as a "sovok", "Shanghaian" Arab Muslim, or refined European - a citizen of the European Union. Being civilised as the quality of the individual arises exactly in the process of reformation of national consciousness, for it is a natural part of the cultural universe that lies at its base. Neither liberal democracy, nor Keynesianism, nor tolerance, nor the modernization of the economy, "catch" the individual ordinary man, if all these phenomena are not included in his personal spiritual horizons and are not its inherent characteristics. Thus, the formation of national consciousness, contemporary cultural and social capital associated, on the one hand, with overcoming the "peripheral awareness" or the complex of civilisational outskirts, "who are at the tail-end" of strange stories, and thus doomed to be not the creator and initiator of new social perspectives, what actually makes the formation of modern national identity in the country urgent, but rather the recipient of "external" modernization projects, as it happened in conditions of the Soviet Union. Though, despite the fact that Kazakhstan during the Soviet era has undergone a radical reformation as expressed in the rapid industrialization, the creation of an industrial infrastructure of the mining, commodity sector of the national economy, nevertheless, social life and human resources do not constitute examples of the reformational innovative national self-awareness, which is an indispensable condition for obtaining a new, truly "national, social history". On the other hand, the formation of a national cultural identity is becoming a needed social project, as it faces a real prospect of forming its own path of development, social development strategy of the newly formed state with sacralisation and the actualization of new national concepts and objectives. This prospect revealed only with the acquisition of the national sovereignty of Kazakhstan in 1991. It was then that the civilisation and cultural human resources which potentially existed in the past history of the people, really took shape in the country to meet the new challenges of nation building as paramount tasks, for the solution of which also the potential of the whole social capital of the people was mobilized. Institutional changes in the status of human resources of Kazakhstan, aimed at addressing the problems mentioned above, was a kind of challenge to promote and design a new system of social relations built on active social interaction and cooperation for the sake of common development goals. The need to legitimize the new regime of social relations was confirmed by the constitutional sovereign Kazakhstan in various fields, in the political, economic, cultural and ideological field. And currently concepts and horizons of independence are deepened and expanded.

If, at first, it was possible to develop by inertia, specified by centrifugal impulses of the collapse of the former social system of the Soviet empire, and based on a relatively high cultural potential and social standards of the era of the Soviet Union, then now the development by inertia is a more conservative trend, freezing national breakthrough projects and tying them up to the old values and orientations. Kazakhstan's way out to the international arena and the country's search for new prospects, advanced models of development and opportunities of sovereign self-identification, actualize the political, economic and cultural initiatives through which the country can present itself in the international community and express its ambitions and plans concerning development. In this respect, a number of Kazakhstan's foreign policy initiatives were revealed which include the implementation in practice of the status of a peaceful and non-nuclear state, the declaration and progressive action to implement the ideology of Eurasianism in the post-soviet territory, and Kazakhstan's successful moderation of various international forums and organizations such as OSCE, SCO, CICA, OIC, EurAsEC, and others.

The spiritual reformation of Kazakhstan took place over many centuries of active cultural genesis. The peoples inhabiting the center of Eurasia distinguish themselves by a special religious tolerance and their spiritual and cultural manifestations were of syncretic character. Thus, in the spiritual values of the Kazakh people you can easily find traces of different religions (Zoroastrianism, Tengrianism, Manichaeism, Buddhism, Sunni Islam, Nestorianism, Sufism, etc.). Along with the religious beliefs of the nomadic Kazakh society, there always existed also non-religious beliefs about the world and its beings.

The formation of the Kazakh state was accompanied by an active search for spiritual self-identification at different stages of its history. The establishment of the spiritual concept of the Kazakh people was particularly influenced by Islam which was brought approximately in the 9th century to the freedom-loving steppe, first by Arab conquerors and the spiritual mediums of Islam of times of the Arab Caliphate, as well as representatives of the various Sufi orders that have emerged in most of Central Asia. I.e. orders like Yassaviya and Naqshbandiyya which were widely distributed in the urban culture of South Kazakhstan in the Middle Ages. Despite the fact that the cities of the Central Asian civilisations were able to form their own religious centers of spirituality on the basis of Islam and Sufism, the Kazakh steppe always preserved its own unique spiritual identity, based on the free interpretation of propositions of various religious traditions which were adopted by nomads taking into account their pragmatic values and specific character of the nomadic economy and way of life.

Periodic wars of conquest which were carried out on the territory of the Dasht-i-Kipchaks, and the freedom-loving characteristic of the nomads' world view did not form in the steppe stable fundamental religious beliefs in the form in which these ideas were adopted by settled peoples of Central Asia with their devoted faith in Allah, challenging tradition of theological dogmatists and diverse developed ceremonial facilities. Nomadic Islam was deprived of the sophisticated dogma of settled Muslims and in everyday it coupled with the ordinary nomadic law of the Kazakhs.

Islamic influence on the nomadic Kazakhs then was exerted by wandering Sufi dervishes and Islamic missionaries and imams of the central Asian centers of Islamic learning of Bukhara, Samarqand, Khiva and other cities in the region. During the following time, the entry into the Russian Empire, along with direct conquest and punitive actions of the tsar's troops were accompanied by active attempts of forced Russification and Christianization in the first stage. Soon, representatives of the imperial local administration changed the tactic of the region's spiritual colonization from forced Russification and Christianization to a Russian education of the nomadic elites and controlled, by a colonization Government, Islamisation of Tatar mullahs from Kazan, Ufa, Omsk and Orenburg, and through the establishment of mektebs and madrassas, adapted to nomadic life in the steppe. The Arabic script of the Kazakh language communicated by Tatar teachers and preachers enshrined the Muslim ideological orientation in the pro-Russian political interpretation of Islam in the interpretation of Tatar ulema. Moreover, former close spiritual ties to the area of religious education, Islamic theology and justice to the Kazakh steppe with the Central Asian spiritual centres of Bukhara, Samarqand, Khiva and others, have been violated. As a matter of fact, the Kazakh steppe was "separated" from its regional Islamic centres.

The new phase of the modernized Islamisation has been associated with the Tatar Enlightenment of the steppe under Russian dominion. The development of secular and religious education in the spirit of "Usul-e-Jadid" ("new method") became widespread in the steppe. The special feature of the new-method education was syncretism of religious and secular components of training programmes. Exactly on the basis of this education, a Kazakh Enlightenment movement was established in Kazakhstan by outstanding representatives like Abay, Ibrahim Altynsarin, Shakarim and, in following, a brilliant pleiad of social, civil and political activists of the emerging new modernized statehood of Kazakhstan, such as Ahmet Baitursynov, Mirzhakyp Dulatov, Alikhan Bukeikhanov, Mustafa Shokai, etc. It is known that at this time the Kazakh "spiritual picture" was strongly tied to the canons of the enlightened, modernized Islam Jadid spirit.

The representatives of the national intelligentsia linked the hopes of establishing an independent modern Kazakh state mainly with the preservation of the unique identity of the Kazakh nomadic mentality in a time of modernizing the economic structure and reforming the statehood, so it emerges to a similar model as the Turkish Republic of Mustafa Kemal Ataturk for the whole Turkic world.

The reform of the Kazakh alphabet was based on Latin script, the participation of the Kazakh intelligentsia in Russia's State Duma, from the establishment of an Islamic Party and the formation of a national government, the "Alash Horde". To this moment, those were the real steps of Kazakhstan towards gaining sovereignty. But the February bourgeois-democratic revolution and the October Revolution in Russia in 1917, the ensuing civil war and "Red Terror", all this dashed the hopes of gaining state sovereignty and, along with it, spiritual freedom for the Kazakh people. The "Small October" which was carried out in the region, not only claimed millions of lives, beheaded the movement to fight for the independence of Kazakhstan and completely annihilated the national intelligentsia, but also broke the tradition of developing a spiritual self-identification. Despite the declaration of the separation of church and state, state atheism and the cultural-historical annihilation concerning the ownership of spiritual and cultural tradition have been widely introduced. In the territory we are talking about, the Kazakh language, national traditions, education and spirituality existed de jure, but de facto without any possibility of realization. The Soviet period of history was accompanied by a regular migration of various "disloyal" ethnic groups from throughout the USSR to Kazakhstan. We know about deportations of Germans, Koreans, Meskhetian Turks, and others, as well as, exiles of active social and political activists, Jews, and cultural and educational players of other ethnic groups. Along with these migration flows to Kazakhstan various religious and spiritual systems were incorporated which were atypical for the Kazakh national world view. Thus, a rather "colourful appearance" was formed on the territory of the republic and the spiritual guidelines which were totally crushed by the communist ideology.

Only with the collapse of the Soviet Empire, Kazakhstan got the opportunity to gain true freedom, both in institutional and informal terms. It was with the legal formalization of Kazakhstan's state sovereignty when the real story of our national state in its modern international interpretations began. Since that time, all the peoples living in Kazakhstan have started active attempts of a spiritual self-identification, and to revive traditions and rituals, including religious. As we know about this period, Kazakhstan was a multiethnic state with a diverse perspective range of religious orientations.

The proclamation of a new independent state of Kazakhstan as a secular, democratic, unitary state under the rule of law has created a legal basis for the design of these "spiritual" quests, both within the historical tradition (i.e. Kazakhs - Muslims, Russian - Orthodox Christians), and through active external interactions to influence the choice of the spiritual orientation of the people. At the initial stage of independence, basic for the local population, traditional faith groups of Sunni Islam, Orthodox Christianity, Catholicism, and various traditional types of Protestantism and Judaism formed and further developed in the republic. The spiritual revival of the nation after decades of national nihilism and state atheism even increased the number of believers in the world's religions traditional for our territory, and basically grouped people around Sunni Islam and Orthodox Christianity.

But in this period, also a wave of diverse religious communities, sects and new formations, as characteristic of our culture, historical and long forgotten and completely new and unknown, poured into Kazakhstan. The situation became complicated due to the lack of experience in the state's "struggle for hearts and souls of people", and a weak legal basis regulating religious issues. The need of a democratic orientation concerning the legal fundament of these "thin areas" have created a precedent for penetration in the country of a large number of destructive religious and pseudo-religious organizations and their state registration, the extension of missionary work and, accordingly, of the number of their adherents, especially among youth.

Thus, the present confessional situation is characterized by a rather complex structure and a representation of different religions, and also those posing as such. At the same time, since the republic gained independence the religious sphere in Kazakhstan has been characterized by a relatively high dynamism. There are a number of explanations of historical and political nature for this. As it is known, the collapse of the Soviet empire was, at the first stage, accompanied by the destruction of mono-oriented political ideology of communism and atheism, and subsequently by the emergence of an ideological and spiritual vacuum in the minds and souls of the people who, as a result, filled with new poly-oriented content in diverse forms. Moreover, the declared constitutional secular character of the state and the separation of religious organizations from the state in the spiritual realm is not clearly delineated, and nowadays becomes the scene of a complex interaction between state and religious institutions. The lack of a clear state ideology of social development, the widespread and influential set of secular spiritual values creates favourable conditions for an active penetration into the public consciousness of Kazakhstan, religious systems developed abroad with the whole formal complex of influencing the public consciousness, especially among the youth. The line of contemporary spiritual confrontation is now and then not so much between the secular and the religious consciousness, but rather between the constructive and deconstructive spiritual world. The state actively and constructively interacts with the religions traditional for Kazakhstan, but as regards the deconstructive religious influence from abroad, the impact is limited only by legal restrictions which are not always effective and deal with precedents already accomplished. As already noted, today religious tensions and fractures do not take place between Sunni Islam and Orthodox Christianity. Here the normal spiritual religious dialogue has just realized on basis of positive cultural values. The state institutionally supports this dialogue and provides for a constructive and formal interaction, i.e. with the Spiritual Administration of Muslims in Kazakhstan and the Eparchy of the Russian Orthodox Church in Kazakhstan and other official organizations that represent the traditional religions of the world. Furthermore, as it is known, the President initiated the convening of the Congress of Leaders of World and Traditional Religions which is regularly held in Astana. What reveals as problematic is the activation of destructive sects and religious and pseudo-religious organizations non-traditional for Kazakhstan, as they increasingly expand their influence within the country.

In this context, mainstreaming extremism on a religious basis with underlying political reasons represents a real threat to the spiritual welfare of the state and its citizens. In order to streamline state-confessional relations and to displace the destructive sector of the country's religious field, the state founded the Agency for Religious Affairs, and issued a new Law "On the religious activities and religious associations". These measures are intended not only to resolve current problems concerning the development of state-confessional relations which emerge due to internal and external factors, but also to ensure further harmonization of the spiritual sphere of Kazakhstan.

Kazakhstan has a fairly diverse social community, as to its ethnic composition and complex socio-economic and cultural structures. Already in Soviet times defined as a "laboratory of the Peoples' Friendship", our country today is an example of ethnic and cultural diversity and spiritual tolerance. But this does not mean that the processes of nation-building were completed in the spirit of "Soviet multiculturalism". From our point of view, this is only the beginning of the "true history" of modern Kazakhstan. And this story is formed before our very eyes under the moderation of a rapidly growing, in quantity, as well as in quality, Kazakh ethnicity. Today the problem of nation-building is of particular political sensitivity. The emergence of the problem has its origins in the present situation - the presence of various ethnic groups in Kazakhstan, with varying degrees of self-identification and realized statuses. Thus, in our country live different peoples. Some of them have their own statehood and are large ethnic groups in Kazakhstan, such as Russians, Ukrainians, Germans, Belarusians, Uzbeks, Koreans, Jews, etc. These are irredentas (aboriginal inhabitants of these territories) and diaspora (population moved there from the outside). Furthermore, there are also ethnic groups which, due to historical circumstances, do not have their own statehood, and therefore also no possibility of an official identity, such as Uighurs, Dungans, Kurds, Meskhetian Turks.

The Kazakhs, despite the fact that they declared their own state-building essence, have nevertheless not fully realized the potential of a fully-fledged nation, and are on the way of its state registration (because it is a long natural-historical process). For a full self-identification of the Kazakhs as a nation, i.e. an ethnic group which has and realizes its own potential of nation-building, it is necessary to carry out a series of necessary measures for internal consolidation and development, as well as paternalistic political steps of the government which allow the Kazakh ethnicity establish itself as a fully-fledged state-building nation. National patriots insist on this. And also patriots who are proponents of a strong state agree with it to some extent. But how to achieve this common goal can vary.

The national (or ethno-) patriots insist on a "revolutionary" approach to achieving the goals of building a Kazakh nation-state on the principles of the Kazakh ethnic determinism (i.e. defining the role of the dominant ethnic group in the process of nation-building), believing that it is time for the Kazakh ethnicity to "wake up" and "enforce" their own Kazakh statehood on the basis of Kazakh language, culture, political and economic dominance, namely the Kazakh ethnic identity in the formation process of a national statehood. In their view, the priority of national development of the country at the present stage should be the public attention on the development of the Kazakh ethnicity, on strengthening and expanding the scope of application of state language and culture.

Patriots who are proponents of a strong state, with the incumbent President of Kazakhstan leading the way, advocate an "evolutionary" strategy of nation-building, taking into account the actually emerging socio-economic conditions and political realities of modern Kazakhstan, referring to the complex ethno-confessional structure of society, history, and the potential of existing civil and public institutions, as well as the current prospects of modernizing this multi-constituent society and improving state institutions.

The principal difference between these two approaches is the social support of nation-building. Patriots who are proponents of a strong state champion the broadest involvement of all social groups and strata of the Kazakh society in the process of building a national statehood, including ethnic and confessional consolidation of society. Hence arises the idea of a national unity as a consolidation of all peoples regardless of their ethnic origin or religious affiliation, mainstreaming the civil identity upon the ethnic identity. The national (or ethno-) patriots mainly rely on the primary, state-forming ethnic group which is, from its own point of view, the bearer of the national identity, and therefore should be of first priority in the national state politics.

The efforts of the Kazakh ethnicity to state nation-building through the priority of developing the Kazakh peoples clashes with the interests of other ethnic groups in Kazakhstan. Thus, the first ethnic group which was already mentioned above, does not need state formation on a foreign territory, and will understand and accept all forms of Kazakh developments as a nation, if it does not infringe their fundamental interests (the sphere of communication in Russian does not shrink, and there will not be legal, political, economic or cultural discrimination.) The representatives of these groups have the opportunity to choose as regards their self-identification (either as irredentas in Kazakhstan or as a state-building ethnos in their homeland). The situation is more difficult with the people who by will of history live in this area, not having the opportunity of building their own state. In the active process of Kazakh nation-building they can be in a state of "increased vulnerability", because "the progress of the Kazakh territory" will be carried out mainly at the expense of their cultural space. This, under certain conditions (i.e. deterioration of the socio-economic situation of the people, ineffective and ill-advised national policy), may lead to the emergence of a seat of tensions which in general has been observed in a number of events in Kazakhstan in recent years.

However, at present, on the territory of Kazakhstan has formed a unique model of intercultural communication which is related to the different ethno-cultural processes, as to orientation and energetics, in a united area of nation-building of the Republic of Kazakhstan. At present, our state is confronted with the urgent task of institutionally designing a creating statehood model.

This statehood model meets the current needs of the dynamically developing, democratically oriented state, in which all the conditions for the free and legally realized right to free development of representatives of various ethnic groups living in Kazakhstan. Despite the multicultural nature of the population's ethnic composition, based on democratic principles, ensuring the guarantee and priorities of the Kazakh ethnicity's development, as a system-forming, "supporting structure" of modern Kazakhstan. After all, the Kazakh ethnicity has the full legal and historical responsibility for the competence of modern statehood of Kazakhstan. However, it should be noted that the Kazakh people itself is in a process of forming its own identity, both on formal and informal levels. It still has to be fully aware of its historical mission to the multi-ethnic people of Kazakhstan and to clearly define and practically implement the democratic prospects of future development of the whole country. And here it is unacceptable to directly adopt foreign models of cultural identities, characteristic of multicultural, civil and even non-ethnic communities, even with the most advanced experience of its implementation. Kazakhstan needs a new positioning in the international community as a democratic, legal and multicultural community with a stable tolerant and social environment, having significant constructive power for the implementation of high humanistic tasks of overall harmonious development of the personality.

It is necessary to mention that under the conditions of transit to a democratic state structure, the processes of national identification run along with the registration processes of the civil identity. These are interrelated and interdependent processes. And the attempt to be in opposition to one type or level of identity of the other is absolutely erroneous. These are complementary factors of the very same process of finding an acceptable form and content of national (i.e. state) identity of Kazakhstan at the present stage. This identity is demanded to answer fundamental questions about people's own existence: Who are we? What unites us? Where do we go? What are the goals and results we want to achieve in the future? And anyway, what are the social contours of our future prospects? An incorrect making and interpretation of the self-identification model may lead to irreparable and tragic social consequences. Though, the making of Kazakhstan's model of identity is a lengthy process which in other countries needed centuries, and we are only at the beginning of this journey. An important aspect which influences the processes of national identification and, therefore, the building of a statehood model corresponding to the requirement, is the current process of globalization which disturbs the usual trends and speed of nation-building and destroys not only the established national interstate boundaries, but which is especially important, also erodes the cultural, linguistic and spiritual "borders" between nations, "hastily" marginalizing the global territory outer space. Under the conditions of a still evolving and growing national identity, this process has a destroying, deconstructive power which undermines the very foundations of the ethnicity and the ability and capacity to its survival, value, and sometimes physical regeneration of it. That is, in this situation for a growing ethnic group arises the question of ethnic consolidation and the formation of a unifying ideology. And here the fully justified slogans of "nationalism": inherent worth and uniqueness of this or that people, the protection of "native land", the language, "faith of the fathers", etc. After all, they put quite a positive task of preserving ethnic and cultural uniqueness of the people under the conditions of the offence of "a faceless globalization" with its omnipresent media culture.

Another negative factor in the process of nation-building is, generally, the negative historical memory of the people, cemented in the minds of the growing, only emerging ethnic group, the old stereotypes and clichés of the "constant struggle" for the people's own survival which complement the "negative background" in the process of forming an adequate identification model. For example, under the circumstances in Kazakhstan, such a "negative background" is: the experience of the Russian tsarist colonialism, repression of the Kazakh intelligentsia, the Holodomor in the 1930s, unequal socio-economic development of Kazakhstan during the Soviet period, the lack of an unambiguous assessment of the events of 1986, and the activity of leaders in these events, priority participation of foreign capital in the process of privatization of state assets of Kazakhstan and preferences in doing business, lack of goal-oriented state (central and regional policy) in terms of reviving the state-building Kazakh ethnicity in the field of socio-economic, demographic, linguistic, migration, information, cultural and educational policy, etc.

Uncertainty and red tape as regards the solution of a number of current practical issues in the field of interethnic, cultural and information policy of the state will be an "illusion", and sometimes also the reality of opposing an ethnic and cultural conflict revival of the indigenous ethnic group from the various "hostile forces". In Kazakhstan, the problematic issues are making the law "On State Language"; an effective strategy for the demand of the Kazakh language in various spheres of public life in Kazakhstan with a list of specific government actions and demands, "reformatting" the activity of the Assembly of People of Kazakhstan out of cultural and representative organizations in the public bureaucratic structure which develops and puts into practice the national government policy concerning interethnic and interfaith relations, implementation of the strategy for the formation of a sovereign information space in the Republic of Kazakhstan, the establishment of legal guarantees ensuring equal rights and freedoms of citizens regardless of their ethnicity and religious affiliation, etc.

Therefore, the strategy of nation-building suggests the definition of some common development paradigms which are understood and accepted by all social, ethnic, confessional and political groups which make up the full range of popular will. This classical paradigm may be a conceptualization of the nation as a historically emerged stable community of people characterized by their community on its territory, economic ties, language, mental characteristics, culture and self-consciousness. Thus, in this case the concept of "nation" is not identical to the categories such as "ethnos" and "nationality", and built on the basis of general civil and supra-ethnic, universal criteria which, however, include the whole diversity of its deep, polycontextual content. It can be noted that the nation identifies the whole of the country's citizens, regardless of their social, political, ethnic, religious or other affiliation, as a united people on the basis of common citizenship. In this connection, in the process of ensuring national unity, one should not only emanate from the ethnic and religious, but from the whole range of social, political, cultural and other diversities of the Kazakh society. Moreover, such a requirement dictates not only the theory but the real state of Kazakhstan's contemporary society. Here, the cornerstone of forming a national identity model, in our view, should act as a system of values. The basic values, including values of civil society, of any State, like territorial integrity, a national language, a historical destiny, national symbols, moral code and code of ethics, as well as a vision of national development prospects which have a very concrete carrier, namely the ethnic group, who built the source of state identity, and is directly responsible for the further existence of the state. Under the conditions of forming of a young Kazakh statehood, it is necessary to be clearly aware of the historical mission of the Kazakh people to be the "cementing" basis and source of our state as well as the carrier of our people's core values.

The adoption of the Doctrine of National Unity, in the spirit of being aware of the Kazakh ethnicity as a system-building beginning in the formation of a modern identity in Kazakhstan, marks the acquisition of the real meanings and its own historical perspective by our country.

Finally, it has to be mentioned that Kazakhstan has built a unique model of social cohesion, which allowed our country to pass the transition period without any social conflicts and political cataclysms of racial, ethnic or religious strife. The ideology of cooperation, social cohesion, tolerance among representatives of different confessions laid the foundation for a peaceful and evolutional nation-building. The country has established important institutions of civil society, that allow for solving current issues concerning the modern national identity and interreligious harmony in a constructive way. The singularity of the country's state policy is the establishment of real conditions for an adequate development of all ethnic communities living in the state, and even the development of the ideology of mutual understanding, interdependence and tolerance in society. The Kazakh society today is a "living organism" which is in a constant and dynamic development with its problems and, doubtlessly, also its achievements. The social model of Kazakhstan which was created in the last 20 years, is certainly not perfect, but, at the same time, it represents an intermediate result of the constructive interaction between the state and the whole society.

Valikhan Tuleshov, Characteristics of the Political Modernization in Present Kazakhstan

I. Since the formation of sovereign Kazakhstan, the country's political system has evolved in accordance with the conditions which the state found in the early days of independence, when the Constitution of the Kazakh SSR was still effective which was adopted at the extraordinary session of the Supreme Council VII of the Republic IX convocation on 20 April, 1978. It consisted of one preamble, 10 sections, 19 chapters and 173 articles. According to it, all the power belonged to the people which were divided by classes into workers, peasants and the working intelligentsia. Over the system of authorities and administration was placed the Communist Party of the Kazakh SSR (Art. 6). The state and cooperative kolkhoz property, as well as the property of trade unions and other public organizations were announced as the basic economic system of the republic.

In the Constitution of 1978 the national-state and administrative-territorial structure of the republic, the competences of higher and local authorities and administration authorities (Art. 78-83, 97-139), the principles of the electoral system, the legal status of People's Deputies, the institutions of the state plan for economic and social development, the state budget, judicial power, arbitration, prosecutors supervision, etc. were defined.

After the declaration of independence on 16 December, 1991, the Supreme Council of the Kazakh SSR was the supreme legislative body, elected still during Soviet rule. Then, in December 1993, the Supreme Council dissolved itself. The first parliamentary elections were held in 1994.

Therefore, in the early 1990s, in the Kazakh SSR, and then in the Republic of Kazakhstan several laws were adopted which made significant amendments to the Constitution of 1978.

According to the Law of 20 November, 1990 "On improving the structure of state power" the provision that the President is the head of the executive and administrative power was included in the Constitution, and the Council of Ministers was converted to the Cabinet of Ministers. According to these amendments, the President of the Republic of Kazakhstan is President Nursultan Nazarbaev, who has been in office since 24 April, 1990. Among other laws adopted in this time of transition were the Law of 15 February, 1991, "On local self-government and local councils of people's deputies of the Kazakh SSR", the Law of 10 December, 1991, "On change of name of the Kazakh Soviet Socialist Republic", the Law of 16 December, 1991, "On State Independence of the Republic Kazakhstan", the Law of 20 December, 1991, "On Citizenship of the Republic of Kazakhstan" and others.

The first Constitution of independent Kazakhstan was adopted at the IX session of the Supreme Council of Kazakhstan XII convocation on 28 January, 1993. Structurally it consisted of one preamble, four sections, 21 chapters and 131 articles. The Constitution has incorporated many of the legal rules adopted after Kazakhstan gained its national sovereignty: people's sovereignty, independence of the state, the principle of separation of powers, public recognition of the Kazakh language, the recognition of the President as the Head of State, of the court – the Supreme, Constitutional and Supreme Arbitration Courts and others. **The model of a parliamentary republic built the basis of the Constitution of 1993.**

However, within a very short time, the shortcomings of the first Constitution based on the model of a parliamentary republic became apparent. Under the conditions of unsettled private property, the practical absence of institutionalized new owners, economic imbalances after the collapse of the Soviet Union and the chaotic social and political situation, in which it was impossible to expect a stable civil conduct, the country's President Nursultan Nazarbaev and the political elite which supports him, initiated a national referendum on the adoption of a new constitution of Kazakhstan.

The new and current Constitution of the Republic of Kazakhstan was adopted on 30 August, 1995, by a national referendum. This day is a public holiday, named Day of Constitution of the Republic of Kazakhstan. In 1998 and 2007 significant amendments to the Constitution were made, redistributing the powers of the President and the Parliament. Amendments were also made in 2011, as to which the president was granted the right to hold early presidential elections.

According to the current Constitution, the Republic of Kazakhstan is already a unitary state with a presidential form of government. The President is the Head of State and Commander in Chief.

President Nazarbaev took office on 24 April,1990, and has led Kazakhstan since 22 June, 1989 (more than 22 years by the fall of-2012). The first President of Kazakhstan Nursultan Nazarbaev, in accordance with the Constitutional Law, has a special political and legal status: the extended protection of him and his family, the opportunity to speak before Parliament, at meetings of the Government after the termination of his powers, as well as other favourable conditions. The status and powers of the First President of Kazakhstan are defined by the Constitution of the Republic and the constitutional law. The Constitutional Act of 20 July, 2000, N 83-II "About the First President of the Republic of Kazakhstan".

II. Since the declaration of state independence, the President and the ruling political elites of Kazakhstan, while literally balancing between a possible economic collapse and a social explosion, had to rapidly undergo the process of creating and designing an economic and social discourse of the new independent state, an arsenal of political means of the country's governance and a security system and state sovereignty.

In this case, it must be clearly noted, that the very important question of modern history was unswervingly heeded: the establishment of a new ideological conceptual system which by defining the state's attitude to the disintegration of the USSR and the emergence of a new regional entity on the international scene – the CIS – identified the most important domestic priorities of public and social development. However, the understanding of the historical-philosophical process, revised by the understanding of social life in the richness of all its manifestations, began to happen in an evolutionary way. The establishment of a national worldview position, which allows recreating a complete image of the history of the Kazakhs and i.e. also combining it with the country's future project, emerged cautiously. Assessments of the Bolshevik version of the communist ideology and its Soviet model of modernism began to appear gradually, making the impression that the intellectual elite of the country remained infected with multicultural (proletarian internationalism, bourgeois cosmopolitanism) and anti-market (pseudomarket), authoritarian stereotypes of consciousness.

Liberal-democratic ideology came not as a simple and spontaneous rejection of the entire former ideology of life which would be fraught with conflict of millions of ordinary people, but as a model of continuity, not only in the life of the whole country, but above all in the mind of the single ordinary man. It triumphed without loud reports and campaigns. **Freedom of choice was established, because there was a gradual and objective understanding of its necessity.**

At the same time, all former thoughts of life and characteristics were not trampled upon and destroyed in one moment, and thus, also the Soviet society, included in these characteristics, was not destroyed "to the ground", as it was before, the national-cultural nature of the Kazakh society was also not proclaimed as a purely nationalist direction of the Kazakh citizenship. Preserving the tradition and promoting people's tolerant relationship to each other within the society and state, Kazakhstan managed it to come relatively smoothly through this dangerous and critical period of gaining its sovereignty and creating its state-legal and political system.

Today it is hard to imagine how it would be, if everything had happened in another way, as in the days of Mikhail Gorbachev, who literally pushed individuals unprepared for change into the abyss of the unconscious and unrestrained liberal ideology – whose violent collision with the old communist ideology led to the collapse of the Soviet Union.

Today it is hard to imagine how it would be, if at the dawn of our independence a purely nationalist programme of state building had been proclaimed which in Georgia, for example, during the time of Gamsakhurdia, resulted in the isolation of different national ethnic groups and civil war. Finally, today it is difficult to imagine how it would be, if the bare denial of the past would have resulted in a civilisational confrontation with the former "sisters" in the Soviet Union, as happened during the Georgian-Russian conflict in 2008 ..

So, gradually, step by step interpreting the shortcomings of the former obsolete Bolshevik form of modernist cultural orientation, the intellectual elites, without making a fuzz, but also consistently and thoroughly, approached the acknowledgement of the need to build a new post-industrial society which operates on the new post-modern discourse of human existence and on the new postmodern orientation of human culture. On this basis, the Development Strategy of the state until 2030, the State Programme "Path to Europe" and the defined multi-vector foreign policy of Kazakhstan have been adopted.

Thus, also the fundamental achievements of the European social democracy which laid down the basic parameters and standards of public trust as an expression of the essence of social capital, have not gone beyond the boundaries of interest of the ruling elites of the post-Soviet, sovereign and independent state. The point is that the social capital of the Kazakh nation emerges not only as a capacity for spontaneous socialization on the basis of some new, let's say, liberal or democratic trend, but results from the very essence of the tribal organization of life of the Kazakhs, where the unity takes place at the level of family and tribe affiliation and related ethics. The genealogy of the Kazakhs is also based on tribal ties and relationships which are enshrined in the codes of conduct of all people. Therefore, also the national consensus concerning power, forms of its organization and methods of governance in Kazakhstan, was reached not by great social struggles, as it may be wanted by shrewd democrats, but by intra-national confidential communication within the family, clan or tribe.

Of course, in Kazakhstan, fetishisation which was examined by instruments of state governance and authority in general, has led to the so-called authoritarian version of modernization which presupposes the objectivity of value assessment in the objectivity of the governance tools and the power themselves, and not the objectivity of the higher objectives of economic development and human existence, though, the objectives of economic development and human existence did not disappear, and became major landmarks of numerous state programs for the development of the country.

Since independence, the beginnings of a formal democracy have been inculcated in society as real prerequisites, of which, at the dawn of the state's birth, almost all strata of the population dreamed of. Later, when the political elites were able to reach consensus as regards the formulation of a national paradigm of public development, cultural and historical traditions of the Kazakh nation prevailed in the country with new strength which became a powerful factor in political life. We have in mind that actually more than 60% of voters have signed the letter, calling for a national referendum to prolong the term of office of President N. Nazarbaev to 2020, what, perhaps not fully consciously, expressed the will of the nation, its "collective unconscious" (a term of C. Jung).

By the way, more than 95% of voters which participated in the presidential election, voted in favour of a candidacy of Mr. Nazarbaev. To some it may seem like a manifestation of authoritarian power methods of organizing economic, social and political space, of command-administrative management methods.

But it would be easy to call the desire of the majority of the people to keep President N. Nazarbaev in office until 2020 unreasonable under conditions of expanding freedom by simple obedience to it or its individual representatives. Under conditions in which the political opposition at its own meetings cannot bring together at least one thousand of his supporters, it is impossible to call the desire of ordinary people to settle once and for all the issue of Mr. Nazarbaev's presidency until 2020 a simple indication of power.

III. The reason for such a sustained and massive manifestation of the "collective unconscious" is covered in the genealogy of the Kazakhs, reflecting their whole historical path of development as an ethnicity.

The point is that the entire history of the Kazakh nation's path to its current state, in our view, is similar to the historical spiral of cyclical public areas and processes and, in general, is characterized by two defining features. On the one hand, the earliest and also all subsequent forms of Kazakh statehood, right up to the early 20th century, when the Kazakhs fell under the cultural-civilisational influence of the Western rational world view and the liberal-democratic trends of public life, have been characterized as a **martial-nomadic, steppe democracy**, the most stable form of which were, at first, tribal alliances, and then a Khaganate and a horde.

The military-democratic forms of statehood, ruling up to the first quarter of the 20th century, when the Kazakh Soviet Socialist Republic was founded, and indeed later deferred to forms of mass and individual awareness of stereotypes and archetypes of the respective nomadic (Tengrian) world view which were neither completely changed during the time of the Soviet Union, nor will it indeed be achieved in the near future, especially under conditions of an independent Kazakhstan, as natural and historic changes in public (national) awareness will go ahead much longer. In Japan, for example, it took 100 years since the Meiji Restoration until the Japanese nation, by the 80s of the 20th century, had acquired cultural and civilisational stability. It is impossible to correct the "Collective Unconscious", shaped by 5 000 years of domination of the military-nomadic forms of democracy, in one or two generations. Moreover, the Asiatic mode of production was not based on private property traditions and democratic institutions which took shape in the Western world since the time of Solon.

The martial-nomadic society was a hierarchical society, both in terms of administrative processes of social life, as well as in terms of the activity of ethical codes. Customary law of the Turkic peoples (the Kazakhs), originally expressed, formalized and enshrined in the postulates of the ethical systems of Tengri, and subsequently, in the code of Mode,

“Dzhasake” (The Yasa of Genghis Khan) of Genghis Khan, the “Shining path of Kasim Khan”, the “ancient way of Yesim Khan”, “Zheti zhargy” (Seven laws) of Tauke Khan, etc., were transformed into the institutions of the state legal system, where the “steppe democracy” and “the steppe law” were given a character of power and military verticals, what resulted in the creation of a special governance structure, and the appearance of particular features of the state structure.

On the other hand, for the Kazakhs, reflections on the family as a social institution which is characterized by certain social norms, sanctions, patterns of behaviour, rights and duties, governing the relationship between spouses and between parents and children, on the family as a joinder of persons connected, from the economic point of view, by a common family budget, on the family as a territorial unit uniting persons on the basis of living together and on the family as a biological structure, consisting of parents and children, will not endure without further definition of the family as an ethnic community. For Kazakhstan this is everlasting and of highest importance, since in the family and clan structure of the Kazakh society also the nature of the whole being of the life of Kazakhs is enclosed, including all historical types of martial-nomadic democracy and the whole of their cultural and historical order of life.

Cohesion and socialization in the Kazakh society were nothing natural, they were no arbitrary and spontaneous processes, but based on kinship and tribal consciousness. Therefore, as the family and all of its members built the basis of nomadic communities, the relationship between family members was constructed as the relation between interconnected entities, they, per se, were essentially different, dissimilar, but inseparable parts of one family body. All the basic elements of the Kazakhs’ mentality came from the family (tribe) as a nomadic community. In this regard, the main difference between the collective unconsciousness of the individual is that it is common for different people, does not depend on individual experience and history of the individual, and is a certain integrated “common denominator” for different people. That is why all the basic elements of the mentality of Kazakhs came from the family (tribe) as a nomadic community. Kazakhstan’s President N. Nazarbaev, noting this feature of nomadic families, wrote that “the true family of several people, at the same time, was one body, one organism. The different parts of it lived and pulsated in total physical, psychological, and moral mutual relationships. This classical model of the family is the natural basis of the historical composition and of bigger organic communities - families, clans, kins, tribes, tribal population, zhuzes or hordes (literally zhuz meaning “hundreds”; the Kazakh nomadic society was divided into three basic tribal unions: the Great Horde, the Middle Horde and the Little Horde), and finally, the Kazakh people itself – V.T.”. [22]

Z. Sarsenbaeva notes that “the core of the social relations of nomads and the basic pivot of the world view was a kindred tribal beginning which advocated a fundamental principle of self-identification of the individual with the community, and with the natural habitat, especially with the territory as a continuation of his natural life. Accordingly, the central place in the hierarchy of the traditional values held the concepts of “Atameken” (Homeland) and “Ata Konys” (Territories of generic nomades). Although every nomad as to his way of life was self-sufficient, he saw the meaning of his life in the service to the Sacred, and therefore in the voluntary service to the clan. Expulsion from the clan was regarded as a separation from the cosmos, from God and was considered a disgrace”.[23]

In a traditional nomadic society which represented Kazakhstan until the early 20th century, the individual family member was never perceived as a separate, isolated identity, but has always been one part of a united community of any level - family, kin (tribe), horde (national roots) and peoples. Thus, there is a notably well-known saying about the kinship triad: “жігіттің үш жұрты бар: нағашы жұрт, қайын жұрт, өз жұрты” (a young person has three types of relatives: relatives on the maternal side, relatives through the marriage and their relatives). One can imagine what is going on at Kazakh family celebrations, when all relatives of these three sides come together.

For this purpose, as the President of Kazakhstan N. Nazarbaev writes, “the Kazakh people have established within itself a unique body for their sustainable self-assertion in the specific conditions of a nomadic society which allowed it to preserve itself ... as a whole. Its whole historical body is preserved regardless of the presence or absence of the state membrane. It’s about the indispensable knowledge of every Kazakh about the “жеті ata” - seven fathers, seven generations. For the Kazakhs, the steppe genealogy was what the compass was for the sailor at sea. It was what was solely appropriate to the historical, geographical, commercial, political, economic and cultural circumstances in which, by will of the historical destiny, the Kazakh people are.” [24]

In this regard, the President of Kazakhstan N. Nazarbaev very precisely points to the importance of a cultural-anthropological approach concerning the investigation of the given problem. He writes: "A unique kin-tribal, clan-hordal united body of the Kazakh people was spreading naturally over the centuries on the basis of the following principle: all Kazakhs are fledglings of one "nest", the branches of one tree, of one root. This is why the awareness of people's unity which according to European canon isolated nomads would have lacked, is divided into three basic parts, namely the hordes which were, in fact, separated from each other by large distances. And this unity is perceived exactly through genealogy. In this, the genetic unity of Kazakhs becomes apparent by the origin from one common family tree. For Kazakh nomads it was always obligatory to know about their roots and kinship ties. This was built to a single moral and ethical criterion for the entire nation. It was always like this in our history. Therefore, the principle of "*жеті ата*" (knowledge of the seven generations of the ancestors) naturally ensures ethno-biological, ethno-cultural and, generally, spiritual integrity of the whole of the Kazakh people. Knowledge about your seven ancestors allows everyone to trace one's neighbouring branches of the family tree of Kazakhs to an adequate depth and make out the closeness of all Kazakhs in general. Thereby, their inseparable integrity is maintained".[25]

Various phenomena and occurrences of social life, showing their human capital not only in the family, but also collectively and in the state which were based on the Kazakh principle of genealogy – "*жеті ата*" – built the most important, in this context, cultural and civilisational basis for the development of the Kazakh society. Such phenomena and occurrences of social life were faith and religious feelings which, through the institution "*жеті ата*", were passed on from generation to generation.

Firstly, such "a belief, specified by the whole chain of direct ancestors, was the inner essence of man, and greatly expanded the space where he could seek and find a way out when life conflicts occur". Second, such "a faith allows man and the people in hard times not to restrict their options under external pressure, but to keep a clear mind, a pure heart, clear conscience, and, based on them, to find brilliant ways out of difficult historical situations".26 Along with this, the singularity of religious beliefs of Kazakh nomads is their syncretic-pragmatic character focusing on their social and ethical connotations and the search for freedom as the inner and outer harmony. The perception of freedom also has certain characteristics, as freedom is knowledge and adherence to the path specified by the ancestors, by previous social experience, by public practice, i.e. a kind of "recognition of necessity" (Hegel) in the steppe.

Hence, a hierarchy is not merely formal, but also meaningful and practical. "Көп жасағаннан сұрама, көп көргеннен сұра" (translated by meaning "Ask more from those who have seen a lot, than from someone who has lived long") or "*Молданың жасағанын жасама, айтқанын жаса*" (translated by meaning "Do not do what a Mullah does, but do what he says"). So, a nomad acts on social practice, as a kind of criterion of truth and righteousness of the chosen path. In this case, even the perception of religious canons, i.e. Islam, is realized in the light of everyday life experience. Steppe religious tradition took shape of a special kind of syncretic worldview, capable to revise a variety of religious systems, and adapt them to the needs of the moral and ethical nomadic spiritual tradition.

On the other hand, the principle of "*жеті ата*" allowed not only to survive, when, after the Holodomor of the 20s and 30s, only one third of the Kazakh population stayed alive, but, while preserving the primary genetic material (a total of 2 million people from 6 million until the Holodomor), literally "to be reborn from the ashes", having recreated the level of cultural and historical development which, after a long colonial dependence from the Russian Empire and the modernization project of the Bolsheviks (Soviet Union), allowed the Kazakh nation to tackle the task of restoring self-esteem, describing an objective history, with its positive and negative sides, its victories and defeats. The principle of "*жеті ата*", as the President of Kazakhstan writes, when the "Kazakh society in terms of socio-economic and general cultural development was to lag behind the surrounding nations and to suffer defeat against external enemies, when being torn by internal contradictions", played "the role of a storage of defeatist mood which suppressed the will of the people and created over the centuries an apparent consciousness of its backwardness, a national complex which is at least 300 years old.

In addition, a conscious humiliation by eurocentrists, also largely used by Soviet propaganda and science, of the history of the nomads, its interpretation as a history of careless and lazy people lacking of initiative and leading a semi-animal life, had a destructive and disastrous influence on the Kazakh national consciousness." [27] In this era of colonial dependence the institution "*жеті ата*" has become the accumulator of human capital which did not allow attacking an ethnic group, and also did not allow it to neither die physically nor spiritually. Action based on precedent which continued on a large scale for many centuries and millennia, if we remember the 5 millennial rules of the Tengrian nomadic world view in

Eurasia, then, in the course of time, formed a powerful layer of various ritual actions, regulatory behaviour models and practices of responsibility to the ancestors' spirits for their actions and behavior.

"'*Малым - жанымнын садагасы, жаным - арымнын садагасы*" (All my wealth is nothing against my life, my life is nothing when it comes to my honour). This unique psychological basis of the life of nomads has been proven well for centuries and perfected to its limits. The behaviour, rituals, moral motivation, standards and assessment of human communication in the desert are concentrated in it. All the material and spiritual aspects of a Kazakh's life, the whole life was regulated by a strict sophisticated etiquette of intergeneric relations, supported by the principle of "жеті ата". This principle also included a strict moral code of life of the Kazakhs, forming the basis of traditions, rituals, customs and taboos".[28]

Tolganay Umbetalieva notes that "in the nomadic Kazakh society the system of authoritative domination is based on the principle of genealogical kinship which derived from the traditional views of nomads concerning the law of primogeniture and seniority. The genealogical kinship system which fulfills an ideological function in a nomadic society, served as the primary tool for regulating social relations. Furthermore, an important role in the socio-legal ranking of nomads played the historically established terms "senior" and "junior" tribes. Based on these criteria of status, the structure of the political organization of the Kazakhs was built as a genealogical hierarchy of clans and tribes. The strong (senior) clans and tribes in this case built the core of the Kazakh martial-potestary alliances. Around them less powerful (junior) tribes and clans were integrated, and on this basis state foundations took shape. The system of status ranking of various subjects of power relations also resulted from the genealogical criterion of social statuses concerning various potestary-political groups of Kazakhs. Therefore, the degree of influence of the hierarchy of clans and tribes in the decision-making processes of the government depends on the heritage of the institutions of the past and present political calculations."[29]

It has to be mentioned that political decisions in a nomadic community are not solely made by the Khan or Khagan, but demand also the approval of the society or political elite – „ел ағасы", meaning those who have led the clan or by virtue of own qualities (military valour, wisdom, or wealth) were granted the public authority. For the nomadic Kazakh society with a rational not-institutionalized, formal-legal, political system, moral and ethical criteria were the main grounds of political legitimization. And if the Western political tradition has survived breach of morality and law in favour of the law, and corresponding norms and standards of behavior, then the nomadic political tradition maintained for a long time a loyalty to their moral principles established "at immemorial times". The "boisterous freemen and outlaws" of the steppe, representing themselves from outside as a kind of "bandit monastery", actually had a fairly strict structural-functional hierarchy, as discussed above, and a high degree of compliance with ethical norms and taboos, included in political behaviour. The destruction of this heroic ethic of the steppe in Russian and then in Soviet colonialism, led to the leveling of the traditional moral and ethical origin in the political consciousness by replacing them with ideological and class clichés, and then with the Machiavellian principles of the political market. Therefore, in this respect, the question of the revival of the moral and ethical models of political behaviour, already adapted to the new conditions of independence and sovereignty, is very important in the era of the formation of an own independent statehood of Kazakhstan with an independent political culture.

The presence of a high, culturally rich trust of the people to the „wealthy powers" and the social responsibility of the authorities in relation to the common people is an important guarantee of social and political stability and harmony in the country. Though, in fact, the beginnings of a collectivity or spontaneous socialization emerged at Kazakh nomads with the solution of intergeneric or inter-tribal disputes and, to a greater extent, under external aggression, when a collective solidarity in defending family, nation and homeland was developed. During such periods, the ability of people to internal consolidation and mobilization on the basis of shared values, moral and ethical attitudes, became apparent to its full extent, which, in our opinion, is an indicator of the presence of a high moral status concerning the human capital of the steppe, as well as, of positive, high ethical values uniting this human resource.

The transition from martial-nomadic forms of democracy to a form of Western state and public organization in terms of independence took and takes place under the influence of democratic liberal trends (private property, rights and freedom, republican government, etc.). However, as we noted above, in 1995 a significant disharmony (non-compliance) of the "military-democratic" (socialized in a family structure) public consciousness and the new private-owner democratic (individualistic) foundations of state and social development appeared. The political elite which divided the values of a parliamentary form of government, almost brought the country to an endless and useless, in terms of a rapid and efficient removal of threats for the establishment of independence of the new state, debate and splitting of the public consciousness of the people from Kazakhstan upon various political trends. The beginning "dismantling" of the substance of parliamentary democracy and social policy, and the creation of checks and balances of executive power have led to an inhibition of economic reform policies to create the foundations of a market economy and of political reforms to institutionalize civil and social initiatives in the state. Therefore, the progressive part of the political elite which understands the benefits of the presidential government under conditions of a deep socio-political and economic transformation of society, initiated the self-dissolution of the Parliament of Kazakhstan in December 1993 and the transfer of all powers to the president until new elections. It was at this time, when it became possible to adopt important laws and implement economic and social reforms which laid the foundation for the current modern social and economic system in Kazakhstan. And on 30 August, 1995, the new Constitution of the Republic of Kazakhstan was adopted in a nationwide referendum. In the Constitution the presidential form of government was fixed which eliminates the disharmony between the post-socialist, socialized forms of the public consciousness and the new liberal-democratic trends. In a sense, the presidential government led to the socio-political equilibrium and the stability of the whole social system between the carriers of the past "collective military-democratic unconscious" majority and the new "individualistic" oriented, liberal-democratic minority. It was the result of a consensus of the political elites as regards forms of the political system in Kazakhstan which began to meet the possibilities and needs of the state's development, actively trying to overcome the turbulence of the transition period, and effectively solve the problems of its own development not only in the short, but also in the long run.

Thus, in the Republic of Kazakhstan two contradictory social trends are interacting (the „military-democratic" and the „liberal-democratic" („social-democratic")) in public and social processes. These trends have a decisive influence on the formation and development of the political system in the Republic of Kazakhstan.

The significance of this fact cannot be overestimated, because as to the country's achievement of new and better results for economic and social development in pre-crisis time the economic growth rate was of 10%, and today is of 7%, so the interrelation of these trends gradually began to change, too. Inside each of them their deeper trends can be found which often contradict each other. But, nevertheless, the resolution of these contradictory trends are effective, and different groups of the elites interact on a rather high level.

It should be especially mentioned that this effective interaction might also not occur (detected opposite political trends could result in a collision, as examples of events in neighbouring Kyrgyzstan, or in countries of North Africa and the Middle East show which permanently suspended social progress and social development), if there would not be this primary, strong enough, in matter of relations, level of social interaction and mutual understanding which emerges in the structures of family, grows and expands in the structures of kin and tribe, regenerates in social structures of nationality, and blooms in the social, economic and political structures of the nation. Consequently, and this is especially important to stress, in circumstances where the state became the last refuge of the nation, **ethnic (family, kin (tribal), folk-ethnic and national) identification will become the main and basic form of social identification, and without researching it, it is impossible to understand the peculiarities of the political modernization of present Kazakhstan.**

IV. In other words, the "collective unconscious" or "objective psyche" (another term of C. Jung), as a common culture for the society as a whole, as a common historical deterministic phenomenon which is a product of inherited brain structures and national consciousness, and which the Kazakhs passed on, so to speak, genetically by inheritance, was a permanently cultivated tradition, distinguishing the Kazakhs from other ethnic groups in the 20th century, and already in 21st century as well. That is why, in modern times, the collective unconscious, as opposed to individual (personal) forms of the unconscious, is based on experience of no specific person, but of the society in general. This is a deeper layer than the individual unconscious - the word has not only a direct meaning, but also more hidden layers, meanings, comprehensible on an unconscious level. But since this collective unconscious is also the sum of aspects which tie the people of a united community together, it, obviously in its own and special way, culturally and historically created and continues to create the social life of Kazakhstan and influences the emerging political system of the state.

This is a "transpersonal unconscious" (another term of C. Jung), or mentality, to put it in a modern democratic language, and gave rise and continues to give rise to a "military-democratic" content of political trends. It was, as in Soviet times, the force that introduced significant adjustments to life. During the years of the new Constitution of the Republic of Kazakhstan, according to the influence of the military-democratic tradition, there was, from a Western point of view, a disproportionate and unequal, but, as to the universal grounds of the nomadic philosophy and the world view of the Kazakhs, an objective and necessary redistribution of roles of the different branches of power in Kazakhstan, and an institutional, socially oriented, military-democratic statehood was established. The characteristic features and properties of its manifestations today are the actualizing cultural-democratic and social-democratic orientation of the presidential form of government and the Constitutional Council - instead of the Constitutional Court, the representative function of the Assembly of People of Kazakhstan and the legitimation of a multi-party Parliament and of the real multi-party system.

The current state of affairs in the field of cultural and civilisational self-determination of nations developed naturally and historically, especially in the period when the Kazakhs under the pressure of the circumstances (Djungarian invasion), had to look for a "civilised response" to the challenge of destiny. Such a **forced incorporation** of the Kazakhs into the Russian Empire which became at that time (1700-1861) the classic example of the Eurasian colonial empire, and later (1861-1917) the classic example of imperialism (V.I. Lenin), developed under conditions of violent compulsion on the part of the Kazakhs to settle down, and the ensuing Holodomor, comparable to a large-scale form of genocide (1922-1932), political repression (1935-1937), and the tremendous difficulties of war and postwar period (1941-1961), neo-colonial, and later, after the abolition of the personality cult around I.V. Stalin, post-colonial conditions of their future existence and development within the USSR. The two times changed graphical basis of the Kazakh language, the three times changed territory, with a reduction of the historical natural habitats of Kazakhs, the three times changed status of statehood and the three times carried out resettlement of numerous ethnic groups of Slavic and other origin in the territory of Kazakhstan, when "in the 70s the Kazakhs were a minority in the their own land" (N. Nazarbaev), as well as the introduction of new cultural and civilisational patterns, and related to it ideological structures, ensured the spread of corresponding socio-cultural eclectic doctrines (Eurasianism), led to a partial neglect of even such a deep subcortical basis of consciousness of the Kazakhs which is a mythology, a folk epic, being, in fact, the cultural and civilisational "pantry" of national and self-consciousness. In turn, the loss of such an important component of the synthetic **identification pattern**, as to which the Kazakhs were highlighted as a special ethnic kind of mankind, led to the loss of an objective and cultural and civilisational direction of development of the Kazakh ethnicity necessary at that time which was a liberal democracy proposed by the leaders of the Alash Horde in the 1920s. All of them suffered a tragic fate - they all were persecuted and executed. Thus, the natural course of the history of the Kazakhs was rudely and unceremoniously destroyed, and the **natural historical path** of the nascent in the 20th century Kazakh nation was interrupted. As Alma Sultangalieva pointed out: "After the destruction of the traditional economic structure of Kazakh nomads, also the for centuries polished structure of their social ties collapsed, of which the basis made up the kindred relations on the family level, community level, kin level and tribal union level (horde). Despite the fact that the material basis of these relationships disappeared, it did not mean that they were not held in remembrance".[30]

The partial loss of residues of the emerging **spiritual and civilisational union** led to the disintegration of traditional forms of socialization and the subsequent shift of the social consciousness to a multicultural functionality format and, finally, to the development of the foundations of today's "multi-vectorial" or "civilisation latitude" of the Kazakh identity, to the actual dissociation, separation between and opposition of the Kazakhs themselves to each other in confessional, cultural and civilisational principles (the urban "shala-Kazakhs" and the rural "Mambety", "Agashki" and "young Turks", "apashki" and "tokal", etc.). As the President of Kazakhstan N. Nazarbaev has admitted, "this migration pressure which the Kazakhs experienced, perhaps, no nation in the world experienced".[31]

As it is known, "the spiritual future of the individual is impossible without the reformation of the national and self-consciousness, it uncovers in the process of reformation of one's personal spiritual self-awareness and self-identification, based on the correlation of the individual "I" with the reference group which would have a long historical evolution.

It is high time to realize that you cannot just train, teach or compel a Kazakh to feel like a "sovok", "Shanghaian", Arab Muslim, or refined European - a citizen of the European Union. Being civilised as the quality of the individual arises exactly in the process of reformation of national consciousness, for it is a natural part of the cultural universe that lies at its base. Neither liberal democracy, nor Keynesianism, nor tolerance, nor the modernization of the economy, "catch" the individual ordinary man, if all these phenomena are not included in his personal spiritual horizons."[32] Therefore, the formal liberalization shaped a formal multi-vectorial and also a corresponding isolation of the social life of individuals, where the existing paradigms of Kazakhstan's development, such as Islamic, "Shanghaian", "Eurasian", excluding the Soviet, well reposed in boson, and today, after seventeen years of sovereignty, was not up-to-date for the simple reason that they are not in a pure form national identity projects of reforming the national Kazakh self-consciousness, and are not a **project of national of choice**. Thus, the prevalence of eclectic methods of formulation of national and state priorities, and the determination of the core content of the spiritual union of the Kazakhs, led to the fact that "in the late 20th century, language and culture of the Kazakh people were on the verge of extinction".[33]

On the other hand, the spread of **Orthodox Christianity** in the Kazakh steppe, corresponding to the historical stages, and the wave of penetration and consolidation of institutions and mechanisms of **Russian colonialism of the messianic sense** and **Russian modernism of the hegemonic (proletarian) sense**, as well as the preservation of their influence in terms of gaining sovereignty in Kazakhstan, by itself, was an example of post-colonial influence and domination. In 1991 the Republic presented itself as a territory rich in numerous military sites, the main ones were the Semipalatinsk nuclear test site and Baykonur as the main base of for missile and space forces of Russia.

Since then, many years went by, during which the ruling elite which chose a presidential government and the corresponding "military-democratic" tradition of governance, has not done much to leave the road of a market-oriented authoritarianism.

However, for example, the contradictions between the whole economic structure of society and the outdated rational-scientist ("cognitive") orientation of culture (contradiction of civilisational development), between the new productive forces and the old, not recognizing private property, relations of production (contradiction of production methods), between the old production relations and the new orientation of post-modern culture (contradiction between basis and superstructure), emerging out of the new post-industrial nature of modern social development, they all were resolved in an evolutionary way this time.

Of course, it is impossible to implement the solution of these contradictions during the life of one generation, because, if the liberal economic policy, based on classical and neoclassical theories, acts as genuine alternative to the mercantilist economic policy of the state, whose main objective is economic growth, rather than the rights and freedoms of citizens - this real foundation for economic and social efficiency and entrepreneurial spirit, then the still existing selective attitude towards property rights till today remains the characteristic of post-Soviet state system. If, before the global financial crisis, the results of privatization have not been revised, then its individual procedural processes would have been revised, when the property could be seized in case of breach of an agreement with the authorities or on their permanent request in the interest of oligarchy under the pretext of "dilapidation" or "state needs". Rampant forms of then flourishing "raiderism" (a form of criminal expropriation of property), corruption and legal nihilism also clearly confirmed this. Today, many of the things which disturb the institutionalization of private property, have disappeared, but the preservation of corruption, the fight against corruption on a new national level was initiated in the crisis years by the President of Kazakhstan N. Nazarbaev, and suggests that the economic transformation experiences its most critical and intense period. The government makes serious efforts to curb this phenomenon, by improving the investment climate, by reducing administrative barriers and by establishing major reliefs for small and medium-sized enterprises. In this regard, as to its rate of corruption, for example, in 2008's ranking of Transparency International the Republic of Kazakhstan ranked 145th, and in 2010 105th, together with Moldova. From the CIS countries followed Armenia - 123rd position -, Belarus ranked 127th, Azerbaijan and Ukraine ranked 134th, Russia along with Tajikistan and Kyrgyzstan ranked 154th, Uzbekistan and Turkmenistan ranked 172th.[34] According to a study conducted by the U.S. Company Global Integrity Index Research, Kazakhstan already in 2009 ranked among the states with a "moderate" level of fighting corruption, in the list ahead of Russia, Lithuania, Indonesia, Turkey and Pakistan.[35]

Thus, the transition to new production relations in Kazakhstan also clearly demonstrates the struggle of the military-democratic and liberal, and the old and new economic relations, as well as trends, in the essence of the establishment of a new liberal method of production and new cultural and civilisational state of the civil society which become outdated or emerge.

At the same time, modernism in Kazakhstan not yet fully became the dominant cultural orientation, namely because of its false representation as a mere institutional instrument to renew the sectors of the national economy, and because modernism is identified only with economic reforms and the modernization of industrial products. Not propagating modernism as a cultural orientation in the social sphere, including in political relations, the authorities still significantly restrict the intellectual potential and the reformist resource of the economically active part of the country's population. The national economic elite still not independently determines the national economic interests, and thus, will not send a request to scientific and cultural players, who, in turn, do not articulate these national interests in categories of ethics and aesthetics, that is a national form of humanism and culture.

The scope of social, domestic politics expands more slowly than required by the social situation, thereby limiting increase and development of **social capital**, as an expression of institutional relations in society, and instruments, including a coherent national policy of an independent state.

A unitary state, as it may sound paradoxical, is still based on the parameters of the old Soviet model of multicultural modernism, intending to an internationally-oriented, although tolerant, and, as declared by the ruling elites of the country, along with consolidating and integrating the role of the Kazakh ethnicity, interaction of different ethnicities, ethnic and religious groups.

With this somewhat ideologizing approach which continues supporting the functional status quo of the cultural and civilisational pattern of the "big brother" from USSR times, its "civilisational seniority" in relation to other ethnic communities, and the conditions of uncontrolled infiltration of non-traditional religions and denominations began to grade the very essence of the Kazakh **national spiritual union** as the most essential foundation of the state. The Kazakhs, while the authorities maintain the cultural and civilisational impact of the former mother country and the local ethnic Russian community, as well as under the conditions of the penetration of new cultural and religious patterns under the new sovereign conditions, were still not socialized and not consolidated in their own country as a state-building nation, and thus found themselves in a partly disadvantaged, partly discriminatory position in relation to other national minorities which nominated nine of their representatives each from among the members of the People´s Assembly of Kazakhstan to Parliament.

Thus, the relevant cultural and historical civil unification of the Kazakh nation on the basis of a cultural and linguistic union did not take place as such, but **the Kazakh people still not yet became a full core which consolidates the whole society, since there exists still a strong and determining influence of state-administrative structures on the development processes of the civil society. The Kazakh language and**

culture so far did not become the basis of a free socialization of the citizens of other nationalities. Ethnic minorities, that is the diasporas, while preserving the current situation as regards issues of interethnic relations, so far, on behalf of individual members, make, although already quite lukewarm, attempts to claim the status of the state-building entities, creating and offering, thus, different versions of a federal reconstruction organized as a unitary state.

This **imbalance** of cultural-national cooperation which is reflected in the appearance of discontent and protest sentiments of the Kazakhs concerning the symbols existing in a multicultural state - the **Assembly of People of Kazakhstan** – and the domination of cultural-data and cultural-civilisational pattern would have been about to bring the country to the brink of an interethnic conflict, if in 2010 the Doctrine of national unity was not adopted, which put an end to multicultural versions of citizenship and cultural identity of citizens of the Republic of Kazakhstan, and laid the foundations of multi-socioculturalism in interethnic and religious spheres.

The adoption itself, by the way, was accompanied by collisions and substantial contradictions, as its original multicultural version was subjected to severe criticism from the national-patriotic-oriented people and the whole Kazakh intelligentsia. The proposed definitions in this version which wrongly communize the understanding of the subjects of socialization processes to the "melting pot" level, which was an attempt to present the process of consolidation on a spontaneous, purely liberal basis, ignoring history, culture, language and psychology of the state-ethnic group, were firmly rejected. Finally, on the basis of long and intense negotiations, the consensus which was reached between the multiculturalist and national trends of nation building, the Doctrine of national unity, was signed by President N. Nazarbaev. It identified the main objectives for further development of Kazakhstan's society based on the achievement of real equality of rights and freedoms of the Kazakh nation, and into it integrated national minorities in Kazakhstan, and the format creating the mutual recognition and protection of the nation and the minorities (diasporas). So today, undemocratic attitudes and multiculturalism in interethnic relations in the country is grinding to a halt. In this way, harmony within the Kazakh nation is achieved, and gradually the nation is developing an understanding of the perspective balance of the country's ethno-cultural and socio-cultural development, presenting opportunities for citizens of the state to define and articulate independently the preferences of a national and state character, to put the ideology of Kazakh statehood and the Kazakh a socio-cultural phenomenon into practice.

Today, state-owned mass media, television and radio are more and more involved in the translation of modern concepts, trends and principles of state and nation building. This unitarian understanding of the nation which is actually beginning to recognize the relevant institutions of the state, affects the efficiency of the state's counteraction against present challenges and threats, and no longer threatens preservation of a disintegration potential of the state along ethnic lines which it had previously, at the dawn of becoming independent.

Thus, emerging democratism of interethnic relations, characteristic of a multi-sociocultural form of modernism, that is, **civic-oriented multi-socioculturalism**, begins to embody one of the main motives for the existence and development of a young Kazakh statehood, because it counteracts against the preservation of unequal relations between the Kazakh nation and the diasporas not integrated in it.

V. So, the peculiarity of the present political situation in Kazakhstan consists in the struggle of parts of the Kazakh political elite, headed by the President, who are convinced of an evolutionary political modernization and a broad stratum of our fellow citizens, expressing the will of the "collective unconscious" in the stabilization of the achieved status of the political system of the state, and not in the struggle of the government and the political opposition which, in general, is marginalized and so far does not represent true parameters and development goals of the Republic of Kazakhstan.

This is not simply a struggle between liberals and conservatives, because, on the one hand, an authoritarian, rather than an administrative form, apart from its historical origins and contemporary personal parameters, basically and indeed ultimately, is needed only for the education of the owner and the citizen under conditions of creating themselves traditions of private property and democracy, under conditions of a ruling Asian paternalistic view on the development of society, and, dominant in the minds of most of our fellow citizens, Eastern tradition of governance. In this respect, the President of the Republic of Kazakhstan is universalistic: being, in fact, the head of the democratic state (building the formal institutions and saturate them with real democracy), in his appearance he remains, in the political hierarchy of the Eastern tradition, a "khagan" which is exempt from fulfilling the duties which ordinary "horde members" themselves are not going to prepare and, moreover, he was asked to stay in office until 2020. In this consists, as a matter of fact, the traditional meaning of a referendum initiated by a group of our fellow citizens, to extend the powers of the First President of Kazakhstan N. Nazarbaev. And, in this context, the idea of a referendum is a result of the "collective unconscious" of most "horde members".

The reason for the referendum most probably lies in a deep national tradition of respect and an adherence of the people to the institutions of supreme power which ensure the overall safety of society and its stability in terms of the functioning of all its institutions. Due to banning a rapid and uncontrolled entry of a, for the Kazakhs, new tradition of personal political freedom (which broke down one day through the uncontrolled "glasnost" of the USSR) and a liberal system of rights and freedoms (facing systemic difficulties of its implementation in Europe), they never before existed in a systemic form in the Kazakhs social order, if we recall that the Kazakh statehood until the 20th century was actually a horde's statehood, and in the 20th century a control-administrative (it was even called totalitarian) statehood, the vast majority of ordinary citizens (including, of course, the elites), however, do not even realize all the consequences of such a step, just protect their deep mental basis of life by suitable for this, new, convenient for them, even if formal democratic methods.

They choose or agree with the elites' choice of that method of legitimization of power which to them seems the most simple and straightforward. And even the president cannot influence this choice which has a collective, mass character, even if it became so bureaucratized, by simply not risking dissolving parliament and appointing it at the next election. But for this, even the order of parliamentary elections has to be broken which, of course, is not wanted, keeping in mind the criticism of international organizations and countries.

Therefore, a spontaneous idea which was essentially an unconscious objective idea, was easily laid in the bed of an undeveloped democratic society's mind, and mixed thoughts and meanings of rationally understood, but objectively unachievable standards of democratic development. This is the "collective unconscious", and it has become for the opposition as well as for the authorities something that has to be seriously learned by studying the ethnic culture and psychology of the Kazakhs which we have forgotten to understand during the Soviet Union.The famous work of the outstanding Kazakh scientist, lawyer, and academic S. Zimanov, "Bukeev horde", in this respect, shows and reflects the deeply philosophical mentality accumulated in the historical memory and institutionalized in an appropriate manner, of the Kazakh ethnicity as the most consistent nomadic culture as regards traditions and, along with this, it demonstrates classic examples of the functioning of the institutions of statehood, law, and legal consciousness of the Kazakhs of that and, of course, of earlier times.

The traditions of the military-democratic governance and ethical and socio-political hierarchy which embodied the ideas of a fair horde-state - the realization of the **celestial** Otan (Fatherland), firmly formed and implanted the most cherished moral and ethical codes of nomadic ethnicities of Eurasia which could not occur in the conditions of formatting a modern Kazakh democracy (statehood) which in terms of substance stops to be nomadic and steppe, but military in mentality and form (authoritarian democracy or democracy, developing inside, within the framework and boundaries of tradition of respect of institutions of power, authority power).

Besides, the link of authority and tradition, and these are very close concepts as to their origin, is straightforward and natural, because the authority of tradition or the tradition of authority is expressed in the objective ability of the authorities to reproduce the power of its institutions and symbols. Since in the Turks' world view, the idea of statehood ranked first, but the state itself is considered a sacred entity, the nation, experiencing the gain of sovereignty and the establishment of an own statehood, this coming true of his own dreams, additional opportunities to develop their own identity, to strengthen their own subjective characteristics, and functions for a deeper and broader self-identification in the future. And in this respect, for example, it is necessary to rethink the modern understanding of the Kazakh state with all its democratic opinions as the **horde** state, not in the sense of tyranny and the denial of private property (at this moment, it does not make sense to speak about it), but in the sense of cultural tradition of the steppe, nomadic, military democracy, and a deep metaphysical validity of the goals and tasks of the national state. The authorities in the country, where for centuries the traditions of worship were put together, its sacredness, based on the philosophical, methodological and ideological, syncretic unity of the nomads, is and was no opposition in the Western view and understanding of the meaning of the word. Power in the East is either there or is not. The question is posed exactly this way. The rationalism of democracy which divides the rights and freedoms amongst all in equal shares, is just not always universally accepted as cultural and ethical traditions of Eastern societies. This fully applies to Kazakhstan.

So, any idea of sovereignty, national revival and statehood of the Kazakhs without this deeply philosophical history of their national spirit, without a genetically polished formation of national statehood, defining in a concentrated form the essence of their social existence, would be artificial and would collapse under the pressure of recent events, hitherto unknown phenomena. Only eating life-giving sap of the deepest and oldest forms of the phenomenology of the national spirit, the idea of sovereignty, the idea of national revival and the latest statehood of the Kazakhs will find genuine and not fictitious (fabricated in the form of an artificial appearance of an adapted and fitted national idea) basis, will find the true ground of the substantive national ideologemes (strategemes). Exactly this metaphysical, historically and culturally mediated, deeply personal way to the community was formed and expressed in a universal form of statehood of that time – the **horde state**. By the way, this tradition also up to this day defines the cultural foundations of governance in Kazakhstan, where the Residence of the President of the Republic of Kazakhstan, for example, is called, as everyone knows, "Ak Orda" ("White Horde").

Therefore, democracy should not be overemphasized in Eastern society, it cannot be implemented immediately without breaking the cultural foundations and traditions of the nation, but it can be implemented as a process of evolutionary, gradual democratization, not excluding its administrative, centralized and authoritarian functions. As Deng Xiaoping said, expressing in this way the incorporation of market relations and democracy in the essence of life of the Chinese nation, "crossing the river by feeling the stones".

On the other hand, the command-administrative form, as the will of the political elite itself, is not able to evolve towards a democratic form: impulses to the evolution of a political system towards democracy usually arise from "below". But lest this bottom-up process prevent a relapse in the evolution of the forms of a young Kazakh statehood, the President began to establish not a traditional military-democratic political model of governance, oriented towards, figuratively speaking, the creation of a horde, a "nation-army", and the political model of governance oriented at the formation of a new elite that would ensure the functioning of the mechanism of transfer and continuity of power. Today when this political model formally works, the need to fill it with new content of governance requires a new, already more universal political initiative "from above". The point of it is to determine the parameters of the transformation of the old, less efficient authoritarian-democratic (political) structure of the state and governance (power) into a new, more effective. This political initiative should provide an evolutionary and temporal extent of this transformation, as well as a way to institutionalize the new administrative-democratic (cultural-democratic), political structure of power. Here, the main issue of the transfer of power is not a question of legitimacy (power always finds a way to be legitimate), but a question of continuity of policy, the provision and implementation of which is the most important and most difficult of the young Kazakh statehood, where the presidential and parliamentary elections which are conducted on a regular basis, will institutionalize a new, more responsible and more specific form of statehood.

Second, statehood, or as we call it, democracy, as a form of governing and a way of co-existence of cultural and historical individuals, in general, makes sense as a process in which an authoritarian, administrative component in every new moment of the present is in equilibrium with the liberal component.

Therefore, in a state where the sacralized institution of supreme power, let's say, the institution of the presidency, regards the people, on a subconscious level, as a unified army (or as a unified working collective body) which aims to meet the tasks and goals this institution faces, in proportion to the development of the economy, the social sphere of the state and its democratic institutions and instruments which provide the basis of social equality and partnership, the military-democratic and even imperial (imperialistic), absolutist manifestation of spiritual leadership which denies all dissent, will be transformed from a supra-constitutional structure and status of political power to a constitutional, civil-democratic, cultural-democratic structure, supported by the spiritual leadership of the First President. As a rule, the provision of such a transformation falls to the lot of the head of the country. Defining the parameters of the functioning of public and political spheres in the vital activity of the country, in the subsequent postwar-democratic, cultural-democratic period is also the task of the First President of the Republic of Kazakhstan, the Spiritual Leader of the Nation. He sets the historical format of state and social development, controlling the course of its deployment and implementation exclusively with cultural and spiritual means. The next president, subject to such an algorithm and the speed of political modernization, is likely to remain only the head of the executive branch, blessed with deep metaphysical foundations of the historical person of the First President, the Leader of the Nation. Therefore, the President, without imposing his election on the elites, without forcing to obey his will mindlessly and uncritically, demonstrated commitment to the statehood model which is based on the evolutionary political modernization and which supposes a gradual, based on the preparedness of political institutions and instruments, establishment of democratic foundations in the vital activity of our state and society.

Another thing is that the next president must be a successor not only by kinship, by blood, but, above all, in spirit and in his power and strength. The succession of political, economic and social policy means that the next president must not only to the same extent, but much more harmoniously, if it could be expressed like this, act in this fundamental field. The scope and format of the philosophical understanding of the country's mission in the 21st century, defined by the first President of the Republic of Kazakhstan, can neither be reduced, nor narrowed, because the country will inevitably start to lag behind the gathered momentum of development, format and scope of the movement, and stays on the way of civilisation thrust. Consequently, first of all it is necessary to maintain the highest level of thinking and understanding the problems and tasks of the state and the society which has been reached by the first President of the Republic of Kazakhstan. The universalism of thinking of the First President which necessarily has to be maintained at a high level, consists in acting consistently and harmoniously in a traditional, so to speak "hordal", and in a new, democratic dimension of life, in order that these dimensions do not disperse, and gradually interlock and penetrate into each other. In this respect, the next president, for the nation and its mentality, has to establish himself in the mentality and in the historical and cultural traditions of the Kazakhs, first of all, as khagan, as khan, in order to be in the following able to establish himself as a "constitutional Khagan" - as the president of the republic. In this regard, by far not all members of the political elite and the entourage of the First President have such a universalistic understanding and thinking. Consequently, government technocrats and national companies and holdings, like sophisticated policymakers, who do not have experience in governing the administrative units of the country, in fact, cannot be ranked among the cohort of potential successors of the First President. Only a person truly included in the traditional and, simultaneously, in the new democratic hierarchy of the Kazakhs can become the political successor of the First President of the Republic of Kazakhstan.

VI. The fight for human rights in various countries cannot be identified with the fight for the elimination of social inequality, and, consequently, must rather be understood as an element of stability of the social system of the state, balancing opposite social trends (wealth and poverty, dynamism and conservatism, democratization and centralization, etc.) for a long-term and sustainable social progress which is expressed in the harmonic (consistent, mutually complementary), if you will, ethical and aesthetic nature of the combination of personal, collective and public interests, and the appropriate nature of an individual's life.[36] The tradition to adhere to the public demand of state control is the same objective aspect of any more or less sovereign statehood in ancient times, as the tradition of "demand for one's rights" in a democracy.

Now, the moral responsibility of the individual towards the society under conditions of a post-industrial development, when the very foundations of social antagonism are destroyed (class inequality), becomes a dominant political factor. And if the culture and moral of the nation get along with the authoritarian institutions (more than administrative, even military) of democracy, if such an authoritarian model implements basic social rights (labour, housing, ...) and, only in accordance with this, gradually expands the scope of personal freedom, then demanding even more from this nation still does not seem worth it, if you do not try to become the enemy of the state.

Educating the citizen as an owner of political rights and freedoms in this vein is possibly the process of an approach of the "Eastern" mental orientation and the "Western" democratic tradition.

The Kazakhs will not achieve this without presenting themselves as a horde-nation-army uniting general civil values, without having, in respect to the internal structure, principles of democracy – a democracy of a national philosophy of strict disciplines, military discipline and, therefore, not having a deep ideological and metaphysical ("hordal") kernel of state governance.

On the other hand, the horde as a principle of Kazakh statehood, as a source of national power, conceived as a universalist, metaphysical, deeper form of a modernizing Kazakh statehood, not denying or disparaging modern democratic standards (as in fact it was in former times, with the first Turks, and later, with the first Kazakh khans), but gradually, in accordance with the development of private property relations and civil initiatives leading to prosperity and restoration of places of nomadic culture and philosophy in the world, is able to help identifying the role and importance of the Kazakhs as philosophical and spiritual unifiers of representatives of different ethnicities in their own country, and as initiators of the new multi-sociocultural identity and spatio-temporal (meaningful) security structure in Eurasia, and along with this, in the whole modern human civilisation.

The phenomenon of spiritual, social and political leadership, being a modern interpretation of leadership, first in animals, in the biological world, and later in an imperial (hordal) spiritual phenomenon, in a transition period, under the conditions of the development of democracy within the authoritarianism, within such a traditional "imperial" relation of power to the opposition and leadership position of the Head of State in relation to other institutions of the political system, of course, will undergo changes. In proportion to the development of the economy, the state and its democratic institutions and instruments which provide the basis of social equality and partnership, the military-democratic and even monarchical, imperial (imperialistic), and absolutist manifestation of spiritual leadership which denies any dissent, will be transformed from a constitutional-democratic military (authoritarian-democratic) structure of political power to a constitutional civil-democratic, cultural-democratic spiritual leadership. Through such a cultural and spiritual leadership of democratic nature, by the way, not only opposition relations to power, but the imperial relation of power to the opposition, will be transformed by not all developed countries of the world, but only by universal states. The synthesis, the synergy of a deeper channel of unity of society and the state, will allow such countries to fully call themselves universal. So, deeply metaphysical personalities will interact and the need for recognition will be carried out in the service of common goals and ideals, and not in opposing these general goals and ideals by individuals or their communities (the opposition in the old sense of the word) these common goals and ideals. As Yoko Ono "learned with the love" of John Lennon "to see the good in bad", also Kazakhstan's way of an authoritarian (administrative military) democracy should subtly and humanely, diligently and patiently educate and teach, but not tame and force, all to see the development of a culture of democracy within authoritarianism, a culture of universalism, by means of the Eastern universal tradition.

An education by the use of philosophy, ethics, ideology, as well as education by the use of hierarchy of values - this is the way of development of the Kazakh democracy on the trajectory of its evolution from military to social, and thus, deep metaphysical state, to a new, globally conscious state of universality. This path concentrated in time and space like a compressed projection of the development of nomadic mankind, represents itself as a model of a dynamic modern social development, merging and combining within itself different conflicting and sometimes contradictory traditions. Otherwise, democracy as a way of organizing universal human existence will not be understood as part of one of the ways of life, as one of the basic and the main forms of social life. A true democracy cannot be built (reached), if its rationalizations are all the time limited which oppose the rights of children, for example, to the rights of parents. Liberal democracy, in this respect, much more destroys the institution family, than Tengrianism ("shamanism", as it was nicknamed by the same Westerners and Slavophils) or Islam, since legal individualism is the first destroyer of the old indigene (maybe genuine or universal?) family, marital ethics. The big family of "undemocratic Muslims" and the little family of "democratic Christians" long ago became metaphors of time.

Therefore, **the phenomenon of democracy can be understood and realized only as part of a world-wide, human-wide universality of life, in which Eastern metaphysical and Asian universal statist traditions are the main aspects.**

Because of this, it makes no sense to speak of democracy in Kazakhstan in a purely Western sense, since neither private ownership initiatives, nor free state-policies together with the civil societies have been implemented since the time of Solon. The institutions of democracy in Kazakhstan are still not in an adult state, though this year marks the 20th anniversary of independence, they have developed under the auspices of the former military-democratic "horde" tradition, the bearer of which unconsciously is our entire nation. And therefore, from a political point of view, it does not matter, if an election or a referendum will take place. The result is foregone long before it.

For the President, whose spiritual importance as leader of the nation is increasing day by day, the ethical point of the election (which is why he issued a decree canceling the referendum) is important, because in reality he is the engine of political modernization and would not play in his own hands (his self-respect forbids unethical action), the format and course of which, as the situation shows, can neither be increased, nor accelerated artificially. And hopefully, someday, his view on what is happening will become dominant and it will be shared the 3,6 million signatories to initiate a referendum. Here in this format, we believe, it is necessary to interpret the question of a referendum to extend the powers of the First President of the Republic of Kazakhstan till 2020.

In lieu of a conclusion

In over 20 years of independence, Kazakhstan has established itself as a democratically-oriented and, at the same time, institutionally developing state. In this short, as to historical standards, period, the country achieved to get far away from totalitarian and purely authoritarian forms of government and to build the necessary foundations for a democratic political system, to create a basically market-based model of economic development, to establish prerequisites for the formation of a tolerant civil society and to define for itself its main directions of development. The three directions of Kazakhstan's concept of development are economic reform, political transformation and democratization of the society which gradually and steadily become one integrated form of strengthening and developing Kazakh statehood and nation-building. Meanwhile, as to developing state sovereignty, they face also new tasks, new challenges and global threats emerge, and to be aware of them is our duty to the country and its citizens, to the history and future.

Aygul′ Solov′eva, The Civil Society is an Indicator of Democratic Progress and an Effective Partner of the Government Concerning the Country's Social Modernization Processes

Formation story: Since its first years of independence Kazakhstan has adopted a course to build a state in which the civil society plays the most important and significant role. The degree of development reflects the progress made in the field of democratic reforms, and the non-governmental sector which is a full participant in this process, serves as a distinctive indicator of occurring changes. NGO activities cover a wide range of social problems, as called-for by the society and also individuals. October 2000 can be considered the official date of the political recognition of citizens' associations (NGOs) in Kazakhstan, when President N. Nazarbaev in his message to the people of Kazakhstan "Towards a free, effective and secure society" mentioned the term NGO (non-governmental public organization). In this message it was pointed out for the first time that „non-governmental public organizations already today play a great role in Kazakhstan, both in law-enforcement and realization of special group interests of the population and social stabilization of the society".

In his message „On main issues of domestic and foreign policy for the year 2003"the President gave a direct order: „The government also has to initiate the development of **a law on the status and rights of NGOs**". As a primary issue in the field of "state-building and democratization of the society" "the legal introduction of a mechanism of state social order for services of non-governmental organization" was designated.

Those basic principles and governmental policies to support non-governmental organizations have been enshrined in the adopted **Concept of State Support of NGOs** of the Republic of Kazakhstan, in accordance with the Government decree of the Republic of Kazakhstan No. 85 of 2002. The ideas embodied in this Concept formed the basis for the **Program of State Support of NGOs for 2003-2005**. Targeted public funding of NGO projects started in 2005 with adopting the law of the Republic of Kazakhstan "On state social order".

The **"Concept for the development of civil society in the Republic of Kazakhstan for 2006-2011" (hereinafter - the Concept)** which was developed by the working group of the State commission for development and concretization of the program of democratic reforms in Kazakhstan and approved on 25 July, 2006, by a presidential decree, was a significant development in 2006, and the fundamental document which triggered the dynamic development of NGOs. This concept was the most comprehensive and important in terms of the subject and the inclusion of various public institutions and defined the main directions for the development of civil society institutions and the possibilities of realizing civil initiatives. As a fundamental and strategic document it became the basis for the development of targeted programs, for the adoption of legislative and other normative legal acts aimed at creating favorable conditions for the functioning of civil society institutions, and also served as the basis for a social partnership of authorities, businesses and NGOs.

The objectives stated in the Concept are achieved through clearly outlined basic principles concerning the activity of state bodies and the development prospects of the "third sector" which are reflected **in the final third phase. Its realization will start in 2011:**

- The development of civil society institutions will be of a systemic character. Introducing corrective measures in the relationships with businesses and state bodies to optimize the cooperation with each other.
- Publication of annual reports and conduct annual hearings on problems concerning the development of Kazakhstan's society.
- The development of civil society which is an ongoing process, based on changes of public needs, on trends of world development and on the challenges of the time.

One of the very important things this document particularly focuses on is the identification of the main ways and mechanisms of how to implement tasks which significantly enhance the national program of democratic reforms. In addition, any subject of civil society is embodied in the sections related to its activities. The trends and principles of civil society development in our country which are defined in the concept, as well as outlined objectives, made it possible to establish the tasks aimed at an implementation in three stages.

At present, the legal regulation of the activities of the non-profit sector in Kazakhstan is realized by the Laws of the Republic of Kazakhstan: "On public associations", "On non-for-profit organizations", "On political parties", "On trade unions", "On freedom of religion and religious associations". Certain rules are included in the Civil Code of the Republic of Kazakhstan (General Part), "On state registration of legal entities and record registration of affiliate companies and representative offices", "On state of emergency", "On the national security of the Republic of Kazakhstan", as well as laws governing certain types of professional associations (i.e. the Law of the Republic of Kazakhstan "On advocacy" and others).

The legal foundation, established for the existence of the non-profit sector during the time of independence:

- Formulated status laws regulating the main organizational-legal types of NGOs;
- Established system of tax incentives and preferences for the activities of NGOs;
- Adopted and widely applied in practice Law "On state social order".

Positive changes made:

- Lifted ban on state financing of public associations in the Constitution of the Republic of Kazakhstan;
- Funds received by non-governmental organizations (NGOs) under agreement of the state social order are exempt from VAT and corporate income tax;
- Ratified the International Covenants on Social, Economic and Cultural Rights and on Civil and Political Rights. The first Optional Protocol was signed.

In the conclusion of the International Centre for Not-for-Profit Law which operates in all CIS countries, it is noted that concerning issues of tax laws it is one of the best for Kazakhstan's NGOs. However, this does not mean that all problems have been successfully solved and the legislation of Kazakhstan concerning NGOs does not need to be improved, but it should only be matched to its nearest neighbours. It is necessary **to approach and orientate towards the most economically developed countries in the world, not only in terms of regulation of business, but also in terms of non-profit interests**. It was revealed that a high level of mistrust on the part of the state towards NGOs and their consideration as a risk area which is characteristic of some countries of the former Soviet Union, reflect some of these existing trends inherent in them and lead to unreasonable confrontation.

Current situation: The speed of the nonprofit sector's development in our country shows an obvious increase, according to quantitative, as well as to qualitative indicators, and also in terms of geographical coverage and areas of activity. According to official statistical data, currently there are more than 40 thousand NGOs in Kazakhstan, but it should be mentioned that they also include entities which cannot be definitely identified as public associations. This is due to the fact that, according to the legislation, also organizations with "state property" are considered NGOs which, within a period of 3 to 5 years hold a stable share rate of 45-43% of non-governmental.

Furthermore, if you take into account that among the NGOs are many so-called "sleeping" organizations with zero activity, and a great number of them have a rather short "life span" which stops more practically than legally and is accompanied by registrations of new ones, then these numbers will decrease dramatically. This assumption is confirmed by a study conducted by the Civil Alliance of Kazakhstan which shows that 48.7% of organizations have a short activity period, 25.8% exist 6 to 9 years, while "long-living" organizations, created back in the 90s, account for 21.8%.

Compared to the survey of 2007, the attitude of the population to the areas of NGOs' activities showed that the range of the services provided is growing and is becoming more and more diverse. Experts point to the predominance of operational and informational, and to a lesser extent, of educational services, and also to the reduction of research services. Many experts, representatives of NGOs and target groups tend to believe that in general the capacities of mass media in the country provide for the information needs of NGOs.

At the same time, many of them think that, in future, the area which allows intensively expanding the existing channels of constant information together with modern sources of feedback for a broad awareness of the population about their activities has to become the main and basic direction.

Many of those asked, and especially members of NGOs, are of the opinion that several types of mass media should be set up by NGOs themselves or their organizations. Setting up such publications and magazines, in which the scientific and applied issues of the activity of NGOs should be reflected, received little support. Respondents noted that the approach of Kazakh NGOs to concrete and certain types of activity gained a stable character, due to the high demands of the society for them. On the scale of activity, NGOs are more often associated with the youth, followed in descending order by public organizations dealing with problems of people with disabilities, gender issues, a healthy lifestyle, families, children, education and others.

In general, the evaluation of NGO activities in the community also significantly increased in a positive way, characterized by a list of standing orders for the products of their activities. It was revealed that in addition to government agencies at various levels, major clients for NGOs are various international organizations and funds, some of the responses indicate a wider range of clients, sponsors and investors. There is a tendency that when domestic organizations and business companies, are also interested in their services, other funding recipients are represented to a much lesser extent. This analysis clearly demonstrates that the state was and still is the largest client and financier of Kazakhstan's NGOs, and prevails as partner and beneficiary of public organizations. There is an obvious increase in positive evaluation of NGOs from almost all respondents, a fact which could be called unprecedented. For two years, the average evaluation of the functions and conditions relating to the activities of NGOs improved by an average of 10 points.

Despite the positive trends in the development of NGOs in Kazakhstan, a number of challenges and obstacles still hinder the promotion of their role in society. The project for the introduction of changes and additions to the law "On the social order" which was discussed for some considerable time in public, requires serious and conceptual amendments which may solve problems associated with its implementation more successful. Compared with the survey of 2007, the demand of members of NGOs and citizens engaged in the third sector to ensure greater public participation in tender procedures grew. According to the respondents' evaluation, gaps and shortcomings which exclude negative phenomena in the formation of orders and realization of competitive tenders, have not been eliminated over the past two years. It is noted that no new effective methods of combating corruption have been built, and many of the proposals of NGOs that contribute to the improvement of their implementation procedures have not received support. Therefore, compared to the 2007 survey, the confidence in the transparency and fairness of their results, especially the confidence of experts, declined.

The above-stated notwithstanding, all groups having participated in the survey, generally evaluating the practice of introducing a system of a state social order, recognized it as a fact that it had a large and positive impact on the enhancement of NGOs' activity opportunities. The respondents stated that consequences of its introduction were the expansion of social assistance coverage for the population, the establishment of cooperation between NGOs and government agencies, the opportunity to effectively solve urgent problems of the society, the emergence of additional sources of funding for the third sector. Some of the respondents clearly expressed their opinion about the loss of independence of NGOs due to government funding. Other contrary findings were the independence of NGOs from funding by international organizations. A survey among employees and members of NGOs, revealed that the majority of them deny the possibility of the alleged misuse of funds or abuse. However, according to some, this phenomenon, objectively, also occurs in the practice of adopting the social order. In the latest survey the topics for the state social order which reflect the urgent problems of Kazakhstan's society, were more clearly outlined. First of all, they deal with questions of assistance to socially vulnerable groups of society, fight against corruption and drugs, environmental protection, human rights, gender projects, and youth problems. At the same time, almost all groups of respondents ascribed education for active citizenship, patriotism and political modernization to the primary tasks.

Based on the foregoing, the non-governmental sector of Kazakhstan believes that to reach and fully realize the tasks identified in the Concept **it is necessary to completely and cardinally renew the legislative basis**. **Recommendations of Round Table participants, conferences and other dialogue platforms clearly demonstrate that the society is concerned about the inadequacy of the** current **legislative framework** and the processes taking place in society.

Prospects for Development: It is symbolic that the achievements defined in the last stage of the concept and gaps tolerated during the time of its implementation will be discussed at the **fifth Civic Forum**, in the year of celebrating **20 years of Independence of Kazakhstan**.

The main theme of the first and for subsequent Civil Fora is a partnership of **"State-Business-NGO"**, therefore it has to be considered from a position of reflecting various types of legal relations which it includes. For the purpose of better understanding the indicated, it is important to broaden and separate first of all the relationships between the **state and society**, then **businesses and NGO**s. In the **first case**, by determining their **evaluation criteria** in accordance with the declared intentions which are outlined in the Concept, chief among them, for state use, has to become a "public benefit" from the activities of one or another organization. The application of this criterion makes it possible to determine, whether NGOs are suitable to receive government support and to what extent, (and not the kind of activities of NGOs, such as the provision of services or the promotion of interests). Depending on the extent to which the NGO serves a "public benefit", as defined in the **law "On Public Benefit"** (or equivalent legislation – i.e. tax laws), organizations providing services (service), as well as organizations advocating specific interests or ideas (advocacy) can have the **right** to receive direct and indirect state funding. The above listed organizations which generally provide services to citizens and qualify themselves through and fall under the concept of "publically beneficial activity", may fulfill a publically beneficial activity which deserves state support. Based on the criterion of public benefit, NGOs are usually subdivided into two types:

- Public benefit organizations (PBOs)
- Mutual benefit organizations (MBOs

The difference between the PBO and the MBO usually manifests itself in determining the appropriate level of indirect government support (i.e. tax incentives). In the case of direct support the main question is whether there is a **legislative basis** which **would prescribe** which types of NGOs are suitable for direct state support and for what kind of support. In the absence of legal regulations, the state itself takes the decision and often do not provide financial support on the basis of NGOs' performed functions (i.e. services, advocacy or mutual support), but on the basis of whether the activity of NGOs **helps to implement state policies**. With this in mind, the government decides that a NGO is engaged in any activity that is worthy of state support - for example, in Hungary even self-help organizations - such as "Alcoholics Anonymous" – receive public funding, since, thanks to its activity, the organization promotes the improvement of the whole society. Such an approach is justified, as far as the tasks and the request of the Head of State, arising in terms of priority and importance from his annual messages to the people of Kazakhstan and from the "Strategy 2020", even more aim the whole society concerning the application of joint efforts for their effective realization. However, without a clear legislative consolidation it would be difficult to enable the third sector to fulfill tasks outlined in it. **First**, education, healthcare and the social component. **Second**, rural development, micro-crediting, employment and self-employment, improving the housing and communal services system, and even the IDF, in which the concept of socially important services is already specified. **Third**, public monitoring, combating and preventing corruption, as well as the prevention of offences, together with crisis, adaptation and rehabilitation centers, also for repatriates, etc. When considering them as a whole and their interdependence, it is, first of all, necessary to define the term social service which has to be realized through tendering procedures by a state procurement system, though, the term NGO which we often use, is defined only in the law on social order and only for the aims of its implementation. Under the bill, introduced by the Government, this may be a way out, but subsequently it might also lead to the stagnation of the process. In this connection, the **division of these terms** to build a **broader** funding base deserves one's attention. The field of public relations requires a broader and more comprehensive approach, taking into account the level and prospects of its development based on the existing situation.

Therefore, it is necessary to improve the bill **"On state social order"** in combination with other laws, including the **tax code**. In addition, perhaps also one of the priorities in the near future will be the question of **local self-government,** upon **which** the **President** touched at the last **extended** meeting of the **Government**, because it is **directly connected** with the public sector. In this connection, interaction, built on the **confidence of the local authorities,** should be carried out by entering into contractual **agreements with NGOs** for the provision of social services, as it is done all over the world. The process of decentralization of power for the benefit of local authorities will lead to a transfer of **public services** in certain **essential** areas to the local community. It is obvious that many of the services that used to be in the portfolio of the state, will force local authorities to set up again NGOs or public associations, although, the existing legislative **budget constraints** will impede this process significantly. Governments and intergovernmental organizations of developed countries have developed various, including also new, funding mechanisms for public organizations which i.e. also include the provision of grants to NGOs. Given that a "partnership" implies a wide range of organizational measures and contractual mutual

Relationships, then for receiving assistance it needs the most diverse laws which reflect all aspects of such a partnership and give reasons for its creation. The currently existing legislative basis, not accidentally is subject to criticism by NGOs and raises justified doubts, whether it is possible to fully realize the settled tasks on this basis. Not many volunteer social activists supported the claim that through the activity of associations established by the citizens, they get a real opportunity to have a targeted influence on public life and state policies, based on their perceptions and beliefs. It is stated that the reason for this is the **lack of le-**

gal consolidation in accordance with the views of civil society and the formal attitude to it, and also the **compulsory registration of subjects of non-governmental organizations** which does not correspond to international standards.

This topic was brought up in the National Action Plan and there are two suggestions how to solve it: on the one hand, by adopting a separate law on the right of citizens to form associations (i.e. as the experience of the Republic of Poland shows), on the other hand, by an appeal to the Constitutional Council, for subjects provided by law, with a request for interpretation of paragraph 1 of Article 23 of the Constitution of the Republic of Kazakhstan, regarding the part of citizens' rights to freedom of association in all its forms, including both formal and informal organizations.

The Fifth Civil Forum will serve as a distinctive discussion of the outcomes of 20 years of independence in Kazakhstan, in which the role and importance of the third sector should be assessed through direct and indirect criteria, not only based on quantitative, but also on qualitative parameters, reflecting the contribution to the country's socio-economic development. The special status of the non-profit sector makes it possible to make measurements on the basis of its contribution to the country's GDP through the definition of core indicators which characterize the role of the nonprofit sector. This approach is already widely implemented in other countries with a developed democracy, and the use of their expertise in solving social problems, associated with the use of public funds, increase their efficiency in social services. When it is taken into account that the non-profit sector is an efficient **provider of socially important services** which distinguishes itself not only in the ability to promptly respond to the needs of the population and to new social challenges and problems, but also in low administrative costs, then maybe it would be possible to solve current problems of the society more efficiently. These are issues like ensuring equal opportunities for disabled people, searching for new processes for the placement of children left without parental care, preventing domestic violence, and assisting refugees and IDPs, as well as, protecting the rights of citizens for a congenial atmosphere, social rehabilitation, a set of problems associated with territorial self-government, improvement of the housing and communal services system, microcrediting of self-employed and rural residents etc.

Perhaps, in practice this is technically not an insurmountable obstacle for the activity of a wide range of organizations, such as the various clubs (yard clubs, chess clubs, etc.), but in strict compliance with the legislation, it may be a significant **administrative barrier** for the **performance of useful public** functions which are basic prerequisites for any representative democracy. At first glance, for anybody the norm may seem not that significant against the background of other global socio-economic and political problems, but it is necessary to strictly adhere to the basic norms of international law which guarantees citizens the right to associate with other citizens in order to create public associations.

Non-governmental organizations, the name already reflects the descriptive message about the relative independence from the state and the fact that they are self-defining formations of citizens that can have an **effective influence on the authorities and are able to articulate socially significant interests** in the social and state systems, need the implementation of funding for putting their activities into practice.

The main sources of such funds for NGOs are entrance membership fees and voluntary contributions, donations, also in the form of property via transfer of ownership. Grants, revenues from the participation in and implementation of activities, income derived from legal business; other revenues not prohibited by law, as well as in the form of direct public funding in terms of the state social order, are also widely used in international practice.

The **second** item in the chain of the subjects of the **Civic Forum** is that mutual **business** relations **and NGOs** should proceed from the fundamental principle which is set out in the Explanatory Notes to the basic principles. The activities of NGOs are characterized as not-profit-orientated, and as giving them the possibility of seeking donations of cash or goods. Material assistance of this kind, together with income from economic activities, is vital to NGOs to carry out their defined tasks.

Special hope for reinvestment of profits for the realization of social, economic and cultural objectives was placed in social-entrepreneurial corporations. However, until now NGOs in Kazakhstan have not felt the impact of this institution when it comes to solving the problems of society. Currently, the process of creating a culture of philanthropy and sponsorship goes on with high speed, to which the Zhezkazgan Forum on businesses' social responsibility, in which also the Head of State participated, gave a strong impetus.

Well-established companies with a stable development have already widely implemented corporate social responsibility of businesses within the scope of the Global Compact's 10 principles. **Large companies**, mostly **local economic mainstays**, implement socially relevant projects most effective and most widely, **but** the **implementation** of projects **through NGOs are fragmental** and **not systematic**. In principle, efforts of NGOs aim at promoting systematic and comprehensive improvements in the legislation. Proposals made in the tax code just might be an incentive **to enter the field of charity, without the development** and adoption of new laws. That is exactly the reason why the concept didn't specifically indicate the title of new laws, namely in order to eliminate obstacles for the modernization of existing legislation. In addition, the authors of the Concept wanted to avoid that in the future it is not seen as a guideline to adopt a new law with this or that name, without filling it with relevant content.

The main purpose of the development of a socially useful activity is to focus on a system for encouraging individuals and legal entities which voluntarily make a decision on donations which involves the reflection of the norms of the above listed bills. Furthermore, sponsors and philanthropists may be individuals, but also private businesses, as well as other organizations.

The mechanism of providing assistance is determined by the donor – by the direct beneficiary or through non-profit organization or religious associations which are created and operate in our country in accordance with different legal standards. Furthermore, the prerequisite for this should be a formal system to provide all forms of assistance, recording and reporting of its expenditure for objectives and tasks stipulated by law.

The desire of NGOs to get away from the declarative effect on providing incentives for charity and philanthropy, is conceptually to take a look at this issue by means of amending the new tax code and, as a result, the law "On non-commercial organizations" in terms of granting tax deductions for given donations in the form of cash and property to increase the rate for philanthropy from 3 to 5%. The **introduction of the concept of a sponsor** for the purposes of taxation and the establishment of benefits concerning the payment of individual income tax for individuals, who send in donations, has been unsuccessful.

The government's interpretation that the **incentives for philanthropy** are of fiscal nature and should **be reflected** in a basic **fiscal law** of the country - the Tax Code, whether it would allow to **correspond** with its exceptional status and **contribute** to a charitable activity as **part of a general culture** of the Kazakh society which in the **U.S. reached 70%** of the donations from individuals, and **54%** in the **UK**.

The International practice of public funding of NGOs is executed mainly in two ways.

Through direct support. Allocated funds are transferred from the public budget of the central or local level directly to the organization, i.e. included in the budget expenditures for the given fiscal year. This does not mean that the funds are directly transferred from the account of the State Treasury to those of NGOs - as a rule, they pass through various government agencies (ministries, state and other funds, etc.).

Through indirect support. Indirect financial support does not involve the direct transfer of funds or transfer of property, but instead is a benefit that allows NGOs to use their funds to achieve statutory objectives and not to pay other financial obligations. Such help appears in the state budget not as an item of expenditure, but rather as a not-received revenue (i.e. in the case of granting tax benefits, the taxes which were not provided in the budget, are considered indirect support).

In terms of funding policy there is a fundamental difference between the types of services that **the state has to provide** to citizens **according to law**, and those to which the state is not legally obliged. For example, in every European country, the state must ensure that all children get a primary school education - in other words, the state must give every child the opportunity to learn and thus to exercise its right to education. At the same time, the state is generally not obliged by law to provide access to hippotherapy (therapeutic riding) to all children with spinal abnormalities, even though it is considered one of the most effective treatments for such diseases. In many countries, this distinction is not so clear. For example, in one country, local authorities are legally obliged to arrange care for the elderly at home, and in another country it is not part of their duties. An idea of what is and what is not a duty of the state changes in the course of time, and in most Central and Eastern European countries it varies each year with the development of society.

For example, in Hungary due to the change of the political system (1989), thousands of people suddenly lost their homes since companies closed the dormitories for workers. Because the state was not able to solve the problem of so many homeless, in the first winter of the new democracy hundreds of people froze to death. To provide shelter and assistance to people, who found themselves on the street, several NGOs were established. Because the issue was in the public eye and was widely publicized in mass media, the parliament made it obligatory for local governments to open shelters for the homeless. But since many NGOs had already built such shelters, local authorities simply transferred the allocated money from the budget to these NGOs. Until now, virtually all homeless shelters in Hungary are operated by non-governmental organizations and are funded by local authorities.

Often some kind of service becomes a duty of the state as a result of successful lobbying of NGOs to include the given condition in the legislation. For example, social NGOs which organized the first "meals on wheels", – they began to deliver meals to older people in several districts of Budapest – were able to convincingly demonstrate that, by organizing meals for elderly only in social centers, local authorities discriminate against those elderly who are not able to go to a social center. As a result of a local law, "meals on wheels" were included in the list of services that are required to be funded by the state.

Despite the constant attempts of NGOs to prove that services of that kind can help to implement the constitutional right of patients to human dignity, other services in Hungary, such as hospice (care for the terminally ill, especially for cancer patients in terminal stage), have so far no right to receive public funding. Thus, if a hospice is attached to a hospital, usually they are operated by a fund which attracts external funding (i.e. from the church or private donors).

This important distinction between the state's responsibilities determined by law and those functions which the state is not obliged to fulfill, is reflected in the funding policies of NGOs.

When a NGO provides services which are included in the obligations of the state, this fact in itself does not entitle the organization to receive state support. However, in most European countries there are legally established policies, according to which the state assumes the obligation to fund such services, regardless of whether they operate public or private institutions. Governments of Central and Eastern Europe even increasingly fund private organizations providing services which are considered mandatory and which the state has to fund in any case. There are various mechanisms for direct funding (an overview follows below).

On the other hand, funding of those types of services which, according to law, **are not part of the state's duties**, depends solely on the policies of central or local authorities. In most European countries there are defined areas of policies for social and economic development. Each ministry defines for itself the priorities for the current year (i.e. for the ministry of labour such priorities may be to reduce the number of unemployed in a particular region, increasing the number of companies that hire disabled persons, or increasing the rate of part-time employed women). Among other measures to implement such policies - such as legal regulation or support of employment - the ministry can create a grant program for NGOs for the realization of programs to achieve the objectives of these state policies.

In the European system usually it is difficult to find funding for services which central or local authorities do not consider priorities. For example, supposing a NGO wanted to urgently address the issue of domestic violence in a small Hungarian town, it would not have got public funding for this program and this till the end of the 1990s. The problem of domestic violence is simply not considered a priority at national and local level, but the world starts to change its thinking. Thanks to the efforts of women's organizations, but mainly because of pressure from the EU and its policy of gender equality, in 2004 the Ministry of Internal Affairs of Hungary, headed by a woman, initiated a nationwide campaign for instructing the police on the problem of domestic violence. Today, the same NGO in the same small town will have many possibilities for being funded by the state, when working with women suffering from domestic violence. For NGOs, providing shelter for stray dogs, there were no opportunities for grants in 1996 and still, up to now, these organizations have great difficulty with funding.

As a summary, we can say that the main criterion for direct state support is to provide certain services which are by law an obligation of the state. In addition to these services mandatory by law, priorities for grant funding are influenced by public policies at national and local level. It is very likely that the ability of NGOs to lobby for the inclusion of their activities in the relevant legislation and the state budget or among the priorities of public policy affect the availability of public funding for this organization.

The results of the activities of non-profit organizations have to be considered in the system of national accounts for the purposes of calculation and analysis of employment GDP. These are public and religious organizations, social movements, funds, institutions, non-profit partnerships and other non-profit organizations. In this context a precise percentage structure of the activity area of all non-profit organizations is important. The analysis of this structure will allow for determining the contribution to the GDP through the calculation of the cost of products and services of non-profit organizations. For example, in Russia, in 2002 this contribution amounted to about 1% of the GDP (calculated by the method of final consumption) which is significantly lower than in developed countries. For the period from 1996 to 2002 the output of products and services by these organizations decreased by 43%, while the GDP grew by 11.5%. Post-crisis recovery of this sector has been slower than in other sectors of the economy. This year the employment in the non-profit sector, taking into account only the social and religious organizations (associations), amounted to 0.8% of the total number of employed. In this respect, Russia is ahead of other countries of the former socialist camp.

As to data of the fund "Institute for Urban Economics" and for visualization of the role of NGOs in the Russian economy, indicators like the output of products and services of NGOs (143 bill. rubles) are delivered which is 1,6 times higher than the output of products of the light industry throughout the country (88,8 bill. rubles) and which is comparable with the output of the "housing" sector (172,4 bill. rubles). For this reason, it is important to understand that NGOs are established to fulfill social, charitable, cultural, educational, and scientific and management purposes, in order to protect public health, promote the development of physical culture and sport and meet spiritual and material needs of the citizens. They also aim at the protection of rights and lawful interests of citizens and organizations, the settlement of disputes and conflicts, the provision of legal assistance, as well as at any other purpose to achieve public good.

The non-profit sector directly and indirectly contributes to the economic development. Direct contributions are related to the fact that non-governmental non-profit organizations provide employment, buy and produce goods and services necessary for their activity, and, thereby, stimulate the total demand and increase the total supply. Furthermore, NGOs can operate in niches, in which in a natural position on the free and competitive market the commercial sector is not interested, because they have too small profit rates. Indirect contributions are conditioned by the fact that, when competition is created through state and municipal structures, NGOs increase the efficiency of social service delivery system as a whole. Non-profit organizations can work on order of the state, implementing government orders for the provision of socially important services on a competitive basis. They may also independently determine the types and amount of their social services, both paid and free (funded by donations from businesses and individuals). Summarizing the stated, it is important to define the role of public organizations in a society which is "**a strategically important link in the search for middle ground between businesses and the state**". Studies of the John Hopkins Institute among 22 countries have shown that NGOs make a significant contribution to the GDP. For example, in developed countries, their share amounts to 5.7% of GDP including volunteers (4.6% without volunteers), and together with religious organizations reaches 8.5% of GDP.

Economic impact: 4.4% employment of the whole working population (in 36 countries, 156609 bill. USD in revenue (from 1995 to 2002 among 22 countries)), in the U.S. it reaches 3.94%, in Germany 2.56%, France 3.21% of GDP.

Largest employer: 40 962 million jobs, 25 135 7 million wage earners (the largest corporation has 3,5 million), 15 826 3 million full time jobs which are executed by volunteer workers (study conducted by the John Hopkins Institute among 36 countries).

The economic effect of public organizations:

- 55.4% of all public organizations in 36 countries engaged in the scope of culture, education and health.
- Developed countries have the most advanced public sector and the biggest economic impact.

Income sources of the third sector: 53.4% are made up by income from business activities, 34.1% come from government grants and contracts, 12.5% come from philanthropy (according to studies of Johns Hopkins Institute among 34 countries). On top of that, NGOs bring the element of competition into the production and distribution of socially important goods, and consequently increase the efficiency of this sector. Increased efficiency means that, for the realization of the same amount of social functions, fewer resources from the economy (i.e. because it will be possible to reduce the tax burden) will be confiscated which means that more resources will be invested in ensuring future growth. Thus, **a strong non-profit sector is an important factor for ensuring social and political stability, improving living standards for the population and, finally, an important factor for the country's economic development.**

Zhangazy Karimovich Kunserkin, The Judicial and Legal System in Kazakhstan: Modern Requirements and the Approach to International Assistance

Introduction

The Republic of Kazakhstan gained independence on 16 December 1991, and, at the same time, complex and institutional-political, and socio-economic and legal reforms took place in the country.

Earlier, in the period of the USSR, Kazakhstan had a legal system which was based on the communist ideology, and the priorities of this legal system were the interests of the socialist state and the ruling communist party. Furthermore, human rights and the principle of rule of law were ignored.

The Soviet legal system and socialist legality were characterized at various stages of its history of mass extra-judicial repressions of citizens on class, religious, political and ethnic grounds. There is no doubt that, under certain historical conditions, the Soviet system of justice, taking into account the previous negative experiences and challenges of the time, did not permit large-scale violations of laws and human rights. I.e. a system of effective crime prevention which ensures judicial and prosecutorial control of compliance with the law upon the administration of justice, was provided, which guarantees citizens protection from unlawful prosecution. However, the Soviet system of justice was inherently vicious and does not provide for impartial, objective and fair trials. There is no doubt that, with these starting conditions, the new Kazakh national system of legal proceedings and court organization is in need of a speedy reformation and radical change in the fundamental principles. The purpose of legal reforms was the formation of a judicial system which would be based on generally accepted international standards, including the principle of independence of judicial authorities, the rule of law and respect for human rights. The main direction of the state's legal policy is currently defined by the Concept of Legal Policy of the Republic of Kazakhstan for the period from 2010 to 2020 (approved by the Decree of 24August 2009, of the President of the Republic of Kazakhstan No.858).

However, it has to be critically noted that such objectives of legal reforms, as the independence of the judges and the rule of law, up to now still have not been achieved, and this is clearly evident in the work of the

Supreme Court of the RK and all courts of the country, as well as confirmed by various studies in this area. In recent years, judges and the bench were constantly exposed to public criticism concerning corruption in the judicial system, incompetence, prejudices, and accusatory bias. The corporate solidarity of judges creates, under the conditions of impunity, a fertile ground for misuse, corruption and massive violations of the law.

Past scandals got great resonance in society, one of them was about a criminal case against the President of the Supervisory Board of the Supreme Court and a number of Supreme Court judges, and the second case was about the facts of corruption and criminal activities of organized criminal groups in the customs house of Khorgos, involving senior officials and officers of the Customs house and NSC.

In recent years more egregious cases were made public which occurred in the judiciary, and include judges and prosecutors discrediting their high public status with their acts.

Furthermore, in cases of big scandals the Supreme Court remains either silent, or makes lengthy and unprincipled statements, thus, only encouraging a climate of impunity and permissiveness which has developed among the judges. Moreover, it should be borne in mind that a judge in Astana and Almaty is not a judge somewhere in the outback, where he just administers justice and where he really represents local power.

Some of the courts' verdicts are, by their nature, just anecdotal, i.e. a judge has ruled to ban some of the suras of the Koran - the holy book of Muslims.

The mentioned examples illustrate the rise of negative trends in the judiciary and the system of justice.

Such cases raise legitimate concerns and criticism among society and even may, under certain circumstances, really destabilize the political situation in the country and cause social unrest.

However, the population and ordinary citizens, first of all, don't even worry about those criminal cases and scandalous examples anymore, but about the fact that they often cannot obtain justice in courts. Ordinary citizens often suffer the arrogance of judges, neglecting and ignoring their concerns. The human rights situation still up to now remains unresolved, accusatory bias in the administration of justice adopt mass character, even in administrative courts, in some cases entire departments of law enforcement agencies are interpenetrated with organized crime, as in the case of Khorgos customs.

Among the most pressing problems of Kazakhstan's justice ranks also the large gap between existing legislation and enforcement practice at all levels of administration of justice. The pronounced judgment of courts often not only directly contradict the law, but also the published Normative Resolutions of the Plenum of the Supreme Court of the RK, and the arguments of an appeal in the higher judicial instances are not considered and not taken into account when making judgments.

In addition, our judicial system has become extremely cumbersome and inert. The administration of justice does not correspond to international standards and to the challenges of time, it does not adapt to changes in the world and in society, but, quite the opposite, a politicization of a series of court verdicts and of the judicial system is quite obvious.

Yet, one cannot state that the government does not see the problems and shortcomings of the legal system created by exactly these authorities. Having said that, to overcome this crisis the fight against corruption has been declared and put into practice. Corruption had already reached the overall national level. However, we should recognize that this fight is aimed at the consequences and results of the established system of state governance.

As problematic remain the status and situation of public prosecutors and lawyers as the most important institutions of the legal system. On the one hand, prosecutors which have real leverage of power in controlling legality, cannot provide legality, including upon administration of justice, but, on the other hand, advocacy which actually is not an equal part of the system of justice, but instead infringed in its legal status.

Because of Kazakhstan's presidency in the OSCE and the numerous statements in the press about the progress of democratic reforms, a real reformation of the country's legal system can be expected. This was confirmed by expectations in connection with Kazakhstan's adopted political commitments, as reflected in the National Human Rights Plan of Action of the RK for 2009-2012. However, in the year of the presidency, and much less a year later, Kazakhstan, in fact, has not confirmed the commitment to democracy, human rights and progress in the field of justice. Having said this, it is obvious that the political will for change in this area is minimal.

Progress in Legal and Judicial Reforms 1991-2011

In the years of 1991 to 2011, real systemic reforms of the court organization were carried out in the country. I.e. on the initiative of the judges, people's assessors were excluded from the main trial, in criminal proceedings trials by jury on certain categories of cases were introduced, justice was administered by specialized economic, administrative courts and juvenile courts, and the competence of appeal and cassation instances was defined.

However, at present we cannot say that the judicial-legal reform took place to the right extent. Quite the opposite, the promotion of reform leads to serious problems, and a number of trends have, frankly, negative consequences.

All these processes have been defined, in general, with the adoption of brand new legal documents in 1998, i.e. the Law "On judicial system and status of judges of the Republic of Kazakhstan", the Code of Criminal Procedure, Code of Civil Procedure, and the Code of Administrative Offences.

It has to be stressed that the worst for many judges and prosecutors was the introduction of trial by jury in 2004. According to the latest official reports of the Supreme Court, in this category of criminal cases, acquittals reach 20% of the total number of cases reviewed. In trials by jury basically only cases of very serious crimes, like murder, are considered. Concerning other categories of cases, a jury court first convened in a criminal case on charges of former Health Minister Doskaliev.

At the same time, the courts of general jurisdiction have little or no practice of acquittals in criminal proceedings, but the insignificant 1.5% of acquittals causes reasonable doubts about their objectivity, for the persons involved in such cases are usually well-known high-ranking officials or their close relatives.

However, the Supreme Court of the RK sees positive trends in this process of justice. So, the Chairman of the Board on Criminal Cases of the Supreme Court of RK, Abdrashit Zhukenov, said at the enlarged meeting of the judges on the results of 2009 that Kazakhstan is experiencing a positive growth trend of acquittals in criminal cases. According to him, in 2009, of 75 accused persons in criminal cases, more than half were acquitted (in 2008 there were 538 acquittals, in 2009 there were 613). The percentage of acquittals is 1.5%, in 2008 it was 1.4%, and in 2007 it was 1.2%. So, a trend of increasing acquittals can be observed.

However, according to A. Zhukenov, in 2009, higher judicial instances like the appellate and supervisory board overturned 0.4% of verdicts for 253 persons, compared with 0.5% for 297 persons in 2008, and changed 3.2% of verdicts for 2 055 persons.

In general, as explained by A. Zhukenov, in 2009, the courts of the republic considered 56 601 criminal cases which is 993 cases, or 1.7%, more than in 2008. During this period, the proceedings of 56 620 criminal cases were closed, in 34 677 criminal cases a sentence was imposed against 41 491 persons, which is more than 8.1% compared to 2008.

Therefore, a natural question arises: why does the number of acquittals in jury courts differ so much from that of courts with one professional judge?

There are other legitimate questions: if in our country convictions prevail where actually the indictment is copied into the verdict, then why do we have a court, you can greatly simplify legal proceedings and avoid courts at all, and abolish this protection institution, if it does not work? May the opinion of the investigator be enough, to decide whether one is guilty? After all, in fact, the court's role is now reduced to the final approval of the investigator's opinions! Why do we need higher judicial instances, if they, in fact, only agree with previous convictions and decisions of courts? Maybe the regional and the Supreme Court will be reduced, or a minimum number of judges will be left who will not be required to read the criminal and civil cases, and simply sign their decisions? Of course, I am exaggerating these questions, but the issues of quality and fairness of justice still remain, and now they are still not being addressed. So, talking about fair justice from the perspective of the rule of law is currently impossible, since the percentage of acquittals is very low. Furthermore, I base this conclusion on the undisputed axiom that justice does not exist without acquittals. In 1998, a system of the appointment of judges was determined as a whole by the Law "On judicial system and status of judges". However, as proved in practice, this law did not provide real independence of judges and courts. Quite the opposite, judges were completely controlled and became more accountable to chairmen and -women of higher courts and judicial colleagues, and the judicial system itself became dependent on the executive branch of government, including also local authorities.

Certain difficulties in the work of courts are, of course, caused by the instability of adopted laws, when the newly passed law after some time is exposed to substantial changes and additions. And exactly these laws are actually prepared and submitted to the Parliament by the Government on behalf of the Ministries and agencies, so, they maintain a bureaucratic and departmental interest right from the beginning. These laws, furthermore, suffer from low legal quality, and are often borrowed from Russia and other CIS countries without adequate adaptation to new conditions and specifics.

The Constitutional Council of the RK has already indicated that "some laws are passed without proper conceptual assessment, are often contradictory and unreasonably, often make changes to them which give rise to instability of the current legislation and practice of law adoption".

Unfortunately, in the judicial enforcement practice, courts almost never explore the controversial relationship in terms of the principles, enshrined in the Constitution, as the basic law. For example, in 2000, the Constitutional Council has received six complaints from the courts, in 2001, they received seven, and in the period from 2002 to 2007, they received an average of only two complaints for each year. Moreover, concerning the consideration of cases in court, lawyers and human rights activists have repeatedly emphasized and, for the court, pointed out the unconstitutionality of these or those applied laws, and asked the court to apply to the Constitutional Court for an official interpretation.

Of particular note is the issue of technical support and equipment of justice. Generally, we do not have specialized court buildings. The very sight of the courtrooms does not call for due respect for those involved and citizens, and this provokes contempt of court and justice among the population. Lack of technical equipment of the courts causes difficulties in the work of lawyers, who are in the proceedings deprived of the possibility to provide adequate legal assistance to their client to ensure secrecy of communication during legal proceedings. Most of the defendants in court sit in cell or "tanks", and lack real opportunities to communicate with their lawyers. The relationship between courts and defendants cannot be considered respectful. Quite the opposite, in a criminal trial the defendant is an outcast whose rights are not guaranteed and are not observed properly. The court initially sees the defendant as its opponent in the proceedings, and is prejudiced against him/ her.

At present, the general meaning of the judicial and legal reform is to maximize the decriminalization of economic crimes and the humanization of criminal punishment. For example, there are proposals to include the following mechanism in the criminal procedure law: if, in case of an economic crime, the offender compensates for the resulting damage, s/he is exempted from criminal punishment. It is also proposed, to introduce processes of judicial (procedural) deal, in case of admission of guilt, the prosecutor requests to prescribe a softer or lower penalty and a judge only approves the deal.

I believe that the judicial and legal reform is a complex multi-level and nation-wide step, along with which it is necessary to address not only legal issues, but also budgetary and technical.

International Assistance

Throughout the years of implementing judicial reforms, international assistance from foreign governments and international organizations is constantly provided to Kazakhstan. During this time, many programmes were financed with the participation of authorities and regulatory bodies of Kazakhstan, a large number of measures, involving the Supreme Court, local courts, prosecutors and judicial bodies, were carried out, round tables and conferences were organized, books were published, and educational programmes with the participation of our specialists in other countries were implemented.

However, for quite inexplicable reasons, foreign educational programmes became the most popular form of cooperation between Kazakh officials through international cooperation.

Yet, it is very difficult to determine the positive effects of these programmes, given that the human rights situation in Kazakhstan and the rule of law in the judicial system have not improved at all.

Numerous advices, recommendations and consultations, provided through international cooperation, did not help to develop justice in Kazakhstan, but were of formal and superficial nature. Foreign specialists usually poorly represented the legal system of Kazakhstan, they not at all knew their way around in the local legal system, they were not familiar with the specifics of court organization, and suggested to automatically transfer the positive experience accumulated in their countries to us which brought no tangible benefits and results.

All information provided by foreign and international organizations are actively filtered by our bureaucracy, and further recommendations are efficiently adapted to the needs of our system.

At recent times, a programme for the implementation of juvenile justice was realized, that is, of courts which consider cases in which minors are involved. However, after a short time this programme started to virtually phase out.

Great assistance from international human rights organizations is provided to the local human rights activists, but even here assistance is not provided on an institutional basis, what within 20 years did not result in the creation of a real human rights system.

Paths of Judicial-Legal Reforms

Reformation of the Judicial System

In a democratic society the court is intended to resolve a conflict which arises between the individual and society, on the one hand, and the government, on the other. In this case, the court must be formed and operate in a maximum of independence from the state, from political and financial groups, and, furthermore, the court should not give in to public sentiments. This independence is achieved by a variety of legal mechanisms, such as a system of appointing judges. Most democratic countries do not use a system of electing judges, because it puts the judges into the subordinate position of political parties.

Also unacceptable is the practice of appointing judges from the executive branch, since it generally excludes the independence of the court and the judges as a legal institution.

The most acceptable solution is the appointment of judges as agreed between the executive and legislative branches of government. However, this method is appropriate in the presence of the legislative branch of government opposition and turnover of the executive branch. Unfortunately, in the foreseeable political future, given innovations are unrealistic. If you recall the latest appointment by the President of the Supreme Court, Mr. B. A. Beknazarov, this is an obvious example that the appointment to the highest judicial office in the country is executed by the will of one person and without any actual consideration from the legislative branch.

In any case, it is necessary to start judicial-legal reforms with ensuring the independence of judges from the date of their appointment, and continue throughout their activity through the administration of justice. Moreover, the basic principle in this direction should be the priority of human rights and the rule of law, and not only the goal of strengthening the law enforcement and judicial system.

Openness in Administrating Justice

At the time of the French Revolution, the phrase "You can judge me unfairly, but try to do it publicly" was born. One of the fundamental principles of justice is the publicity of the trial. However, as mentioned above, our courthouses and courtrooms are not fit for public processes. We are facing again a purely technical problem. For the last years, I'm aware of only one construction of a district court in the town Kaskelen in the Karasai district of the Almaty oblast. In Almaty, with a population of 1,5 million people, courts occupy former kindergartens, dormitories, administrative buildings, and some courthouses are in a catastrophic condition. The state must solve the problem of building specialized court houses, where all professional participants will be provided with appropriate conditions to carry out their professional duties. It is difficult to assess the degree of openness of the process of justice at the present time. On the one hand, judges do not object to the presence of the press in court, including oppositional, on the other hand, they cannot guarantee the presence of audience in the courtroom. Under the openness of justice, I even understand the availability of all judicial decrees of the courts of all levels. At this point, we should positively mention the electronic database http://supcourt.kz/rus/acts, where you can find the rulings of the courts in an electronic format.

Overcoming Accusatory Bias

There is the widespread wisdom "It is better ten guilty men go free than one innocent is convicted". My long-term observations show that the convicted not so much painfully react to the fact that they were convicted, but that there are so many innocent convicts among them. This creates a mood of protest in prisons, and is one of the causes of criminal recidivism, as convicted persons will not believe in fairness in court and will find for themselves a moral motivation to reoffend. This is evident in juvenile delinquency. Criminological studies show that recidivism among teenagers is high. Typically, teenagers are put in prison for having committed minor offenses, though a correction would be possible without isolation from society. However, in the colony they already undergo the full criminal process, the psyche of the teenagers gets destroyed, they will become angry because of their destroyed fate. After serving their sentence, such persons increasingly often commit serious crimes.

Accusatory bias is the most sensitive topic of Kazakhstan's proceedings. As already mentioned, acquittals now constitute about 1.5% of the passed verdicts.

The key problem lies in the fact that in the trial there is no guarantee that they adhere to the rule of law. In addition, this causes unjustified cruelty of judges when it comes to passing a judgment. As a consequence, the prison population of Kazakhstan, as estimated by PRI in 2006, amounts up to 49 292 people, which is 340 persons per 100 000 persons of the population. This figure is lower, however, than that of Turkmenistan, Russia and Belarus on the territories of the former Soviet Union[37], but higher than in Uzbekistan, for example, but a comparison with European countries is, in general, impossible.

Furthermore, it became usual that, in the course of the trial, the judge resolves irregularities, accepted during pretrial investigation, does not take into account motions, claims and arguments of the defense, is not guided by the principle of presumption of innocence and uses doubtful evidence against the accused. In private discussions, judges refer to the instructions received from higher courts of the punitive judicial practice.

In theory, the Supreme Court has to exercise strict supervision concerning the observance of legality and justice, and to ensure that the rights and legitimate interests of the accused and convicted are safeguarded. But in practice, the Supreme Court does not comply with even its own regulatory resolutions, which is confirmed by the actual law enforcement, and has never examined the issue of guaranteeing protection of the accused. A fairly common example of accusatory bias in criminal trials is the following practice: during the pretrial investigation, as a result of torture or pressure, the accused admits to have committed the crime. In court, he refuses to give the testimony previously given, and this on the basis of the right granted by Article 245 of the Criminal Procedure Code, however, the court usually takes old confessions made during the pretrial investigation as a basis for a conviction. The court investigates claims of torture and unlawful investigation methods through the questioning in court procedures of the investigator or the police agents. If they do not find evidence of torture and pressure on the accused, the court trusts their testimony, and even ignores obvious signs of beatings, acts of medical examination and medical-forensic examination reports.

At a meeting, the former chairperson of the Criminal Chamber of the Supreme Court R.I. Yurchenko even stated that illegal methods of investigation are no reason to consider the confession of the accused as inadmissible evidence, if it is a fact that the crime took place and this is proved by a set of other evidences.

Courts

Specialized Economic Courts

It is necessary to discuss the issue of the introduction of pre-trial settlement or mediation of economic disputes in the procedure of economic courts. This means that, before going to court or filing a lawsuit, the parties should enter into negotiations and take steps to resolve the dispute.

This practice existed in the Soviet arbitration procedure and was quite efficient. Such a measure would remove the economic burden from the courts.

Courts for Minor Disputes

Concerning legal proceedings, in many countries there are courts for minor disputes which are actively involved in resolving civil legal disputes. For example, in Russia there are justice-of-the-peace courts, whose jurisdiction includes minor property disputes, child support, etc.

I believe that the introduction into practice of such courts will have bright prospects after the example of specialized administrative courts.

The subject of courts for minor disputes was already previously actively discussed and it was proposed to revive the ancient system of "biy" courts, where disputants could appeal to an authoritative judge to resolve the dispute. To these courts citizens whose disputes, for example, did not exceed the cost of 1 million tenge could apply. Legal proceedings in this court could be handled under a simplified scheme, without bringing in a court transcript, and in a shorter period of time.

The court for minor disputes will also have an efficient anti-corruption effect, since in minor property disputes, judges will not tempt, or will be less tempted to extort or accept bribes from citizens. A general comparative statistics allows for analyzing the judicial practice between courts of general jurisdiction and courts for minor disputes. Such an analysis promotes positive reforms in the whole judicial system.

Jury Trials

Widening of the Competence of Jury Trials

It is proposed to widen the competence of a court with a jury including to all types of serious crimes. As experience of jury trials has shown, these cases are dealt with more fairly, the participants of the trials are guaranteed their rights and lawful interests as required. This measure will guarantee a fair consideration of criminal cases.

Changes in the Composition of the Cour

It is proposed to exclude the second professional judge from the court, because his/her role and status is completely unjustified.

The second measure is to change the competence of professional judges and forbid them to participate in a jury verdict in the jury room. This will provide the greatest degree of independence, objectivity and impartiality of the jury, and guarantees to be not put under pressure by the judge concerning the pronouncement of its opinion.

Procedural Deal

A procedural deal is the real mechanism of performing justice, and its introduction into the criminal procedure legislation is long overdue. On this subject, already for a long time there have been discussions among jurists and practitioners. The meaning of this procedure lies in the fact that the prosecutor has the right to give way to the defense in terms of imposition of punishment in exchange for a guilty plea of the accused. This agreement is made in writing and submitted to the court for consideration and passing a verdict. That is, if the defendant faces 10 years in prison, then, as the result of a deal, s/he can get a much shorter period. Such a deal is reached to simplify the procedure of legal proceedings, which implies, without doubt, budget savings. This does not violate the principle of inevitability of punishment for crime.

The attitude among practitioners and jurists in this institution is twofold. Those prosecutors who are involved in real trials, as well as judges, in my opinion, support such innovation.

At present, the General Prosecutor's Office develops and proposes a new edition of the Criminal Procedure Code which provides for such a trial procedure. In this issue the greatest risk has a national (ethnic) specificity with the vestiges of tribal relations. Practitioners know that self-accusation occurs to be responsible for the older brother, father, head of the clan or the family. These facts are seen in law enforcement as cases of very-serious crimes.

Arbitration (Intermediate Court)

The arbitration procedure is, in compliance with the law of arbitration, currently under the actual control of the state system. The arbitration procedure must be completely independent of the state court. The citizens themselves must be aware of and carry the risk of a misjudgment of arbitration and should be denied the right to appeal concerning such decisions.

Reforming the Legal System

Public Prosecution

The role and place of the prosecutor in criminal proceedings and in the judicial system should be clearly and exactly defined. In recent years the function of prosecution has changed, and each time for the prosecution, it was a painful issue, especially concerning the competence of the prosecutor in the pretrial investigation. Experience has shown that the concentration in the hands of one agency of pretrial investigation and the supervision of the pretrial investigation do not improve the situation with the observance of legality, do not ensure human rights, but improve the accountability of prosecution. As an example, the criminal investigation of BTA Bank can be mentioned which was carried out with gross violations of the law, which has already led to the passing of a misjudgment in 2010. The prosecutor should serve as a representative of the state and public interests in court, decide on procedural matters in criminal cases at the stage of bringing the accused to trial.

Furthermore, one of the most important functions of the prosecutor should be the protection of citizens, including the prosecutor's office, should identify unlawful charges, demand an end to criminal proceedings if there are grounds to refuse the charges in court. That is, all those features which we see in judicial practice.

Advocacy

The Institution of advocacy in Kazakhstan is well developed, especially when compared to neighbouring countries. Advocacy groups acquired with a sufficient degree of freedom and autonomy which are possible in our situation.

However, in its mission, advocacy is constantly facing difficulties of systemic and institutional nature.

So, the legislative and executive branch and their authorities made regular attempts to curtail the independence of the advocacy profession and the independence of advocacy groups.

Nevertheless, the injustice of the taxation of advocacy has to be noted.

Advocates bear the statutory costs for the financial support of their professional colleagues, who are required to maintain the office, and bear the costs in terms of record keeping. Furthermore, the costs for maintaining the office and membership fees to the panel may be attributed to the expenses by law. There are continued attempts by the Government, including the Ministry of Justice and local authorities, to limit the independence of advocates. However, these initiatives do not receive sufficient support in Parliament. The problem of principles and rules for the payment of legal aid appropriatioons from the state budget was not resolved to the end, and also is still not resolved. Now, investigators and judges decide on the issue of paying for legal aid. In a number of regions and cases, we can already talk about the effect of pocket advocates, that is, those who sit next to the investigators and receive payment from the state in exchange for a rather comfortable position for the prosecution.

Transformation at Present

Every year, in the reports of the Supreme Court, upon summarizing the results of the activity of the courts of the Republic of Kazakhstan for the past year, it is highlighted in one form or another that the quality of justice in the country remained at the same level, despite all the measures taken to improve it.

According to preliminary data, collected in 2009, the courts of the Republic considered only 906 867 claims and cases, of which 555 259 were civil cases, 295 007 were criminal cases and 56 601 were administrative cases, that is, 76 358 or 7.8% fewer cases than in 2008. This reduction in the total number of cases is, in the first place, the result of the reduced number of administrative cases, that is, 109 856 or 27% less than in 2008. This is due to the fact that the number of road traffic offences and offences against the safety of communication decreased by 50%.

All in all, 772 576 cases were closed (discontinued), 476 111 were civil cases, 239 845 were criminal cases and 56 620 were administrative cases. There was a significant increase in the number of trials in civil cases in the economic court. Courts of Appeal, because of cassation complaints, annulled 1% of all decisions that were made by these specialized economic courts. In the economic courts of the Mangystau, South-Kazakhstan and Zhambyl oblast a significant shift in the review and closure (termination) of cases was recognized.

A significant event occurred in November 2009 - the 5th Congress of Judges took place, which examined issues relating to the status of judges, as well as the further development of the judicial system.

In order to improve the judicial system, in December, the President of the RK signed a law on introducing amendments to the Criminal Procedure and Civil Procedure Codes. This was a step towards the streamlining of procedures, the reduction of regulatory authorities, the strengthening of the independence of the judicial system and a significant increase of the importance of district courts. The new law was passed in January 2010. The main purpose of this law is to regulate the provisions of procedural legislation, as amended by the Constitutional Law and the provisions of the law on the judicial system and status of judges of the Republic of Kazakhstan. In particular, in accordance with the law, a three-stage-system is created, in which all matters relating to the "first instance" will be considered by district and other competent courts.

Bibliography

The Concept of Legal Policy of the Republic of Kazakhstan for the period from 2010 to 2020.

Presidential Decree of 4 May 2005 No.1568 "On measures for further using the potential of the Constitution of the Republic of Kazakhstan".

National Action Plan for Human Rights in the RK 2009-2012, approved by the resolution of the President of the Republic of Kazakhstan No.32-36.125 on 5 May 2009.

Information of the Constitutional Council of the RK to the President of the RK "On constitutional legality in the country (1 July 1996)".

Message of the Constitutional Council of the RK to the Parliament of the RK "On constitutional legality in the country" (according to the results of operations in 1997).

Message of the Constitutional Council of RK of 29May 2007, No.01-4/1 "On constitutional legality in the Republic of Kazakhstan" Kazakhstanskaya Pravda. 2007, Nr. 85 (25330).

Elnara Baynazarova, Kazakhstan in Global and Regional Politics: Conceptual View and Development Issues

I. Central Asia was and remains to be the key element in world-wide political and economic processes. Being in fact a strategic ground where the interests of the leading world players coalesce, the region increases its potential in the field of transit of raw materials, goods and services, and in that manner revives the concept of the Great Silk Road in the new, 21st century.

Actually, not a single "serene harbour" remained in the world where countries and nations could image themselves safe. In that regard Central Asia is not an exception. In light of new unconventional challenges and menaces, not one state is in fact able to single-handedly provide its own security. All that brings the issue of creating an integral collective security system into focus, of whose necessity Kazakhstan tries to convince the international community since its first days of independence.

When the question of post-crisis integration of Eurasia appears on today's global agenda, then Kazakhstan, situated in the heart of the continent, can become the initiator and co-ordinator of the necessary processes. Such integration is not only possible provided the strengthening of collaboration between countries, but given the realization of carefully considered internal reforms. It is necessary to highlight that Kazakhstan is an active stakeholder in the system of geopolitical and geo-economic co-ordinates in the Eurasian space. Kazakhstan's ranking in the Index of Globalisation bears witness to that fact. In the ranking of 2010 Kazakhstan was placed 61st in economic globalisation and 95th in political globalisation[38]. Without doubt, these results serve as an additional stimulus for Kazakhstan to develop perspectives on further, more substantial involvement both in world-wide and regional integration processes.

At the dawn of independence Kazakhstan chose the path of a multi-vector foreign policy, whose success is held up to the present day. The equilibrium of all the lines of action in foreign policy obviously enables the state to adroitly manoeuvre between the national interests of regional and global players. Kazakhstan's initiatives in the international arena within the last couple of years allow attesting an evident activity increase in the sphere of creating new security structures as well as improving the functioning of existing ones in the Eurasian space. In this regard the role of the republic of Kazakhstan as a carrier of the message of peace and security in Eurasia must be paid attention to. Thanks to deliberate and effective foreign policy strategies elaborated by the country's President N.A. Nazarbaev the country's transition from **geopolitical vulnerability to successful geopolitical adaptability** was accomplished by now.

The aspiration of the young state to play a pivotal role for the security nets in the region results from the cultural-historical and geographic background of Kazakhstan's location and position. At all times the territory of Kazakhstan was the centre of the intersection of the main transport and communication arteries of the Eurasian continent, where the cultures and ethnicities of the West and the East met and enriched each other. Not incidentally the discourse of "Kazakhstan as the connecting link between the East and the West" is a recurrent theme throughout all foreign policy declarations and initiatives. The belt of steppes and deserts where great nomadic states were formed takes a central place in the large Eurasian continent. Exactly on the territory of today's Kazakhstan and its contiguous regions a manifold of civilisations emerged that exerted determinant influence on the development of many nations of the world. The great nomadic empire, that stretched from Siberia to Hindustan, from Western Europe to the Far East, combined the cultural identity and the way of living of the Eurasian people, and thereby bore the unique spirit of "Eurasianism" which is the leitmotif of Kazakhstan's policies regarding the promotion of peace and harmony. As the President of the RK N.A. Nazarbaev states in the book "V potoke istorii" (literally: In the stream of history; note of the translator) the steppe has formed a particular spirit and mentality, where the Turkic spirit draws its dynamism from. Since the beginning of the 21st century the changed nature of global relations calls for transformations of traditional methods and procedures of pursuing policies as well as of approaches and notions of the own position in the world and national interests. All that brings us to revise some stereotypes and reconsider the complex structure of the world order in the 21st century.

It is necessary to regard Kazakhstan in context of the role that countries of Central Asia could possibly play in the relationship between the European-wide and the developing Asian security systems, and thereby **create a new joint cluster of the concept "indivisibility of security"**. The given expression developed along with the formation of such structures as the **Conference on Interaction and Confidence Building Measures in Asia (CICA)** which to a large extent is based on the history of the creation of a European, Euro-Atlantic security system. As President N.A.

Nazarbaev notes, "... cooperations like the APEC, SCO, CSTO, CICA and others will become institutions for the partnership of civilisations. It is through them regional integration centres and partnerships of civilisations can be established, and conflicts overcome. Kazakhstan actively participates in the work of a couple of global and regional partnership institutions, and is willing to promote their development on principles of a multi-polar world order on behalf of humankind"[39]. The factors above mentioned allow drawing conclusions on the expediency of rethinking the dimensions and geography regarding the scope of the global security net. Together, all the parts of the mosaic that add to each other render it possible to include the most troubled security clusters of a region into its global dimension. Today we can acknowledge with certainty that Kazakhstan begins to administer the Asian security vector in a global context.

II. According to the general opinion, each state should act on its national interests when it comes to the prioritisation of the different directions in foreign policy activities. In this regard the criticism of foreign experts is remarkable, with which the expediency of the multi-vector foreign policy of Kazakhstan was met. All too often, the term "multi-vectorial" itself which is equated with a "dispersion" of the state's endeavours is incomprehensible and vague for outside observers. In order to understand, however, the philosophical constituent of Kazakhstan's positioning in the world, it is necessary to comprehend the cultural-historical background and geopolitical position of our state. The philosophy of nomadism is the marrow of the Eurasian universalism which manifests itself in the striving for dynamic assimilation and adaption to new conditions, flexibility and pliability to modernization changes. That means the very notion of "universalism" is not product of capriciousness on part of Kazakhstan but springs from the state's objective reality. As was mentioned above, Kazakhstan is situated on the intersection of the civilisations, thereby constituting the civilisation hub of the Eurasian nations. Such a position entails the huge opportunity for Kazakhstan to act as an administrator of processes regarding peace and security within the scope of the Eurasian continent. According to the laws of physics, any intelligent system seeks the state of minimum potential energy which guarantees its maximum stability. Hence, Kazakhstan's current dynamism in terms of pushing forward new initiatives for the reformation and enhancement of activities of international organisations for security and cooperation as well as of international monetary and financial institutions turns out to be nothing else but a manifestation of the underlying power of nomad philosophy.

Every day we learn about new theoretical concepts, doctrines and interpretations of the notion "security", about concepts regarding the formation of systems of global cooperation, global centres of force and so on. Like a kaleidoscope the given assertions present a colourful picture of today's world order which at times leads to false judgements and the escalation of international tensions.

The notion of "security" proves to be ephemeral, and at the same time touches the life and fate of humanity. The recent cataclysm in Japan, the transformation of the former world economic system, regional conflicts, challenges of ecological security and so on bear witness to the instability of the world system.

Unfortunately, the last year did not bring a decrease in the potential for conflict in the present-day world. We experienced the rise of new centres of instability including one in geographical proximity. It is necessary to acknowledge that the countries of the region, just as the world as a whole, face ambivalent and multi-factorial security challenges and menaces, whose solution is in need of joint efforts of politicians, diplomats and the scientific community. The reasons that impel Kazakhstan to elaborate new approaches of foreign policy include the end of the transformation period in Kazakhstan, the strengthening of Kazakhstan's role in a regional scope, the changing geopolitical conditions in the world as well as the emerging new security challenges and menaces.

Since the geopolitical realities are changing, so will the priorities of Kazakhstan in foreign policy. In this regard wrong ideas may not to be nourished - the republic does not strive to become a global player in international relations. Kazakhstan concentrates its energy on fulfilling the function of a process administrator on a regional level and on solving urgent problems of military, social, economic and production security within the realms of its possibilities and in accordance with its national interests. In practical terms Kazakhstan realises the multi-vector approach by actively participating in international cooperations and by securing strategic relations with its neighbours and the main centres of force. In this context the focal areas of Kazakhstan's foreign policy can, for the purpose of discussion, be divided into global, regional and national dimensions of guaranteeing security.

- It is necessary to look at the global tasks of Kazakhstan in the light of the country's specific contribution to the improvement of international conditions, the guarantee of progress in settling the many problems the international community has to face, the removal of existing tensions and the provision of a peaceful and constructive cooperation between organisations. It's not by coincidence that Kazakhstan actively develops the theory on the **necessity of a unified structure in order to guarantee security on the Eurasian continent. After the OSCE summit in Astana the international community not only operates with categories of Euro-Atlantic security but also with Eurasian.**

- On a regional level the main efforts must be directed at actively rising to today's challenges like terrorism, religious extremism, illegal migration, drug trafficking, economic backwardness and the low rate of cultural-humanitarian components in regionalism.
- The national constituent in foreign policy advises to maintain stability along the borders and develop the transport-economic potential of the country. According to the data of the WTO, Kazakhstan's share in world export in 2009 accounted for a total of 0.34%, and the structure of export is to a large extent determined by the orientation on raw materials40. The development of international organisations on an economic basis is to the advantage of Kazakhstan since the latter needs to strengthen its export dynamics. This primarily concerns areas like investment cooperation (in non-primary and innovative sectors), the development of transportation and transit possibilities as well as modern information and communication technologies, energy cooperation, development of new technologies in agriculture which also have to be brought into focus.

The amplification of geography regarding infrastructure projects in the framework of the Eurasian structure, too, is to the advantage of Kazakhstan. In this regard it is necessary to mention the transportation-logistics project "West Europe – West China". Therefore, one of the manners to react to the menaces will possibly be the active transformation of bilateral projects into multilateral ones, with due consideration of the interest of the parties involved.

III. One must also direct attention to Kazakhstan's role in processes of disarmament and creating a nuclear weapon free zone. Both on a regional and on a global level Kazakhstan appears to be an active adherent in the battle for a nuclear free zone, being that as of today it is the only country on whose territory 456 nuclear and thermonuclear explosions were set off. The state, having experienced hardships throughout its history, learned about the price and the value of security the hard way. In his work "Epicenter of Peace" President of the RK N.A. Nazarbaev writes, "Kazakhstan was not only the site for strategic nuclear weapons and delivery systems. The monstrously huge military-technical complex was a well-oiled machine, a kind of state within a state."[41] During Soviet times Kazakhstan functioned as the mere supplier of human and natural resources.

In this regard it's not without reason that the leading politicians on the whole world recognise the valuable contribution of Kazakhstan on the way to disarmament and to the creation of a nuclear weapon free zone. Notably, on the last Nuclear Security Summit in Washington, DC in 2010 US-President Barack Obama highlighted the key role of Kazakhstan that voluntarily ceded its share of the Soviet nuclear arsenal. Moreover, on the suggestion of Kazakhstan at the session of the United Nations General Assembly, 29 August was declared International Day against Nuclear Tests. All things considered, the choice of a nuclear-free status is the result of catastrophic consequences of the imbalance in the system of global security in the 21st century. As of today Kazakhstan advances the view of the necessity to strengthen mutual trust when pursuing the path of guaranteeing nuclear security, as one of the elements of a global security belt.

IV. Concurrently with the declaration of the nuclear-free status, Kazakhstan's initiative for building a security structure in Asia – the CICA – was announced from the podium of the United Nations General Assembly. Nearly 20 years passed since the declaration of the idea to create such a network to its practical realization in dimensions of an authoritative international Conference which in institutional terms has real chances to become an effective international organisation.

Until then joint approaches were limited to a couple of sub-regional mechanisms as ASEAN, SAARC, ECO and others. The CICA operation is unique because it is aimed at creating a security space that envelops the whole Asian continent with cooperation of, dialogue and confidence measures between the member states. CICA comprises countries from all over Asia, and its territory and population makes up around 90% of the whole continent.[42]

Since CICA discusses a wide and manifold spectrum of security issues which endows the Conference with potential dynamism, it appears to be one of the most promising structures. The fact that CICA is able to accord different approaches and interests is reflected in its success to draw up a number of integral documents as well as to take sizeable steps in realizing confidence measures in a rather short time. All this bears witness to the interest of the member states to further advance the CICA operation.

Adopted in 2007 within the CICA, the "Cooperative approach" contains detailed mechanisms for the realization of measures. 8 countries, namely Azerbaidzhan, India, Iran, Kazakhstan, the Republic of Korea, Russia, Tadzhikistan and Turkey voluntarily acted as coordinators or co-coordinators in the realization of confidence measures with regard to human dimensions, new challenges and menaces, the development of secure and effective systems of transport corridors, counter-narcotic actions, the dimension of national disaster management, information technologies, energy security cooperation, the development of small and medium sized business and tourism.[43]

From the time on when the idea to convene the given conference was proclaimed it turned into an internationally sought-after dialogue platform where issues of peace and security could be discussed and possible common grounds on diametrically opposed positions could be found. In that way the conference constituted the first institutional basis for Asian security in international practice.

The fact that the number of member states is increasing has to be considered as one of the main advantages of the CICA operation. The geographical coverage symbolises the beginning of a new branch in the institutionalisation of security structures in Asia. Today the CICA counts 20 member states, with the tendency to rise.

In the cosmos of the CICA the term "**indivisibility of security**" emerged, meaning the eschewal from territorial isolation of regional unions and the acknowledgement of the fact that security challenges and menaces are transnational. European security therefore stretches into the Asian dimension, and turns out to be part of the Eurasian security belt. The given holistic approach to the structure of the global security system is the **most implemented modus operandi in the new geopolitical realities**.

As the Norwegian scholar Johan Galtung notes, in near future we will become witnesses to the weakening of the role of states and to the strengthening of the regions that can serve as a kind of adaptive "umbrella" as the increasing influx of people, traversing national borders, brings them more and more together.[44] Therefore it is important to understand the gist of the ongoing processes in light of the methods of guaranteeing global security. Given the accruing uncertainties of the global system, the last resort is the rapprochement of approaches and the instrument of global structures, the creation of one general philosophy of the existing cooperation in Eurasia. With reason, one of the mottoes during the Kazakh chairmanship in the Organisation for Security and cooperation in Europe (OSCE) was security "from ocean to ocean". This idea was met with support amongst politicians, and keen response in the hearts of millions of people in the Eurasian space and in the Western world. Because at the bottom of the beautiful metaphor there is the deep philosophical thought on the identity and community of methods to rise to the security challenges. The results of our OSCE chairmanship bears witness to the fact that bridges for mutual understanding and friendly dialogue can and have to be built. In the last years Kazakhstan shows the international community in practice that it is necessary to find and apply new approaches for the examination of different international issues. Without doubt, it takes time for the world to steady itself against the background of a new order. But **it is important to begin the quest for a mutually acceptable solution, the quest for generally recognized rules already today**.

In this respect, the prospective on a development of an Eurasian geostrategical space is to a decisive degree dependent on the rational use of the advantages that the geopolitical and geoeconomic position between the Euro-Atlantic and the Asian-Pacific super-regions offers Kazakhstan. This will also to a large extent determine the order of global power in the new century. Today, the failure of the existing security structures to surmount the confidence crisis and to create a basis for effective dialogue as well as for an ultimate refusal to participate in the zero-sum game presents itself quite clearly. This trend will persist until new, that is common and clear rules of cooperation between the players of "the big game" are set. This has fundamental meaning, given the perdurance of globalisation's impact which proves to be a determinant world trend. At the same time the role of regionalisation processes grows, too which the Asian region substantiates. In a world that becomes more polycentric, new regional players begin to exert increasing influence. In accordance with the theory of equal development, the possibility of constructive forms of mutual influence and completion in international relations is put forward, and proposes the alternative paradigm of a world renewal under the premises of maintaining autonomy and the variety of forms of development.[45]

The Swedish political scientist Björn Hettne identifies a number of differences between new and old regionalism. While old regionalism developed under conditions of a bipolar world, **new regionalism is a more spontaneous process whose impulse derives from the very countries of the region that require the solution of security issues**.[46] New regionalism is directly linked to globalisation, and therefore may not be regarded in context of only one single region. **As a constructed phenomenon regionalism can not be separated from its discourse context**. Hence, regionalism is closely coupled with the creation of ideologies on integration, notional tinging of cause and on the necessity to form organisations.

The cooperation results in other regions did not follow the pattern of the Euro-Atlantic security model, and therefore did not allow researchers to step out of the framework of the general theory of international relations and to elaborate a complex approach on the definition of regions that would include factors of security, economy, identity and integration.[47] Thus, due to differences in the functional determination a security region can substantially diverge, for instance, from an economic region.

Accordingly, it is to expect that **such a world order can not be established with only one global centre**. Under these conditions the **idea to create an Eurasian security belt gains renewed momentum**.

V. The last three years were marked by a range of chairmanships of Kazakhstan in leading international organisations like the OSCE, SCO (Shanghai cooperation organisation) and the OIC (Organisation of the Islamic cooperation). During a chairmanship the state can more efficiently announce and facilitate initiatives for reforms and for the optimisation of one or the other structure's functioning. The intermediate results of Kazakhstan's foreign policy initiatives can be viewed by means of the method of "sectorality" of security and "securitisation". Every international structure can be regarded as a "link" in one single chain of the global security belt. Therefore, the practice of Kazakhstan's chairmanship, aiming to increase effectivity of international cooperation, is the premise for Kazakhstan's integration in the Euro-Atlantic and international structures. Thus, universalism appears to be the central concept in the global and regional positioning of Kazakhstan.

Drawing on the very notion of universalism we can confidently assert the mutually beneficial future cooperation between NATO, CSTO, SCO, OSCE, CICA and UNO on the basis of equality and the comprehension of general security menaces, as well as concerning the implementation of the principles of soft and smart power.

Also on the agenda is the question on the recognition of the present-day development potential and current developmental issues of the whole Islamic world in the context of the 21st century by ourselves, as part of the association of Islamic states in the OIC. In the last couple of years, the impact of the "Islamic factor" on world and regional politics rose substantially, and one has to pay careful attention to that fact. The quality of structures in organisations as OSCE and OIC, and their authority render dialogues on different topics possible, be it political, humanitarian and economic cooperation, fight against terrorism or religious intolerance, as well as to develop cooperations with different security structures, like SCO and CICA.

From 28-30 June 2011, Astana hosted the 38th Council of Ministers of Foreign Affairs of OIC, in which around 140 delegations participated, both from member states and from different field-specific and field-related institutes of the OIC. After the last OSCE summit this Council became the most important international forum of 2011. One of the Council's remarkable outcomes is the decision on renaming the organisation from "Organisation of the Islamic Conference" to "Organisation of Islamic Cooperation", which bears witness to the institutional maturity of the organisation.

With regard to the realization of foreign policy projects of Kazakhstan the use of the OIC platform for revitalising the CICA processes and stimulating a Congress of leaders of world and traditional religions lies in near future. As to the first, emphasis might be set on the independent character of security maintenance and cooperation on the Asian continent in order to attract a higher number of Islamic countries to this process.

As to the Council of world religions, it is necessary to highlight the uniqueness of the given forum to the effect that the level of its representativity and effectivity (due to reaching decisions, including, for the process of elaborating and realising them, the involvement of officials and the liable state bodies) increases.

Besides the chairmanship at the Council of Ministers of Foreign Affairs of OIC in 2011, in the years between 2010 and 2012, that is within three years, Kazakhstan will be a member of the Executive Board of the said organisation that is in charge of the general policy formation of the OIC. Using the opportunity, Astana intends to reinforce Islamic solidarity, realise the 10-year action plan of the OIC and expand cooperation with the Islamic world. This was and will be promoted by the following important events, held in Kazakhstan: the 7th World Economic Islamic Forum, the 3rd Conference of Health Ministers, the Conference „Role of the Islam in the CIS countries“ (October 2011), Conference on Islamic women (2012).

With regard to the chairmanship in the SCO, Kazakhstan assumed that the interaction dynamics and spheres of cooperation of the SCO develop in connection with its mission as well as with the necessity to elaborate appropriate responses to the security challenges in the context of a transformation of the world system. It is gratifying to see the association of SCO member states' general awareness of the necessity to introduce new stimuli for the organisation's development. New forms of cooperation in the SCO framework, the definition of a clear identity of SCO as to concept and values on the level of head of state's meetings, and the determination of main priorities are imperative. **It is essential to increase the emphasis on providing social and economic stability in every single member state of the SCO, which will allow to equalise the diametric differences in the dynamics of socio-economic development of the participating countries**.Within the last year the SCO countries acknowledged the necessity to frame a SCO doctrine or development concept in which the mission, principles, ideals and values, standards of interplay, key objectives of the organisation, status and position regarding a complex of international issues will be stated, and the concepts of „SCO region“ and "SCO participant“ defined. There is a vast range of possible development directions of the SCO which offer outlook on yet again a huge number of possibilities. On the other hand, however, the uncertainty of these directions hinders a conciser, richer and more manifest formulation of the description of the SCO's development projects. Without doubt, the SCO action plan for the years 2010 to 2011 was fairly successful and significant. The efforts of the participating countries of the SCO regarding the provision of regional security, the stimulation of cooperation in economic, social and humanitarian domains became the pivotal development mechanisms of the organisation. According to the slogan of the chairmanship „10 years towards security and cooperation“, 110 measures with regard to all vectors of the SCO activities were implemented on Kazakhstan's part. On the Summit papers of strategic nature were signed: the Astana declaration of the SCO, the anti-narcotic strategy of the SCO and others.

On the SCO Summit the leaders of Kazakhstan promoted a number of initiatives that aim at the further progressive development of the organisation, like: the formulation of a programme on multilateral trade and economic cooperation, the elaboration of operation guidelines of the SCO Development Fund, drawing up a document on cooperation in the fight against illegal migration, the creation of a Water and Food Committee of the SCO countries and of an Emergency Council, the picking up of the idea to found an SCO Energy club, Cyperpol services for information safeguarding as well as the constitution of a single scientific-analytical association, the SCO Prognostics Centre.

VI. Nonetheless, the problem evaluating the efficiency of Asian security structure lies in the impossibility to compare the achievements of organisations with other models since the European experience differs from the Asian context of security policies. Notwithstanding the intermediate results accomplished, the further path to constitute a unified security cluster will hardly be even and free of obstacles. The development of organisations is complicated by a number of factors:

- Amongst the countries that geographically belong to the SCO and CICA space, a significant gap in the socio-economic development remains. As organisations like the OIC are evidently spinning wheels, the differing development paces cannot build a foundation for an effective solution of problems;
- The political regimes and systems of the countries are very different from each other. This then projects onto the contrasting notions of solving security problems and of approaching the definition of menaces;
- The states of Asia very reluctantly react to ideas of creating inter-state structures, and, in comparison with Europe, the region has no solid foundation of joint objectives and values;
- The rivalry for leadership in the region between Russia, China, India and the USA;
- The vigilant attitude of the USA to the processes of Asian rallying which is driven by anxiety for the emergence of a detached bloc in the region;
- The features of Asian multilateral institutions: informality, consensus and open regionalism. Informality means, that, despite the efforts of Kazakhstan to appeal to the member states to initiate the practical implementation of confidence measures, and not to hold a „dialogue for the dialogue's sake", the participating countries favour personal contacts, and reckon that the very cooperation process is not less important than its specific content;
- The tendency to avoid international-legal mechanisms in solving bilateral disputes. For example, at the end of the Istanbul Summit of CICA

in 2010, Turkey continues its policy to attract attention to the acts of aggression of Israel. Moreover, the participants of the summit called upon Israel to join the Nuclear Non-Proliferation Treaty (NPT), which is remarkable considering that amongst those who extend the invitation are India and Pakistan who are not member of the NPT.48

However, these factors may not be regarded as insurmountable obstacles on the path to building a security space in Asia. The Asian countries are under a powerful external stimulus that encourages regional consolidation – a factor of participation of new world centres of power, namely China and India. In this context, when other countries refuse to develop a joint approach to security, they risk to lose political influence in the international arena.

In accordance with the above listed obstacles on the development path, it is advisable to focus foreign policy efforts on the following directions:

- It is necessary to equate the development levels of the member states. It would therefore be desirable to constitute a mechanism of financial aid, the Development Aid Fund, thanks to which it would be possible to render donor assistance to those countries that are the hot spot of emerging untraditional security challenges (the fight against illegal migration, piracy, drug trafficking, computer crime and more).
- An increase and accentuation of activities in just these untraditional realms of security is necessary: the enhancement of natural disasters prevention control, provision of security in health care, water security and more.
- A high level of development in information technology may foster business and cultural contacts and form a single information space in the region.
- Providing that the principle of „informality“ gives Eurasian security processes a progressive and developmental character, the possibility is given to establish mutual confidence and a sense of community. **Instead of concise and binding legal norms, general principles and rules of conduct, that can be, in the sense of „soft law“, flexibly interpreted, are given priority.**
- **Following the principle of „open regionalism“, the formation of a detached and closed bloc is circumvent. Eurasian structures may not substitute for global institutions like the UNO, but complement and support them.**
- Mending interactions with other organisations and forums: Following the example of the Asian regional forum ASEAN (ARF), the coopera-

tion with expert communities of the member states is to be intensified. The event „second path“ of SCO and CICA should be held on a regular basis.

- The number of different forms of dialogue and cooperation with other region and interstate associations (Asia-Near East Forum, CICA-OSCE Forum, ASEM and more) has to be increased. Without a strategic partnership of military-political and functional organisations (including the NATO, EU, OSCE, CSTO, SCO, CICA) it is impossible to solve the many issues of regional and global security.

The cooperation between CICA and OSCE has to be intensified. Along with that, a progressive realization of the idea on the creation of a fully-fledged organisation for cooperation and security in Asia should be developed.[49]

The „cooperative approach“ suggests further work on drawing up confidence measures, the development of preventive diplomacy, the elaboration of conflict solution measures.

It remains to be said, that ARF which persisted as a consultative forum, did not become an organisation, apt to solve conflicts. Furthermore, the assessment of the organisation's efficiency differs significantly depending on the expectations of the participants. The fact that since the foundation of the organisation in East Asia not a single serious interstate conflict occurred, and that the participants conceptualised and realised a complex of confidence measures, can be reckoned among the positive outcomes. Following this example, further development of the Asian security link shall be pressed ahead, during which failures and negative evaluations are inevitable. Both assessments allow to substantiate the role of Kazakhstan in matters of international security, and the given velocity of institutional changes provide for structures to remain relevant for issues to be solved. As A. Vlasov noted, Kazakhstan must simply evolve from its role as an administrator of large international PR-projects to the role as an intermediary in conflict situations.[50]

Without doubt, Kazakhstan begins to position itself more clearly as an authoritative foundation in the system of providing international security, and thereby more and more countries regard our country as a positive source of mutually beneficial cooperation and, possibly, as a creative approach to the solution of problems in Asia. In connection with that, Kazakhstan needs to reinforce the conceptual and ideological elements of international organisations' being, to promote measures regarding the further institutionalisation of structures, to determine the functional specificities of the subdivisions and to avoid a redundancy of functions.

Not just a surge in fierce problems, but also the evolvement of ground-breaking innovations and the realization of new global opportunities belong to crisis developments in politics and economy. Moreover, contrary to the common perception, **the Eurasian space is not object of a "chess match", it is rather a constructive "draughting board"**.

Kazakhstan, as the incumbent chairman of OIC and former chairman of the OSCE and SCO voices its certainty about the fact that only after having united the strength of the regions, it is possible to react appropriately to present-day challenges. For that it is necessary to get the effective cooperation between regional security structures, having many points of contact, on track. A strategic objective of such an integration on the continent appears to be the facilitation of building a Eurasian union that would enable cooperation with other parts of the world on a fair and equal basis.

As a matter of expedience the underlying principle of the existence of international organisations is to be specified as "**security constellation**" which unifies a whole complex of traditional territorial and untraditional space security. The creation of multilateral approaches to the provision of security in Eurasia has to become the hallmark of the international process.

Kazakhstan demonstrated its capability, having created a new cooperation platform in the realm of regional security in Eurasia and having laid the foundation for an interplay between SCO, OSCE, OIC and CICA, integrating the principles and ideas of regional organisations. The uniqueness of the security platform proposed by Kazakhstan lies not only in the fact that the given complex integrates in itself huge territories, including states with a high, predominantly economic and demographic potential, but also in the swiftness, in which structures of security provision gain influence and authority.

Within a rather short time, for example, SCO and CICA created an image of being fundamental structures in the international information space that play a serious role in administrating processes of security maintenance in the region. In this connection, the scope and rationality of objectives and tasks, without doubt, attracts the attention of many other countries that showed their willingness to be observers and, possibly, fully-fledged participants of the given organisations. Despite the development dynamics and scope of activities, Kazakhstan is still a young state. This being said, problems of overcoming a number of serious interior faults and the quest for the ideal for all parties involved development paths of organisations certainly becomes inevitable in the near future. Thereby, all opportunities are at hand for an **evolvement into a pivotal system-relevant security structure in Asia, around which subregional unions and initiatives will group**. Every organisation has, just like all the others, interior development trends and quite diversified positions of the leading players. But Kazakhstan, combining different approaches, acts as the administrator of the given processes, and has its worthy share in the process of building a security belt in Eurasia. Today there is probably no one who would doubt that the Eurasian continent will actually become the world centre of the 21st century. And it will be there, where the future post-crisis configuration of the world's political and economic system will be determined in many respects.

The effectivity of Kazakhstan's foreign policy depends on the quality in which the adopted documents come to realization. This, again, implies the involvement of all participating politicians, business representatives, scientific communities, mass media, agents of culture and the youth in this process with interest. The Asian world is the key element of the mosaic of the civilised world. Today it is important to send this message along the right channels in order to attend to cooperation and development of our nations.

Gregor Legeland, Kazakhstan and the European Union – Challenges and Prospects for a Close Collaboration

This article highlights the current status of Kazakh-European relations in the light of present security issues in Greater Central Asia and Europe's continuously growing energy security concerns. Additionally, special attention from the Kazakh perspective will be paid to the recent turbulent events in Kazakhstan and the uprisings in North Africa and the Middle East from the Kazakh perspective. Moreover, core risks and prospects of the ambivalent relationship between both, Kazakhstan and the EU will be elaborated in the context of mutual security matters as well as in terms of political and economic cooperation.

Introduction

Kazakhstan, Central Asia's economic powerhouse, is emerging as a player in the global arena. After 20 years of independence from the Soviet Union, president Nazarbaev still rules the country in an authoritarian manner. As a result of the richly gushing petrodollars, the overall economic performance of Kazakhstan over the last decade was extraordinary. With its seemingly inexhaustible natural resources, situated in the middle of the Eurasian landmass on the crossroads between Europe, Russia and China, the country provokes international attention. Indeed, it appears as if the Kazakh regime knows how to deal with this attractive situation in a self-confident manner.

Due to a variety of reasons, one part of Kazakhstan's outspoken multi-vector foreign policy is its "Path to Europe" component[51]. Europe is by far the biggest foreign investor in the country and its the major trade partner. The EU-27 account for more than one third of the country's total exports, totaling almost 12,6 billion Euros in 2010[52]. The European markets are to this day the most lucrative and accessible (via the Russian Federation) outlets for the country's resources, despite increasing Chinese demand and new pipeline projects. The Kazakh side is hoping for more investment and technology transfers from Europe in order to modernize its business environment including strengthened transparency, governance and institutional quality.

On top of that, both sides have a strong interest in pushing for Kazakh WTO-membership and a rapprochement of Kazakhstan towards EU standards and regulatory systems in order to create a common legal framework together with increased trade flows and facilitated investments.

The Europeans, on the other hand, are keen to diversify their energy suppliers and transit routes, especially in the natural gas sector, in order to decrease their dependence on Russia. Within the scope of this strategic approach, the countries of the Caspian Sea region play a decisive role, especially Kazakhstan. Another important concern for Kazakhstan and the EU is the regional stability in Greater Central Asia, in the context of the current situation in Afghanistan and the fight against terrorism, drug trafficking and organized crime. In this realm, Kazakhstan has a prominent role for the EU, having been the most stable, developed and reliable partner among its Central Asian neighbours for a long time.

However, in 2011Kazakhstan experienced a series of incidents which seem to question its stability, including the first suicide bombing which happened in May. This attack was followed by a car explosion in Astana and several armed clashes between security forces and armed combatants, primarily in the country's energy hub. Some of the insurgent forces were suspected to have links with an unnamed terrorist organization based in Pakistan.[53] Simultaneously, a long-lasting organized strike of oil workers occurred, mostly because not everybody has profited from the country's energy boom. Social tensions are rising.

The EU, on the other hand, has to reconsider its policy toward enduring authoritarian regimes in general. As with the "Arab Spring" and the cries for help to the Western world by the protesters demonstrate, the stakes are high.

Having said this, Kazakhstan should not be an exceptional case, despite its economic potential and its alleged stability. All well-respected organizations dealing with good governance and human rights issues denounce the current situation in Kazakhstan on different levels. Human Rights Watch[54] and Amnesty International[55] report widespread torture or other ill-treatment and massive restrictions of fundamental human rights. Freedom House confirms these bad findings and compares Kazakhstan's Political Rights and Civil Liberties Score with that of countries of the Middle East[56]. According to the results of the Corruption Perceptions Index 2010 of Transparency International, in terms of public sector corruption Kazakhstan ranks on 105 out of 178 states, behind states like Tunisia, Egypt or Algeria.[57] Another ranking, the World Press Freedom Index 2010 of the Reporters Without Borders, excoriates the state of media freedom in Kazakhstan, since it only ranks 162th out of 178 countries.[58] Although these figures should always be regarded with caution, they underline the fact, that Kazakhstan is still an authoritarian regime, highly corrupt, with strong political repression and huge democratic deficits.

The latest demonstration in this context was to be observed during the early presidential elections in April 2011 which extended the term of incumbent President Nazarbaev until 2020. The OSCE/ ODIHR Final Election Observation Report revealed serious irregularities and shortcomings, similar to those in previous elections.[59]

Ever since the "Arab Spring" began, the EU had to deal with the question, to which extent it is justifiable to cooperate with authoritarian regimes and have intensive business relations with them.

From TACIS to an "Advanced" PCA: Kazakh-European Relations at a Glance

For an evaluation of the current situation of Kazakh-European relations and their possible prospects, it is necessary to review their development.

Shortly after the collapse of the Soviet Union, the EU member states recognized the independence of Kazakhstan without delay in 1992. Soon thereafter, the country became a recipient of the EU-funded TACIS programme, an instrument aimed at promoting the transition to a market economy and to reinforce democracy and the rule of law, and allocated 166,2 million Euros until the programme expired in 2006[60].

The first bilateral step was the EU Partnership and Cooperation Agreement (PCA) - signed in 1995 and ratified in 1999 - a-non-preferential agreement, in which the parties grant each other "most favoured nation" status, hence prohibiting tariffs and quantitative restrictions in bilateral trade. The agreement also provides for regular bilateral meetings at the foreign minister level in Cooperation Councils and at the senior official level in policy specific committees.[61] In 2006 a Memorandum of Understanding on cooperation in the field of energy was established, followed by a similar memorandum on the transport sector in 2009.

Moreover, the country was included in several ambitious programmes, covering the whole Central Asian region, e.g. the infrastructure oriented initiatives TRACECA[62] and INOGATE[63], or CADAP[64] and BOMCA[65] for security issues. After the TACIS programme had expired in 2006, and while the Eastern European and Caucasian states had been integrated into the European Neighbourhood Policy, Kazakhstan together with the four other Central Asian countries was addressed by the EU's Central Asia "Strategy for a New Partnership". Under the German EU Council Presidency in 2007 this regional approach was signed, elevating the relationship to a new level and ending the years of neglect of this important region by the EU.

Against the backdrop of sky-rocketing oil prices and the foregone energy crisis between Ukraine and Russia, which led to tremendous shortages in some EU member-states in the midst of a cold winter, energy security became a paramount issue on the European agenda and an important part of the European Central Asia strategy. Moreover, the strategy was influenced by the stagnating situation in Afghanistan and an increasing number of terrorist assaults on NATO's main supply route through Pakistan. As a result, common security issues became a pivotal interest, including the implementation of a supply distribution network leading through Central Asia to Afghanistan from the north. Furthermore, the events in the city of Andijan in 2005, where Uzbek security cracked down on a national uprising, killing hundreds of protesters, caused a strong emphasis on the development of human rights.

Other priority areas were the transport, educational and environmental sectors, the Rule of Law Initiative, the promotion of economic ties, as well as combating common security threats and challenges.[66]

However, after being in place for four years and despite high-level talks and direct contacts at unprecedented levels, the "core of the problem is a deficit within the EU in defining and articulating its interests in the region. The EU has not visibly integrated, or even reconciled, its various agendas: normative (human rights, good governance, cultural dialogue), technical (education, environment, economic development) and interest-based (energy, security)."[67] Likewise, it is criticized that the European Central Asia strategy is incoherent and has too many priorities and interests, backed by too little means to have a sustainable impact.[68]

Compared to the other four Central Asian states, Kazakhstan enjoys the most attention from the European Union and is thus being treated as "front-runner" of the states of the region, due to its domestic stability and profitable business prospects. In addition, it is the Kazakh perception with its "Path to Europe" state programme, which shows that the country is very eager to maintain and expand its pro-European stance, since the EU is one of its most important strategic partners. It was the first country in Central Asia with a permanent fully fledged Delegation of the European Commission, and always had the most stable relationship with the EU. That applies even to the level of nation states, since 18 EU members honoured Astana with the opening of bilateral embassies, whereas for example in Tashkent, the capital of more populous Uzbekistan, just ten diplomatic representations of EU countries operate. Recently, after the 11th meeting of the EU-Kazakhstan Cooperation Council in June 2011, it was envisaged to negotiate a new, even more advanced bilateral framework agreement, being the first among its Central Asian neighbours. The first round of substantial negotiations on October 12th 2011 was "progressive and fruitful". Both sides agreed on better political cooperation, including chapters on justice, freedom and security in addition to a chapter on trade and investment. The main areas of outcome of this particular meeting were the agreement to enter into consultations to facilitate Kazakh citizens' mobility to Europe, an important transition period granted to European companies concerning a new Kazakh law on work permits for foreign workers, as well as air safety issues, concerning civil aviation. Furthermore, the European side declared its expectation, that before the next common meeting "Kazakhstan will fulfil its commitments, and hold all-inclusive parliamentary elections with fair competition among political forces".[69] The sequel for further negotiations is scheduled for the beginning of next year. However the aforementioned point, concerning the commitment of holding parliamentary elections according to democratic standards, possibly proves to become the crucial question and indicator for sincerity of a sustained future Kazakh-European partnership.

Common Fields of Interest in International Security

The EU and Kazakhstan share a number of security concerns emanating from Greater Central Asia. Both sides are concerned with similar security issues, such as international terrorism, organized crime, drug and human trafficking. Nevertheless, the unstable situation in Afghanistan represents by far the most imminent and direct threat to both Kazakhstan and the EU member states.

International Terrorism and Security in Afghanistan

Despite having no direct border with Afghanistan, Kazakhstan is confronted with immediate implications from the precarious situation there. First of all, it is situated along several routes for illicit drug trafficking. Additionally, Kazakhstan is exposed to slow but rising Islamic infiltration. With an unstable "buffer-zone" out of Kyrgyzstan, Tadzhikistan, Turkmenistan and Uzbekistan the danger of an external "spill-over" is at hand.

The EU, since most its members are part of the ISAF-mission, has quite similarly a vital interest in stabilizing the security situation in Afghanistan.

Since the ISAF mission is "celebrating" its 10th anniversary, the gap between the naive anticipation of a short and uncomplicated deployment at the beginning, and the current security situation with immense casualties among the civil population and combatants alike, becomes quite obvious.

Currently, there are 130 thousand international soldiers from 48 countries fighting in Afghanistan. However, the current situation on the ground, with fierce attacks on a regular base, is everything but satisfactory.

Most electorates in the ISAF states are at the end of their tether with the long-lasting, unpopular mission, which is why a troop withdrawal until 2014 is being debated. The Taliban should have enough patience until then, as the Afghan security forces which have to guarantee for security by that time, have huge problems in dealing with Islamic infiltration, nepotism, self-enrichment and indiscipline.

Kazakhstan and the Central Asian states are realizing that the planned departure of ISAF-troops in the coming years will not just be a challenge for their geopolitical environment, but for their domestic stability as well, since they are situated right on the "front-line".

The mutual collaboration with the ISAF started with the beginning of the mission in 2001. In the early stages, Uzbekistan functioned as a deployment ground for the international troops, and granted overflight rights. The airfields in Kyrgyz Manas, Tadzhik Dushanbe and Uzbek Termiz are of considerable importance for the ISAF-mandate.

In recent years, the Central Asian countries became even more important in terms of supply routes. For a long time, main ground supplies for the ISAF started at the Pakistani port of Karachi, where solely non-lethal goods were loaded on local trucks heading to the north. The most dangerous region on this route is the Peshawar valley with its Khyber-Pass on the border to Afghanistan, a region, the government in Islamabad can hardly control. With increasing pressure by Taliban insurgents and numerous attacks on supply convoys, the ISAF-command had to search for alternative routes.

The outcome was the recently implemented Northern Distribution Network (NDN), a railway scheme divided into three different distribution lines, connecting Baltic (Riga), Black Sea (Poti) and Caspian (Baku, Aktau) ports with Afghanistan, while Kazakhstan is the only intersection of all three routes. In 2010 NDN supplied about 35% of all ISAF-cargo for Afghanistan and will probably reach 75% by the end of 2011.[70]

Kazakhstan is already engaged in Afghanistan on bilateral terms, and the only Central Asian state which has an Assistance Programme for the Reconstruction of Afghanistan that includes projects related to infrastructure development, water supply and the delivery of construction commodities[71].

Another sign of a credible Kazakh contribution to the ISAF-mission is an agreement to deploy a four-person group of military officers, being the latest ally of the NATO-led mission in Afghanistan.

Obviously this agreement did not pass unnoticed by the Taliban who announced in a statement, that “the Muslim people of Kazakhstan should stand against this wrong policy of their rulers and should not let their Muslim sons fight against their Muslim brethren”. That warning came in a mysterious combination with two foregone attacks. On 17 May, a suicide bomber blew himself up inside the local headquarters of the domestic security agency KNB in the western oil-city of Aktobe, being the first suicide bombing ever in the history of Kazakhstan. A week later, a car exploded outside a KNB facility in the capital Astana, killing the two men in the car. Government officials denied that the attacks might be the work of radical Islamists. However, the parliament, usually a rubber stamp for president Nazarbaev, rejected the Kazakh contribution to the ISAF-mission.[72]

In August and after a series of deadly clashes between security forces and armed combatants, law enforcement officials announced that they had foiled a plot to carry out terrorist attacks in the oil-rich area of Atyrau in western Kazakhstan. This official announcement of a terrorist plot differed from former explanations, that the string of suspicious incidents had no terrorist background. These incidents left a total of 19 people dead, including five members of the law enforcement agencies, eleven suspects, one suicide bomber and two perpetrators of the car blast in Astana.[73] Just like the rest of the region, Kazakhstan experienced a rebirth of Islamic consciousness and identity after the communist repression. Nowadays around 70% of the Kazakh population consider themselves Muslim, the majority being Sunni. Hundreds of mosques sprouted in the country, while the doctrinal interpretation of Islam is rather moderate, when compared to the likes of Afghanistan or Pakistan. Up until now, the country was spared from Islamic fundamentalists, as there is no tradition of radical Islam in Kazakhstan.

The most active organization is Hizb ut-Tahrir (HuT), a pan-Islamic movement aiming to create a Central Asian caliphate, uniting all Muslims of the region including the Xinjiang province in Western China. Its leaders disavow any form of violence. Nevertheless, the organization is feared at the same time, particularly by the governments in the area which have detained more HuT-activists than any other "radical" opposition group.[74] They try to recruit followers all over Central Asia, since they offer enticing promises to desperate citizens, who are used to governments and regimes that have alienated their citizens with corruption and repression.

However, as in Kazakhstan social distortions are less distinctive when compared to its southern neighbours, the danger of a strong Islamic movement was for a long time not present. Nevertheless, Kazakhstan was facing probably the most turbulent summer in a decade, as besides the aforementioned rising of domestic extremism, first signs of social unrest emerged which are to be discussed.

With regard to Afghanistan, the worst case scenario for all parties concerned (virtually the entirety of the international community, as well as the people of Afghanistan) would see the country falling back to civil war and shelter once again internationally acting terrorists, after the withdrawal of the international forces is completed. In the event of a simultaneous further destabilization of Tadzhikistan, Kyrgyzstan or Uzbekistan, a possible spread of Islamic extremism in Central Asia could not just impair the region, but the whole world. Concerning this security issue, Brussels and Astana are standing side by side.

International Terrorism and Security in Afghanistan Drug Trafficking

Furthermore, Kazakhstan and Europe are affected by another global security challenge stemming from Afghanistan: illicit drug trafficking. Terrorist organizations like the Taliban or the Islamic Movement of Uzbekistan (IMU) rely on the distribution of drugs in order to finance their actions.

Although the potential production of opium decreased in 2010, compared to 2009, by 48% as a result of a disease in opium plants, Afghanistan still produces 3 600 metric tonnes, accounting for 74% of global opium supply.[75]

Because of successful opium seizures in Iran over the last years, the northern routes via Central Asia became more relevant for drug traffickers to reach the lucrative markets in Europe, Russia and, increasingly, China. Thus, Kazakhstan is situated on the "front-line", as trafficking of illicit drugs and the related cluster of problems increase. Local addiction, violent crime, corruption, social and health problems harm the society. According to the World Drug Report 2011, the annual prevalence of users as a percentage point of the population (aged 15-64), consuming opiates is in Kazakhstan with 1% among the top ten of the world. Moreover, drug-related mortality is rising, among users of injected drugs the infection rate of Hepatitis C is around 60%, that with HIV approximately 10%.

Europe is a key market for a variety of illegal drugs, including opiates coming from Afghanistan. In the EU-27 the annual rate of opiate consumption among the adult population (aged 15-64) has reached 1.59% in Scotland, and 1.52% in Estonia, whereas the average EU consumption is between 0.40 and 0.50%.[76]

The economic aspect of drug trafficking is massive. In 2009 around 25% (at least 50 tonnes) of Afghan heroin entered the Russian Federation through Central Asia into the Russian Federation. It is estimated that the value of opiates trafficked through the Afghan-Central Asian borders, is around 350-400 million USD annually. This amount increases several times on its way through the region via the main hub Kazakhstan, since it is estimated that Russian opiate users pay around 13 billion USD per year to drug dealers.[77] This "dirty" money accumulated through smuggling creates a vicious circle that distorts a country's economy by pushing it into a criminal or semi-criminal direction.[78]

At the beginning of the chain in Afghanistan the Taliban and linked insurgent groups like Hizb-i Islami or the Haqqani-network, are involved in the drug trafficking and earn through smuggling and taxation. According to calculations of UNODP, the Taliban could be drawing around 10-15% of their funding from the Afghan opiate trade. Figures from some ISAF-officials ranged from 20-40% of the Afghan Taliban's total income.[79]

To combat these common challenges it is necessary that transit and destination countries of Afghan opiates work together. However, the sheer size of Kazakhstan, as well as the border length (the Russian-Kazakh border alone measures 6 800 km) and topography make anti-trafficking efforts very difficult. Kazakhstan is willing to fight drug trafficking and participates in several programmes. One of these is the EU funded Border Management Programme in Central Asia (BOMCA), implemented by UNDP. The focal point of the programme is to strengthen counter-drug capacities at borders, mainly by means of regional and bilateral workshops and training-sessions regarding the detecting of drugs, apprehending suspected drug traffickers as well as collecting and analysing information on illegal drug trafficking.

The Central Asia Drug Action Programme (CADAP) is aimed at encouraging Central Asian governments to commit to sustainable strategies in the field of drug addiction and to bring current systems of drug addict prosecution into accordance with international strategies and standards. The new EU Action Plan on Drugs between the EU and the Central Asian states wants to intensify the collaboration with the states of the region, as "limited cooperation between Central Asian countries, insufficient domestic inter-agency coordination in the region, and limited coordination among the major international donors as well as between the donors and the states in the region, complicate the establishment of a more efficient border management in the region and fight against drug trafficking through Central Asia to Europe"[80].

However, it remains to be seen how this re-evaluation will be implemented since the fight against drug trafficking has to go along with the struggle against corruption, as a huge amount of trafficking is done by people with ties to Central Asian law enforcement agencies. Therefore, it has to be mentioned openly that the Kazakh government with its partners in Central Asia has to engage in domestic reforms.[81]

European Energy Security Issues Encounter Caspian Resource Wealth

According to the 60th issue of the BP Statistical Review of World Energy, global energy consumption was rising by 5.6% (an almost thirty year climax) in 2010, taking place in all parts of the world and making China for the first time the world's largest energy consumer. Despite all environmental concerns and the fastest increase of CO_2 emissions in four decades, oil remains the global leading energy source at 33.6%. According to this aforementioned report for the end of 2010, Kazakhstan has a stock of 39,8 million barrels of proved oil reserves, which is around 3% of global reserves, and produces 1 757 thousand barrels per day. The confirmed Kazakh natural gas reserves account for around 65,2 trillion cubic feet, equalling about 1% of total global reserves. Estimating coal, the country's proved reserves accumulate for 33 600 metric tonnes (almost 4% of the world share)[82]. Beside hydrocarbons, Kazakhstan has the second biggest known exploitable resources of uranium and significant deposits of iron, ore, copper, zinc, rare earths and gold.

To sum up, Kazakhstan has vast, very profitable and extensively unexploited natural resources.

Needless to say, that the highly developed European nations with their energy hungry economies are keen to gain access to the rich resources of Kazakhstan. Especially, since EU prosperity and wealth depends on accessible mineral fuels as the supplies in Europe and the North Sea are shrinking, and are by far insufficient for the Union's energy requirements. Energy dependency (imports divided by gross domestic consumption) of the EU-27 amounts for 53.8% in 2008. Except for Denmark, every EU country is a net importer of energy. Even big member states like Italy (86.8%), Spain (81.4%) and Germany (61.3%) are much more dependent on external energy imports than the EU-average, and therefore quite vulnerable.[83]

Moreover, the demand for natural gas will increase further due to the disaster at the Fukushima nuclear power plant in early 2011 and the decision to abandon nuclear power production in some European countries, most notably Germany.

In the year 2000, with its Green Paper "Towards a European strategy for the security of energy supply", the EU Commission put the energy issue on the European agenda. The urgency of a common energy policy was mentioned quite bluntly, since the main weaknesses were demonstrated. "If no measures are taken, in the next 20-30 years, 70% of the Union's energy requirements (...) will be covered by imported products", and that "in geopolitical terms, 45% of oil imports come from the Middle East and 40% of natural gas from Russia".[84] The main measures to deal with this considerable vulnerability, were at first the diversification of energy sources in favour of renewable energy, an energy efficiency initiative, and a diversification of energy suppliers, to decrease the strong dependency of particular (and partly very unstable) countries. Already during this time, the littoral states of the Caspian Sea were considered as major potential suppliers, especially in the natural gas sector.

In line with the Interstate Oil and Gas Transportation to Europe programme (INOGATE), the Baku Initiative in 2004 which set out the parameters of future engagement on energy issues, was the first attempt to bring together all key supply and transit countries east of Europe, including littoral states of the Black and Caspian Sea, Central Asian states, Russia and Iran. During the follow-up conference in Astana in 2006, the number of participating states narrowed, due to interstate disputes in the meantime (i.e. Russia-Ukraine), but a Road Map set out detailed objectives, on how to transport Caspian gas through a Southern Energy Corridor to European markets, bypassing Russia. This corridor consists of two pipeline projects, with the Nabucco-pipeline (from Erzerum in Turkey to Baumgarten in Austria) being the centrepiece which would transport up to 31 bcm per year to central European states. A second arm is the Turkey-Greece-Italy Interconnectorpipeline (TGII) which would be expanded to supply 3,5 bcm to Greece and 8 bcm to Italy.[85]

However, Kazakhstan recently refused the restated invitations of the European Commission to participate in the Southern Energy Corridor, after the EU agreed to begin talks with Azerbaidzhan and Turkmenistan about delivery guarantees and a Trans-Caspian submarine pipeline. The Kazakh Minister for Oil and Gas stated that the country currently does not have sufficient gas production capacities to join the Nabucco project, but as soon as high-potential gas fields are developed, a cooperation could be possible.[86]

This setback for the EU stands in line with the generally doubtful viability of the whole project. As the current gas supply commitments are by far not sufficient, the beginning of the construction is constantly postponed and the costs are rising, which makes the project hardly profitable.[87]

The Kazakhs are simply not dependent on transporting gas to the West, as they have a variety of possible outlets. If the EU wants to get a large volume of gas from Kazakhstan, it's going to have to put in quite a lot of effort, in order to encourage the Kazakhs, with European assistance, to make the necessary investments in gas infrastructure and in upstream gas production. The still existing problem for Kazakhstan is its landlocked position and the imbalance between production and pipeline capacity, as well as the need for unlocking export routes. Accordingly, Kazakhstan's strategy is to have a multi-vector pipeline system to diversify transit routes, to match international demand and decrease the long lasting, exclusive dependency on existing pipelines to Russia.[88]

Essential steps towards this direction have already been made. Since 2009, an oil pipeline from Western Kazakhstan to China has been completed. A gas pipeline, following approximately the same route, is planned for the near future. Other options are in the planning stage, i.e. a southwards pipeline project through Turkmenistan, to reach Iranian harbours on the Persian Gulf, or an upgrading of the existing pipelines to Russia to extend the volume transferred to Europe.

However, the Europeans fell far behind in the race for Central Asian resources, and are described as being "much better at making policy declarations than at taking policy action". Although China was not a significant actor until the late 1990ies, now it is by far the most important new actor. Russia, together with Iran, restored its regional influence, not least in oil and gas transit.[89]

The EU-Central Asia Monitoring (EUCAM) report on the EU's Central Asia Strategy, notes this quite explicitly: "This is a classic example of how the EU and its member states have to negotiate and decide faster on elements of a common energy policy, or see the world leave it behind."[90]

Implications of the "Arab Spring" and Domestic Challenges: How Stable Is Kazakhstan?

As mentioned before, Kazakhstan achieved its economic prosperity as a result of both its wealth in natural resources and its political stability over the previous decade. For the Europeans the investment climate is favourable, especially in the field of energy, and as they cannot be so sure about other parts of the world, the EU considers Kazakhstan as a reliable, economically stable partner.

But especially in the crucial energy sector, growing civil unrest is taking place. Since May 2011, thousands of oil workers are on an unprecedented strike in Western Kazakhstan. The blow-off happened in August 2011, when thousands of protesters marched on to the ruling presidential Nur-Otan party's headquarters in the western Kazakh town of Zhanaozen to officially quit the party, as none of their strike demands had been met. In their strike, lasting onward from May, the workers claimed equal rights with foreign workers, no restrictions on independent trade unions, a pay rise and the immediate release of their lawyer Natalya Sokolova, who provided legal support to them and was jailed for six years. From government officials the incident was downplayed. Instead, official statements indicated, that hundreds of people had joined the party since the strike had begun in May.[91]

Consequently, and together with the aforementioned rising terror attacks, the reputation of Kazakhstan as a socially and politically stable country is currently widely questioned.

However, thus far the political stability had been the bargaining chip. Consequently, the country was able to acquire most foreign direct investment in the region and to make prolific business contacts with all major players in the past. President Nazarbaev always understood quite well, how to boost the international reputation of his country, stressing the image of stabilization, in every direction. In short progression, the country was holding the chairmanship and high-level summits of the OSCE, the Shanghai Cooperation Organization (SCO), the Organization of Islamic Conference (OIC), the Cooperation Council of Turkic Speaking States (CCTS), several high profile economic and financial conferences as well as the Asian Winter Games 2011. In line with the multi-vector foreign policy, the president intensified relations with NATO over the last years. He is eager to push the Eurasian Union, a single market together with Russia and Belarus, and is warmly welcomed from Beijing to Brussels.

On the one hand, big appearances on the international parquet help to polish the Kazakh image abroad. On the other hand, it is intended to show the domestic audience that the country's leadership enjoys strong international support, and is accepted as a peer by leaders of Western democracies as well as all other major players.

The incumbent president still enjoys a high level of popularity among the Kazakh population after more than 20 years in office. His person is an identity creating element for the young country. The regime in Astana was able to showcase the stability of the country, particularly to demonstrate the competence of the Kazakh president Nazarbaev to its own people. By pointing to the precarious political instability of its Southern neighbours, for example the bloody civil war in Tadzhikistan, severe terror attacks in Uzbekistan, and civil unrest in Kyrgyzstan with deadly street fights and two revolutions, the Kazakh regime always justified its restrictive policy.

Under the reign of the "leader of the nation" the peaceful coexistence of the many ethnic groups in kazakhstan could be maintained, and the country managed to get through the bad economic crisis of the 1990ies, leading it to the current economic prosperity. The unemployment rate decreased over the last couple of years. The country developed a huge allurement for workers from the other Central Asian states. Poverty was reduced significantly, the educational expenditures increased, and the GNI per capita rose from 4 460 USD in the year 2000 to 10 610 USD in 2010[92].

Despite being now in the club of "medium-income countries" according to the Human Development Index, social tensions and grievances are growing. One of the country"s most conflict-ridden and contentious issues is the significantly rising disparity of income levels within the society. The rise of social polarization has several implications, starting with growing regional disparities in the standard of living, since only the cities of Almaty and Astana and resource-rich regions in the west of the country attract investment.

The regional growth dynamics started at approximately the same level in 1998, but within only 10 years they differ by a factor of almost 12, which means that only a few regions are extremely rich while most of them are quite poor.[93]

The economic imbalances are deepening, so that these sharp distortions may lead to broad social and political dissatisfaction. A significant incident was the revolution in neighbouring Kyrgyzstan in spring and summer of 2010. The government's assessment, that similar uprisings could spill-over to Kazakhstan, led to discussing a "People's IPO" (Initial Public Offering). The official announcement by President Nazarbaev followed in February 2011, in which he heralded the participatory model which states that minority stakes of the country's largest state-owned companies will be sold at a discount price exclusively to Kazakh citizens[94]. The start of the programme is scheduled for mid-2012, so it remains to be seen, as Nazarbaev had stated, wether this is a "real opportunity to raise [sic] well being of common citizens (...) to strengthen [sic] bridge of confidence between the business and people at large (...), giving them a new tool for investments and savings"[95]. However, it is questionable whether these measures will be satisfactory, since there is a basic middle class approaching, which is requesting actual political participation and pluralism.

Nevertheless, compared to current uprisings in the Middle East and Northern Africa, it would be far-fetched to speak about an approaching "Kazakh spring". But as it happened in the Arab World, the danger of an external spill-over, for instance from struggling Tadzhikistan or Kyrgyzstan is present.

There are some similar preconditions in the other Central Asian states that led to the ongoing uprisings and the "Arab Spring". Both regions are characterized by a high and obvious level of corruption and nepotism on state level, in the economy and the public administration. Moreover, the regimes are constantly accused of various forms of repression and fundamental violations of human rights. The long-lasting presidents and potentates in both regions facilitated the perception of a certain unreformability. The share of the 15-24 age cohort is disproportionately high, with huge unemployment rates among the youth and a general lack of prospects.

While in the Arab world one leader after another was overthrown or at least confronted with severe uprisings, the Kazakh regime proclaimed early elections, probably being afraid of similar developments in Central Asia.

With the early presidential elections in April 2011, resulting in a landslide victory of over 95% of the vote for the incumbent president and a turnout of 89%, the regime, notwithstanding huge democratic shortcomings, wanted to proceed its way as a bastion of stability, extending Nazarbaev's mandate until 2020.

But with recent events, the picture is crumbling, and officials are anxious of domestic upheavals which could unsettle foreign investors. The great unknown remains the unresolved succession of president Nazarbaev.

In July 2011, officially on vacation, the 71-year-old ruler allegedly received medical treatment in Germany. However, political analysts such as Timothy Ash believe that, while the succession is a "key risk" for Kazakhstan, the elites should be able to implement it orderly. "Kazakhstan is so strategic to Russia, the US and China in terms of energy supply, transit and, in Russia's case, the Baikonur space station plus a large ethnic Russian population that I have some confidence that we would see a pretty smooth transition of power to someone in the inner circle."

Conclusions

As demonstrated in this chapter, Kazakhstan and the EU share similar interests in various fields where further cooperation would not only be desirable but is indispensable. The political will on both sides is at hand, as shown with the ongoing negotiations about an enhanced Partnership Agreement.

However, a positive outcome of a deeper convergence is up to domestic developments in Kazakhstan, concerning radical Islamism and social upheavals as well as the governments reaction, and how fast the EU will recover from the ongoing debt crisis. If Europe remains stuck in its worst crisis in history, and national unilateralist leanings prevail, a deepened common foreign and security policy would be in danger. In case the situation worsens on a political level, e.g. with the expansion of the labour unrest to other areas and escalating danger of Islamic assaults, the ordinary way of tightening repressions may very well lead to a vicious circle.

The following dissatisfaction could drive, for instance, more Muslims into the arms of extremists. As long as no real political opposition exists, the extremists could act as a collecting pool for any oppositional movement. The political measures taken by the government after the uncharacteristic outburst of Islamist-inspired violence go towards this direction. The Prosecutor General's Office announced that an Astana city court "recognized the content of 51 international websites as illegal and ordered them to be blocked to prevent further promotion of religious extremism and terrorism in the Republic."[96] Moreover, the Kazakh parliament approved a restrictive religion law, in which the existing religious organisations have to dissolve and register again through a procedure that virtually will exclude smaller groups due to a predetermined minimum number of members.[97] If these restrictions will be continued or extended to other areas, e.g. employment rights or possibilities of political participation, people will be looking for a way out, which could lead to riots and more violence. Especially now, as Kazakhstan is faced with certain domestic turbulences and is at the beginning of negotiations about deepening the mutual cooperation, Europe should regard the security situation and the official reaction very carefully. The EU should not repeat its mistakes made in North Africa and the Middle East by considering authoritarian regimes in the Muslim world solely as guarantors against further expansion of Islamic extremism. For way too long, the EU collaborated with these regimes, neglecting the demands for human rights in favour of its economic interests, and placing more emphasis on regional stability than on democratic development.[98] It is a thin line between rolling out the red carpet and signing contracts with potentates, consequently supporting the established system, and losing its credibility among local democratic forces of a value-based and normative European foreign policy.

Kazakhstan, on the other side, is heavily dependent on the Europeans as trade and investment partners, despite the general dependence on energy imports and the corresponding vulnerability of the latter. This applies even more to the sphere of security, as demonstrated by the war in Afghanistan, to which, with a few exceptions, currently only NATO members are deploying troops, doing the "dirty work" on the ground. As a consequence of the elaborated mutual interdependence, there is wide scope for a fruitful Kazakh-European collaboration.

Nevertheless, for the sake of not again being accused of a hypocritical European foreign policy, the EU has to stipulate clearly and precisely that the Kazakh authorities need to adhere to the human rights commitments of their OSCE-membership, and make timely democratic reforms from above to facilitate further cooperation.

Magbat Spanov, Gulnara Kairbaevna Akhmetzhanova, The Economy of Kazakhstan: Myths & Reality

Historical Background

In order to evaluate the socio-economic development in Kazakhstan, it is necessary to distinguish some periods, differing both in the intensity of the transformation of economic relations and in the general directions of reforms:

The period between the end of the 1980ies to the year 1991: Initial reform period within the former USSR

As we know, the deterioration of the economic environment in Kazakhstan took distinct form at the end of the 80ies which was tied to the general crisis of the previous system: errors in economic policies, arms race and state paternalism in the social sphere under conditions of a non-market economic model of self-sufficient nature led to a gradual decline of the real economy and the ambient spheres. In this period reforms were undertaken on the principle of khozraschet (literally: economic accounting; note of the translator) in economy, which did not actually result in changes of the economic interrelations between businesses and the state. Funds, thresholds and the control of governmental offices were diminished. Product flows were continuously regulated by means of a state plan, and product prices remained fixed. The financial system was extraneous, businesses worked under conditions of soft budgetary restrictions and centrally allotted credit resources, and the mechanism of budgetary financing was even more reinforced. Therefore the business profits could not be directed to investment objectives, severe limitations of salaries existed as well as foreign economic activities were controlled, and the rouble was convertible.

Starting with the year 1988, a continuous slowdown in the growth of the gross social product began. In 1990 the decline of growth rates faded to a total drop in production, the national income in the Kazakh SSR dwindled down 0.4% and in 1991 even down 4.9%. By 1991 the budgetary deficit exceeded 12 billion roubles in the KSSR and accounted for 13% of the republic's gross national product (GNP). In general terms the production volume was decreasing rapidly and production efficiency sank. Both the population and businesses had liquid assets at their disposal, while the quantity of goods was in deficit, hence the inflation rate increased. As a result barter trade developed, money basically ceased to fulfill its function as a general means of payment and the country's financial system broke down.

Period, Lasting From 1991 to 1993: Economic Reforms Under Conditions of the Rouble Zone

In December 1991 Kazakhstan declared its independence, whereupon economic reforms took a completely new shape: the proclaimed reform agenda aimed at the realignment of property relations and the restructuring of the financial system. However Kazakhstan, belonging to the rouble zone, did not have any financial institutions, that would have allowed to pursue effective money and credit policies and effect a macroeconomic stabilization.

In the course of "orthodox shock" reforms, that began in January 1992 in Russia, Kazakhstan, staying in the rouble zone, continued to receive credits from the former centre. This, along with high yield of grain in agriculture averted a sharp slowdown of production in 1992. The collapse of the system of centralized planning, coupled with a lack of market regulation and a weak financial sector led to a disruption of economic relations, having formed, and an intensification of the slump. Furthermore, businesses that initially struggled with budget limitations began to circumvent them, amassing debts onto each other, which turned out to be the origin of a non-payments crisis. As a result of the termination of tax revenues (around 80% of the GNP) from the former centre, the disorganisation of trade and payments, the disruption of inter-republic relations and loss of orders, the efficiency of labour declined dramatically and social tensions developed, which together with the active money creation and credit accommodation fuelled the rise of the inflation rate up to 30% to the end of the year 1992.

In 1993 the biggest contraction (16%) in business activity took place, since the beginning of the crisis in 1990. The annual inflation made up 2265%, and the number of officially registered unemployed was 13,5 times higher than in 1991. The national income dropped down to the level of the year 1976. In 1993 the pace of reforms in Kazakhstan also slowed down because of windfall losses in foreign trade, that were brought about by a fall in world prices for raw materials and by the country's dependence on Russian pipe lines regarding the transportation of crude oil. A serious demoralizing factor for the economy were the difficult and protracted talks, followed by a breakdown of negotiations about the Kazakh membership in the rouble zone. The introduction of a new rouble ex parte in July 1993 in Russia then extremely quickened the pace of inflation. The reluctance of legislative powers to the policy of radical market reforms, corruption in administration and local Government, as well as the more and more forfeiting social orientation of social politics, the factor of the impending collapse, experts have projected for the economy of Kazakhstan in spring 1995, exerted substantially negative influence on reformed processes.

The priod between 1994 to 1997: Course towards financial stabilization and economic Ggowth under conditions of a self-sufficient monetary system

Due to the dissolution of the rouble zone the Kazakh leadership forfeited technical credits and other financial support from the former centre, and therefore did not have the possibility to consider choices regarding strategies and models of economic reforms. Choosing the radical model, the proximity to Russia, that pursued policies of "shock therapy", brought its influence to bear. Hence, at the beginning of the year 1994 this policy and its pursuance became the reality in Kazakhstan. The choice of the given reform model was also exceedingly influenced by failures of preceding efforts to lead the country out of the crisis and the recent success of financial stabilization in Poland. In a similarly quick manner the reformers intended to transform the relations of planned economy into market relations. A choice had only to be made regarding the kind of shock brought to bear on economy: either by means of control over the distribution of products of fast-declining production or by means of an immediate conversion of the conditions into a standard system of market value including free price and free flow of goods. By that time reformers became aware of the fact that a high inflation narrows the final demand and slows down the output growth. Nonetheless, they continued to bind the exit from this scenario to the braking of the excessive inflation, and the withdrawal of economy from a redistributive dead end.

Despite the complications in the plan to switch to reciprocal payments in hard currency between the countries of the former USSR, the disruption of economic relations, the cessation of orders for output of union subordinated businesses the introduction of the national currency tenge gave Kazakhstan the opportunity to pursue autonomous policies with orientation to financial stabilization. At the end of 1993 the Agreement on a standby loan with the International Monetary Fund (IMF) was signed, which stipulates restrictive measures of monetary policies, targeting the inflation drop. The main goals of this policy in Kazakhstan were the decline in inflation to 7% per month until the end of the year, the provision of a stable balance of payments, the strengthening of the national currency, the deceleration of the drop in production, and the maintenance of the population's standard of living.

First and foremost, these goals were sought to be attained by the realization of a strict monetary policy, meaning increasing the rate of interest, the sale of Government security assets, the solution of debt problems, the constant exchange rate of the tenge and the remittance of currency gains by export businesses. Thereby the credit limitations proved to be the key element in the stabilization programme and the money supply was not to exceed 11 722 million tenge countrywide.

The result of pursuing such a restrictive monetary policy was the decline in inflation down to 1 258.3% in 1994 in contrast to 2 265% in 1993. The biggest increase in inflation inevitably fell in the second quarter (157.2%), which was the consequence of the liberalization of prices for energy sources, as well as the corporate debt financing within the frame of the conducted mutual offset of debts. However, already in the third quarter a decline was recorded down to 55.8% and in the fourth to 51.2%, at which in December it went down 10%.

Furthermore the package of measures included the requirement to reduce the "fiscal deficit" of the Government or the "borrowing requirements of the public sector" by means of cutting government grants and increasing the prices for basic public services. During 1994 the limit for the budget debt was determined for a 4% range of the GNP, whereat the deficiency payments were intended to be effected through means not exposed to inflation, that is mainly through the sale of government bonds and the attraction of external financing sources.

In addition to a "quantitative rationing", that is the scope limitations of loans granted by the financial sector, the package also included the requirement for a „price rationing“ of credits, meaning a high interest rate. This measure was regarded a double-edged weapon. On the one hand it was assumed that it would encourage the growth of private savings and thereby reduce the overall demand for loans by the banking sector; on the other hand it was expected that the measure reduced the demand for loans at the banking sector due to the increase of costs for loan funds.

Furthermore the Government rendered select support to businesses by means of extending targeted loans, that were given out in the amount of 14 063,7 million tenge in 1994. But notwithstanding the rigid return basis as of 1 December 1994, approximately 2 300 million tenge were added.

The measures adopted in the framework of the stabilization programme should have tightened the credit policy and raised their returns in the real economy. In this case, however, due to the lack of discipline and order in the banking system and in the very businesses, the said targeted loans of the Government were irretrievably used for other purposes in most instances.

An utterly undesirable effect of the above mentioned super-drastic measures to reduce the credit demand lay in the fact that these measures were simultaneously accompanied by a sharp drop in supply given the liberalization of prices, the past-due debt of businesses in the CIS and Baltic States, the impossible high costs of interest payments as well as the shortage of working capital. In 1994 the majority of businesses in Kazakhstan suffered a chronic deficit in current assets.

In accordance with the programme, the increase of net savings, that then had turned into investments and stabilized in progress, should have become the ultimate result of all measures taken. Nevertheless, the expected increase of savings did not set in. Over the period discussed the retail deposits increased merely from 606,9 million tenge on 1 January, 1994 to 1 673,5 million tenge on 1 July, 1994 and the balances of current, transactional and deposit accounts in banks underwent a corresponding change from 4 154.1 million tenge to 12 473,0 million tenge.

This resulted de facto in a destabilization of real economy along with a production slump. In the year 1994 alone, Kazakhstan lost more than a quarter of its industry.

The subsequent aim of shock therapy was the measure adopted in order to improve the balance of trade, which is to be attained by the cheapening of export, as well as the appreciation of import for foreigners and the appreciation of import for locals via depreciation of currency. After the introduction of the tenge in November 1993 in a 4,64 ratio to the USD, whose settlement exchange rate is determined weekly on the foreign exchange interbank market, the ratio from tenge to dollar accounted for 12,02 in the first quarter, 33,63 in the second, 45,78 in the third and 51,05 in the fourth. Such a rapid devaluation of the tenge paved the way to lower the Kazakh balance of trade deficit from 1 546,6 USD in 1993 to 1 398,3 USD already by the end of the year 1994.

Moreover, the stabilization package in Kazakhstan included the utilization of two nominal anchors averting the development of an inflationary spiral in economy. The stability of the exchange rate of the national currency over a certain period of time served as the first anchor. To that effect the Government and the National Bank pursued a policy (until 16 April, 1999) stipulating the prevention of sudden fluctuations of the exchange rate of the tenge.

The second anchor was the policy of limiting nominal wages, when wages are indexed as usually by a coefficient, that but partially compensates inflation. This rule means that real wages will continuously decline as long as inflation is effective.

Not only the precipitated world economic crisis or the failures in implementing shock therapy and/ or other reasons may explain the formal macroeconomic stabilization, achieved in the years 1996 to 1997 and the subsequent and repeated decrease of macroeconomic indices in the Republic of Kazakhstan, but also the miscalculations that to a great extent were connected with the latter, and were tolerated in the process of structural transformations.

Structural measures – the second objective of shock therapy – are aimed at the increase of supply, and constitute the marrow and one of the main goals of the whole complex of economic transformations. However, it was exactly them that turned out to be the least effective in Kazakhstan.

When the breakup of economic relations between the republics appeared as the main reason for the drop in production in Kazakhstan before administering shock therapy, then money and credit restrictions, ultimately leading to the breakdown of the country's financial system, became the determining factor as of the second half of the year 1994.

With no regard to the maturity of market relations and to the specificities of the given transformation stage, policies of denationalization and privatization, that bear no relation whatsoever to the tasks and issues of structural reorganisation and increase in supply, have the only objectives to quickly establish a business and proprietary class and to achieve the necessary structure of ownership types, not knowing which established indices to consider. The artificial development of property relations – property, for which instead of a real one an intermediate proprietor was appointed, who due to the lack of an operative equity market is not able today to control the property at his/ her hand – and the lack of institutional investors cause the low capital mobility, and impede the improvement in efficiency of existing investment resources. In the end the shortcomings of the structural reforms led to a serious lack of investment capital and basically disabled the reproduction process.

The course towards the realization of the presidential strategy „Kazakhstan 2030: Prosperity, Security, Enhancement of the Living Standard of the Kazakh People"

The objective of the years 1998 to 2000 work was to guarantee economic growth by recovering real economy, restructure the public sector, and increase investments in the country's economy. These goals were to be attained under conditions of pursuing active social policies and reducing the macroeconomic stability through solving the following problems: the reinforcement of national security; the increase of inner-political stability and of social cohesion on basis of achieving the objectives of the Presidential Strategy; the acceleration of economic growth; the definitive implementation of a concept for the world market's provision with energy sources, project planning, ground-breaking and completion of works on individual sections; in the main, the end of reconstructing and building key communication and transport facilities, that guarantee the development of international trade; the creation of a fundamentally new system of state administration. The realization of the given development strategy of Kazakhstan was destined to conduce to the end of the transitional phase and the country's taking the path of sustained development.

The development of a new economic system in Kazakhstan presupposes that already during the transition of economy not only the latest trends of the modern diversified society's social development should be fully taken into consideration, but also the national characteristics of each country and people, of their different levels standards of social and economic development.

Until the dissolution of the former USSR the Kazakh people, in comparison with other republics of Middle Asia, enjoyed a higher standard of living. Therefore the average annual revenue per head in Kazakhstan amounted up to around 2 470 USD, and even in relation to Western standards the social indicators were regarded as high. Nevertheless, the republic suffered a decrease in the standard of living, and in 1989 approximately 15% of the population were living below the poverty line, whose threshold was assessed 77 roubles at that time.

The features of Kazakh economy with its regional differences, well-developed tendencies towards public forms of appropriation, scant real mentality, traditions of state paternalism both in economy and the social sphere are an objective foundation for directing the transformation towards actually solving society's vital matters.

At the beginning of market reformations in Kazakhstan the notion of social orientation in market economy precipitated the extensive release of labour in national economy and its redistribution.

However, the ongoing transformation of post-socialist economy into a diversified society led to radical changes in the entire social sphere. The transition from hierarchical stratification, in which the rank of individuals and of social groups is determined by their position in the structure of state power and by the proximity to sources of centralised distribution – a proximity that is a dominant in the civilised world of class stratification -, comes to pass with exceptional velocity. More and more importance is attached to relations of power and less to proprietary conditions.

Initially the reform in the social sphere in Kazakhstan, that had been conducted since 1993, premised that social security ought to play a decisive role in the process of restructuring economy. It was a known that in the course of that restructuring unemployment rates would increase, actual wage levels would decrease, subsidies would be cut and businesses would be exempt from social functions, alien to them under market conditions. It was also expected that all this would lead to a low average standard of living and to a rising amount of socially unprotected people in the country.

In order to foreclose irreparable losses of human capital it first and foremost was necessary to protect the most vulnerable citizens from the impact of change, and spare the unemployed, children and the elderly poverty and hunger, meaning maintaining a suitable system of social security.

In the course of these transformations provisions, that included the substitution of the current system of social benefits with subsidies for the most vulnerable strata of society, were made in 1994 for the implementation of highly targeted social security actions. Intentions were articulated regarding the elaboration of a system of social protection, that consists of republic and local levels, as well as the regulation of retirement benefits, the provision with payments out of the pension fund of labour pensions, the institution of a compulsory and private insurance to retirees to be.

With an increasingly targeted approach within the system of social protection provisions were made for re-assessing the minimum salary. Government's policies aimed at establishing a dependence of salaries from the level of production.

However, as part of the said policies from the year 1994 onwards the Kazakh Government practically brought the standard measures of the "shock therapy" package into action, including steps in the social sphere. As we already mentioned, in doing so, two nominal anchors were used in order to avert the emergence of an inflationary spiral. The stability of the exchange rate intending to lower the inflation expectation served as the first anchor, the policy of limiting nominal wages by means of their indexation by a coefficient, that only partially compensated inflation, during a stabilization period as the second. The last-mentioned measure was also motivated by the necessity to discipline state enterprises, that in transitional phases are usually more interested in salary increases than in profit. It therefrom becomes evident that both the first and the second measures are explicit and social in nature.

At the same time adhering to policies of inflation decline by monetary-credit restrictions and to policies of balance of payment deficit reduction and of Government budget reductions, the result were expenditure cuts of the latter, concerning especially budget items as regards social benefits. This involved overall dollarization of these small payments and acute falls in production, the increase of the unemployment rate, the decrease of salary level, the consequential cut-backs of social protection, including those for the most vulnerable strata of society. All that led to a dramatic drop in the Kazakh people's standard of living.

In international practice the standard of living today is measured by the Human Development Index (HDI), which is considered to conduct an integral assessment of the level of development and implement "human development" on the grounds of weighting three of its most important components. These are the amount of the real GDP per capita, life expectancy, quality of life and access to education and knowledge.

From the data presented it follows that after a continuous decrease since 1991 the GDP in Kazakhstan underwent a stabilization in 1997 due to the deceleration of the economic downturn.

One of the most important factors for the drop in the population's standard of living in that period was the destruction of the specific government infrastructure as a result of the reforms undertaken. An unequalled curtailment of free services or, as officials would say, an optimisation of public health services, education and special services went on.

Prospects

20 years later Kazakhstan presents itself as a country with a powerful industry, a developed agricultural sector, a high rate of literate and educated citizens. The country's riches, that are land, environmental resources and industrial capacities, belonged to the entire Kazakh society. The Constitution guaranteed every single citizen the utmost assistance and support by the state (the right to labour, education, free medical care, a system of social protection, decent retirement benefits and so on).

During the time of economic reforms the people of Kazakhstan experienced a wide scope of implemented programmes on economic development, ranging from „shock therapy" to forced industrialization. At this the authorities explained the minimalisation of political and social reforms with the need for a prioritised economic development as the basis for procuring a high level of wealth for the population and a successful development of the country. Due to these goals society had to endure a policy of radical cuts in social expenditures, a drastic drop of the standard of living, unemployment, deterioration of health, a rise in crime and lot more.

As a matter of fact the Kazakh people live with the neglected promise of a life in prosperity for 20 years. Despite all the existing possibilities the authorities were not able to make provisions for a dignified development of Kazakhstan, whose **unique traits** embrace:

1) Profitable economic characteristics:

- An immense supply level of resources, due to whose capacity Kazakhstan belongs to the world's top ten of possessor-nations of petroleum and non-ferrous metal;

- A high production rate of agricultural products (the yearly production of durum accounts for 12 to 17 million tonnes) in high and stable demand on world markets (within the five production leaders);
- An economy of agricultural and industrial nature;

2) Unique socio-demographic factors:

- A relatively advantageous geographical position (a transit gateway between Europe and the countries of South-East Asia);
- A small population size (less than 17 million people) on a vast territory (number 9 in the world);
- A relatively young, economically active population (the mean age of a Kazakh is little more than 30 years);
- The multi-ethnicity of the nation.

3) Qualitative social indicators:

- Overall literacy;
- A remarkable rate of graduating from higher education;
- A rather developed infrastructure in the social sphere.

Literally speaking, Kazakhstan appears to be a country where on average 5 tonnes of petroleum are produced and 1 tonne of corn is grown per inhabitant, and only 5.5 people are living per square kilometre. However, since many years around 30% of the country's population live off a living wage that is lower than the living wage determined by the state (approximately 13 thousand to 16 thousand tenge). 12% of the population officially belong to the poor. 60% of the population are not provided with qualitative drinking water. More than 100 thousand families are on the list for receiving living space.

Furthermore, within two decades only foreign direct investments in the amount of over 100 billion dollars were made in the country. Kazakh commercial banks obtained loans in excess of 40 billion dollars. Within a couple of years one could then observe a surplus in state budgets in the country, as long as the means dedicated to the supply of the population's social needs were not tapped or spent at all futilely.

Given the ineffective economic management the country's national debt rose, guaranteed by the Government, and still at the beginning of 2009 accounted to 19 billion dollars. In the last two years the Kazakh Government borrowed an additional 15 billion dollars from the Chinese Government. Futilely spending internal resources and drawing on foreign loans, the Kazakh authorities, despite all promises and possibilities, did neither succeed in diversifying the economy, nor in establishing a competitive processing industry or furnishing the country's food security and even less in laying the foundation for a steady social development.

The Results Obtained

Altogether, within years of economic reformations a huge amount of programmes for long-term development of the country were adopted. Not a single one was however either completed or successful. **On the level of the realization of national economic programmes, whose results are measured by the absolute calculus of macroeconomic indicators, relative parameters attest to the following:**

1) The external debt of Kazakhstan has increased nearly a twelvefold. The loans of second-tier banks have become the main reason for the external debt increment. As a result in 2009 the state had been forced to amortize debts of private banks, after it had extracted 5 billion USD from the National fund for the solution of these issues (the overall amount of debts, second-tier banks were burdened with, accounted for 42 billion USD).

2) For the social sector the share of expenses of the growing state budget sank by half.

3) Above all, despite the adopted state programmes, the increasing GDP, the auspicious economic upswing worldwide and other factors, the main challenges are not dealt with. These directly involve the establishment of a basis for effective economic development, meaning the diversification of the Kazakh economy and the guarantee of full food security.

- Throughout that period suggestions were made to restructure the industrial production, modernise the material and technical basis, implement new technologies (more than 11 billion USD were spent for these objectives). As a result the realization of these programmes was protracted into other periods and took another 50 billion dollars for 144 facilities in the course of 5 years.
- The supply of national food products should have reached the level of food security, that is not less than 80%, but it de facto sank down to 55%.
- Today the country is provided with drinking water resources by 40%,

while the objectives of the national programme "Drinking Water" were tied to the accelerated accomplishment of the 100%-supply of the population with clean drinking water.

In light of the enunciated huge macroeconomic accomplishments the **qualitative indicators of the social conditions in Kazakh society illustrated contradictory outcomes,** namely:

1) The decrease of the population's life expectancy (from 68 years in 1991 to 66 to 64 years (ad interim according to different estimates));

2) The steady eleven-fold increase of regional differences in standard of living and quality of life (11,5 times in 2000 (GRP of Atyrauskaya oblast accounted for 581,7 thousand tenge while the GRP of Zhambylkaya oblast amounted to 50,2 thousand tenge) and 11,7 times in 2008 (GRP of Atyrauskaya oblast came to 3 625,9 thousand tenge while the GRP of Yuzhno-Kazakhstanskaya oblast numbered 310,3 thousand tenge));

3) The intensification of social stratification (the richest 10% earn 8,5 times more than the poorest 10%, with a tendency to rise);

4) The high level of socially conditioned diseases (tuberculosis, AIDS (more than 14 thousand people), alcoholism (more than 300 thousand people, filed by the Ministry of Health, and 126 thousand people according to the Ministry of the Interior), drug addiction (340 thousand drug addicts) and more);

The following issues became practically insuperable in the economic system:

1) The ultimate dependence on raw materials of the Kazakh economy (more than 70% of the budget are drawn from the petroleum and gas sector);

2) The huge amount of external debts, that nearly equals the quantity of the GNP (the debt amounted to 107,7 billion USD, whereas according to the international criteria of economic security it may not exceed 60% of the GNP);

3) The absolute underdevelopment of domestic investments, that would guarantee the protection and development of the economy (experts estimate the capital outflow from Kazakhstan at 3 - 5 bn dollars/year).

4) The high monopolization and deficiency of internal competition in practically all sectors of economy;

5) Corruption and the rise of underground economy (according to official statistic data its share in the GNP is more than 22% and according to different expert opinions even up to 60%);

6) The technological wear of essential means (on average 70%);

7) The scarcity of both professional leaders in management and qualified labour force, especially regarding technical professions.

A couple of **negative trends** that are directly connected with a **soaring economic growth** (2000-2007) and are practically rooted in the present, are subject to special consideration. These are:

1) The excessive financial inflow due to a sharp increase in petroleum extraction (budget proficit)

2) Unregulated foreign loans of second-tier banks on international markets (nearly 50% of the total external debt);

3) Huge consumption expenditures and non-manufacturing overheads (maintenance of the state apparatus);

4) Illegal migration in the years of economic boom (up to 1 million people);

5) The speculative rise of wages, unrelated to the gain of labour productivity and the quality of the work done;

6) The politicization of social and economic needs, that was triggered by the ineffective work of bodies of state administration.

Key Problems of Present-Day Economic Policy

The latest effort – in order to diversify the economy and conduct structural renewals – became the establishment of state development institutions (2004). Based on the latter intentions were expressed to fully retreat from the focus on raw materials in the development of Kazakh economy. Later these institutions were combined into a unified framework, namely the fund "Samruk-Kazyna", whose goals coalesced with the realization of a scheme of so called "breakthrough" or investment projects, that were capable of bringing forward Kazakh production, able to meet competition on world markets. A special industrial and innovation programme (2004-2015) was implemented. Within six years of these institutions' existence several hundred billion tenge were spent on them (for the maintenance of the apparatus, capitalisation and other expenditures). Nevertheless, neither competitive production, nor at least a single commodity item appeared on the world market.

In the same year, 2004, the National Oil Fund was created with the goal to accumulate financial resources that derive from the extraction of petroleum. It was agreed on that the fund's objectives are concerned with the accumulation and capitalisation of financial reserves for the present and future generations of Kazakhs. It literally turned out to be a strategic reserve and fortune for the whole population, since any record of its activity (including the financial) was shielded and barred from society.

It's noteworthy that along with the reduction of social expenditures the country's administrative expenditures sky-rocketed (maintenance of the state apparatus, building Astana, capitalisation of the fund "Samruk-Kazyna").

Starting with the year 2007, the period known as the world economic crisis began. In unison with the decreasing world demand for petroleum and non-ferrous metal the rate of economic development in Kazakhstan dropped dramatically, economic activities of businesses declined, and a shortage of working capital was registered (moreover, nearly half of all the credits, that were granted by commercial banks of Kazakhstan, were irretrievable or dubious).

After a rapid economic growth the country had to face a critical budget deficit of 5.5% of the GDP (according to the criteria of economic security the deficit may not rise above 3%). The first to be exposed to the crisis was the "pride of all reforms" – the banking system – as well as the most dynamically developing sector of housing construction and the businesses of the mining sector (non-ferrous metallurgy). In the course of only one year, 2009, the Government revised the state's budget 3 (!) times with regard to cuts in social and other expenditures. The due-dates of pay raises to workers of the budget sector and the due-dates of payments of social benefits to vulnerable groups of society were postponed or suspended. Many social programmes were sequestered or "frozen" until better times. The standard of living of the country's population sank down to the value of the beginning of 2000. It's noteworthy that the signs of the onrushing crisis in Kazakh economy became only apparent at the end of 2005, when domestic banks began to actively attract uncontrollable foreign loans. As a result the total debt of the bank sector reached the astronomic amount of 42 billion USD. At that time the main investment field of the bank sector became the real estate and housing construction sector. The fast increase in consumption financing led to an acceleration of inflation and to the reduced domestic production of industrial and consumer goods. Already then one could have known that the near future has the amortisation of private business entities' debts in store.

At the beginning the Government denied the influence of the crisis on Kazakh economy for one and a half year, and therefore did not take any anti-crisis or let alone preventive actions at all. But as the socio-economic situation in the country deteriorated and the official international reserves of the National Bank diminished, the authorities' view "changed". The Government lay the blame for all their missteps and failures in economic management and economic policies on the world financial crisis, and for the following challenges in particular:

the failed development of the finance and bank system, when the amortisation of the banks' foreign debts increased the external debt of Kazakhstan by many times;

1) The crisis of equity construction and the fiasco of housing policies;

2) The swift rise in inflation and the increase in prices for the main consumer goods, for housing and public utilities services;

3) The deterioration of the balance of payments and the devaluation of the national currency by 25% as a method of solving the given problem;

4) As well as all social problems, whose solution the authorities proclaimed long before the crisis (shortage of social institutions (kindergartens and schools), shrinking pensions, the growing incidence rate, mortality and crime rate, ecological issues and many more).

The above mentioned problems can hardly be considered inflicted from the outside or by the world crisis. At the beginning of 2009 the Government affirmed the anti-crisis programme. For its realization 10 billion dollars were drawn from the National Fund, 4 billion dollars for the stabilization of the financial sector, 3 billion dollars for dealing with real estate problems, an additional 1 billion dollars for the backing of small and medium-sized businesses, 1 billion dollars for the stimulation of the agricultural sector and another 1 billion dollars for various investment projects.

Altogether 19 billion dollars were spent on the anti-crisis programme, which actually equates the total budget of 2009. Meanwhile the macroeconomic impact of the adopted anti-crisis measures reverberated on an insignificant growth of the GDP (by 1.1%). The key measure, that was realised by the Government, became the financial aid for the above listed sectors. As in all other cases this process was under way without any legislative-normative measures, which led to a freeze of financial assets on accounts for a couple of months, along with the impossibility to financially control its expenditures. As always time was wasted, and money was used inefficiently – a fact that the corresponding dynamics of the GDP proved true.

Altogether, in the period between the years 1997 and 2010 alone, 52 national economic programmes were adopted in Kazakhstan, among which many have not been realized fully. Due to a redundancy of many programmes financial resources were used inefficiently, repeated revisions and amendments of the programmes were conducted and the following essential programmes failed completely:

- Industrial and innovation programmes (economies of agglomeration);
- Programmes of import replacement;
- So called "breakthrough" or investment projects (11 billion dollars were spent);
- Programmes concerned with providing food safety and drinking water (16 billion tenge were spent);
- As well as a number of community-oriented programmes "100 schools, 100 hospitals" and others (more than 1 billion dollars were spent).

Due to redundancy of programmes money was used inefficiently, and a part of it was simply embezzled. Regardless of the fact that different measures on import replacement and forced industrialization were elaborated at the same time in Kazakhstan, mechanisms of achieving a long-term economic growth are still tied to the export of petroleum and metals.

The resources of the petroleum sector determine the specialization of Kazakh economy. That kind of politics inevitably has janus-faced consequences. At best, they manage to expedite economic growth, solve social problems, create the conditions for opening new enterprises, increase the employment rate, reduce the country's external debts, accumulate domestic reserves and create other benefitiat consequences and assets.

At worst, the dependence of the country's economy on external factors increases, when the state budget (in Kazakhstan by 70%) is determined by the world market price for petroleum. Furthermore, the unidimensional development of the industrial sector worsens, the competitiveness of the national economy is constrained, and transnational oil cooperations bring their influence to bear on the dynamics of internal processes.

There is no doubt that in the course of the next 10 to 15 years the severe dependence of Kazakhstan's economy on the changes of the world market prices for raw materials will persist. Hoping for an export growth as to raw materials in the next decade, under a free floating exchange rate of the tenge the economy may have to face the serious problem of a considerable appreciation of currency, which will result in the recurrence of "Dutch Disease", when real economy, focused on the domestic market, is stagnating.

Apart from the last named, the following issues also have to be considered potential risks:

- The segregation of the export petroleum sector that develops at the expense of currency gains and real economy, weakly tied to other sections in a reproductive manner;
- The vulnerability of export-oriented branches in connection with the dependence on market fluctuations of the world market prices for a small range of goods, that appear to be the country's principal exports;
- The increase in competition on the part of producers of similar products in contiguous countries;
- The incremental orientation of industry and economy towards raw materials, the degradation of manufacturing sectors and the impending danger of a de-industrialization of the country;
- The impact on the environment, which is accompanied by the development of resources.

The lack of high-technology high-added value goods combined with the rampant development of petroleum extraction can become a hindering factor for a long-lasting economic development. Kazakh petroleum fields were already open in Soviet times, but the exploitation was limited by a variety of negative after-effects like the potential menace to the economic safety of the USSR. The increase of the petroleum recovery rate already in 35 years, that the Government had predicted, can lead to a depletion of petroleum reservoirs in Kazakhstan.

A substantial negative factor is the deteriorating environment, that the huge amount of petroleum residues and the lack of petroleum and gas reprocessing plants are responsible for (on dumps more than 12 million tonnes of petroleum were agglomerated). Due to the bad ecological conditions the general dynamics of lowering health levels in petroleum regions aggravated by a few times (the incidence rate is twice as high as the statistical average of Kazakhstan).

One of the few positive constituents of the petroleum branch is the provision of a considerable extent of tax revenues, which ought to be aimed at the solution of social issues, the aid for depressed regions, the employment security (around 25% of the workin-age population). Regardless of the highest level of GRP per capita in regions where petroleum is extracted, the total number of poor people is however constantly rising. Moreover, in west Kazakhstan the availability rate of social infrastructure is one of the lowest all over the country.

The present programme of forced industrialization shows weak ties to the competitive advantages of Kazakh economy. The Government laid stress on the founding of assembly plants or capital-intensive production and of initially non-competitive production. In doing so, the petrochemical branch, enterprises of the secondary sector in mining and smelting, the manufacturing industry in the agricultural sector and so on developed poorly.

In the last 3 years the level of innovative activity of enterprises in Kazakhstan did practically not surpass 3%, while even in countries like Estonia or Hungary, which do not have a powerful economic potential, this indicator amounts to 35-50% (correspondingly).

Another characteristic of the innovative sector of Kazakhstan is that in regard to the general structure of innovative production the overwhelming majority (more than 60%) falls within production, that underwent only insignificant transformations. Newly introduced production or production that was notably modified in terms of technology comprise the other part (less than 30%). Due to such a level of innovative activity Kazakh economy can neither expect to reach the leading position in world economy or in South-East Asia, nor compete for instance with the very Uzbekistan, where in the last couple of years dynamics of economic processes and reforms revitalised.

It is necessary to note that policies of diversification and innovative development were not realised fully, owing to the lack of system impacts that characterize resourceful economies of countries with developed markets:

- The market mechanism that was used in that period turned out to be unable to set signals, that would avert the „running hot“ of certain economic sectors, and could not support the state in building a "right" economic structure;
- The economy showed symptoms of „Dutch disease“, facilitating the recurrence of the effect of redeploying resources (investment and labour resources) into the raw materials sector;
- Policies of diversification conflicted with the lack of a necessary critical mass for their advancement.

The dimensions of the allocated state investments on diversification were insufficient and dispersed, and therefore no serious structural change was brought about.

In terms of the key factor of the economy's competitiveness, namely the productivity of labour, Kazakhstan lags behind the average with respect to countries' development, giving Russia way by 1,5 times, Japan by 4 times and the USA by 5 times.

The extensive growth of big business, that aims at gaining quick profit from the export of raw materials, does not allow it to turn to higher process stages and to the domestic market when the world market conditions change.

The Government, that so persistently urges the forced industrialization of economy, finally has to begin to reconstruct already operating enterprises and to revive a number of manufacturing operations. The grouping of domestic investors in the sense of an „economic class“ can become the motor for attaining the long-lasting socio-economic objectives. For this purpose it is necessary to elaborate a corresponding programme which is capable of supporting these businessmen and -women, that not only exhibit a high business activity but are also able to hold social and civil responsibility to the country. The time has long come to negotiate the dependence of foreign investors who are interested in quick profit making and capital export, and are, beyond the borders of the country, all too often uncontrollable. Local, domestic investors seem to be a more feasible basis for the establishment of a middle class and, by its means, of a stable development of the national economy.

In fact, regardless of the vociferous claims to state support, the share of Kazakh small and medium-sized businesses consistently sank from 15% of the GDP until the crisis down to 2% during the crisis.

For a country, such as Kazakhstan, a powerful industry basis, competitive products on domestic and foreign markets, and a full role in the international division of labour are of paramount importance. The realization of efficient economic policies implies the holistic development of the manufacturing, agricultural and the science and technology sector of economy, and their participation in economic processes throughout the world.

Social Stratification

Regardless of the publicly announced total increase of budget expenditures for social needs, the share of expenses on the social front (education, healthcare, social benefits) shrank unswervingly within the composition of the GDP. Within ten years it dropped by almost 1,5 times, while the GDP (in 2010 in comparison with 2000) increased by a couple of times. It is noteworthy that, along with a rapid economic growth, a budget proficit emerged in that period which turns out to be an unprecedented phenomenon in economies of post-Soviet countries. This being said, only in 2009 60 billion tenge (more than 4 billion USD according to the official exchange rate), that were destined for building educational facilities, healthcare facilities and for the drinking water supply, remained untouched. Furthermore, regardless of the vociferous claims to lower the poverty rate in the country, the said issue affects a considerably bigger number of the population than is enunciated in the data of the official statistics. Up until 2010 more than 10% of the total population were officially recognized as poor in Kazakhstan. For the calculation of the poverty rate in the country a method was elaborated that operates with a compound index, that is the living wage (which equals 10 MCI), that radically differs from the common international equivalents.

If the country's Government loves to call on international comparisons when it comes to the achievements of Kazakhstan, then let us consult the American criteria, in accordance with which the number of the poor in the country exceeds the official poverty rate at least 4 times. The overwhelming majority of retirees (75%) lives on a total of 4 dollars per day or less.

A persistent social problem is raised by the two-level issue on how to train labour force, with the unemployed on the one hand and a shortage of skilled labour force on the other. At first this paradox remained unsolved until the beginning of the establishment of market economy, when a permutation of labour force from the manufacturing into the non-manufacturing sector took place, and the wage levels and wage patterns changed as well as the regional and sectoral employment pattern.

Today, almost 20 years later, the situation continues to remain unchanged: the country still needs skilled personnel (especially with technical training), while at the same time the official amount of unemployed reaches nearly 50 thousand people.

Solving macroeconomic problems, the authorities, with reference to the catchphrase of economic freedom, practically shifted the whole responsibility for material wealth on to the very population. Impromptu employment has led to the steady formation of a social group of self-employed throughout many years.

After the whole period of reforms its number amounts to unvaried 2,5 to 3 million people (experts reckon their revenues to reach the amount of 100 to 150 dollars per month). Furthermore the self-employed are not considered unemployed by the state.

From a socio-economic viewpoint these circumstances can be evaluated as follows:

1) The self-employed population does not have a permanent income, and therefore does not pay any taxes;

2) The self-employed are denied the opportunity to access the "social package" that the Constitution guarantees;

3) Practically a third of the employable, economically active population engages in obscure illegal economic activities out of necessity. This turns out to be a solid foundation for a flourishing black market (which according to official statistical data contributes more that 20% to the GDP and up to 60%, as stated by different experts).

From a socio-political viewpoint, the self-employed population constitutes a potentially conflictogenic group with unsolved economic and social issues. The authorities lack direct leverage on this social group. Moreover, the latter exhibits high political engagement, constantly calling attention on its problems whose solution no one is going about to find.

The unemployment, the shortage in skilled personnel, self-employment and the weakness of the trade union movement all suggest one thing: Kazakhstan suffers from a complete loss of control over employment creation, a deficiency in policies regarding state planning and distribution of production forces. Along with that, already in 1997, when the objectives of the strategy-2030 were announced, the establishment of a professionalised state was given top priority in the strategic development of the country.

The problem of professionalisation may not be solved by local measures such as the programme "Bolashak", whose realization does neither satisfy those who developed it, nor those who participated in it. Spending around 100 thousand dollars for the training of one single graduate yearly (!) throughout a period of already 15 years (and several thousand people are trained or study), the authorities, yet again demonstrating their own unprofessionalism, could not meet the challenge of establishing a professionalised state.

Apart from the above mentioned issues, a potential conflict develops between the beneficiaries of the two existing pension schemes, namely the defined contribution plan or the pay-as-you-go pension scheme.

Out of 7,5 million citizens able to work, only more than 6 million depositors pay up retirement accounts. The amount of pension contributions of the self-employed is unknown, since that kind of data is not collected. In the last 3 years nearly all non-state pension funds demonstrate their unprofitability, and those who draw marginal profit can by means of their revenues not cover the losses caused by inflation. After some time the retiring depositors of the defined contribution plan will not be able to receive disbursements, commensurate with their labour activity. It is indispensable to solve these problems. Furthermore the state has to guarantee the support of the beneficiaries of the other system, the pay-as-you-go pension scheme. In that manner already in a couple of years the social burden on the state budget will multiply. By means of single payments this problem cannot be disposed of, and measures are to be taken proactively.

The most severe problem in Kazakhstan remains migration, both internally and externally. Migration processes were triggered by the economic growth in Kazakhstan in the middle of the 2000s, so that a wave of migrants from less wealthy neighbour countries "flooded" the country. In recent years around 1 million people per year are reported illegal migrants. Internal migration which cannot be controlled, exceeds that amount by far. As a matter of course earnings of illegal migrants are miscalculated, and the latter are tax-exempt. Meanwhile, in "economic dimensions" their work is also regarded as participation in underground economy.

Regardless of the Government's efforts to regulate migration flows at least by, for instance, registration institutions, these processes continue to be unbridled. Around big cities whole settlements of illegal migrants arose. After some time it is necessary to take up the inevitable cause of building infrastructure and of officially securing the law to property and occupied plots. As a result a simply economic issue yet again turns into a political matter.

Basically the Government's anti-crisis programme called "road-map", that was realised in order to create temporary work places, does not solve the issue on unemployment. As a matter of fact, the average time of employment that was registered for attracted labour force makes up not more than two months. Moreover, the allocated financial means were not entirely used anyway, and embezzled for the most part. The Government's plan to appeal the self-employed to socially valuable work failed.

Because the state only formally determines the labour relations between employers and wage workers, strong and independent trade unions are exigently required. Slowly but surely these activities gain strength: in big Kazakh enterprises independent trade unions came into existence which seek to safeguard the interests of workers (concerned are enterprises of the mining and smelting production sector, of the oil and gas industry and others). An indicator for the strengthening of trade unions are the increasing conflicts between entrepreneurial and worker collectives, in which not only economic and social, but also political needs come forward. However, issues of the rural population and the development of the agricultural sector arouse alarm the most. Hundreds of communities in the country are not provided with drinking water, lack infrastructure and the supply with gas and the more.

From a total of 7,5 million countrymen and -women more than 2,5 million work directly in the agricultural sector. The rest is either involved in subsistence farming or, without regulations, forced to migrate within Kazakhstan in pursuit of work. In all big cities of Kazakhstan it has become nothing out of the ordinary that in ecologically wealthy places hundreds of villas and cottages of functionaries are built and in ecologically poor areas thousands of shanties and hovels arise.

The agricultural sector is traditionally an economic outsider, characterized by low labour productivity, dependence from state subsidies, an imbalance between the price formation in industrial production and the price formation in agricultural production and a sharp cut-back of capital investments in key domains of agricultural production.

Every year subsidies up to 1 billion dollars are granted for the development of the agricultural sector. Once even a special three-year programme called "Aul" was adopted, destined to raise the efficiency level of agricultural production, develop the agricultural sector, increase the export of agricultural goods, minimise migration of rural population, develop infrastructure and more. But the outcome of this programme was deplorable. In the main, the effect of this programme was equal to zero (the yield remained on the former level, the amount of live-stock animals did not increase). As a result all benefits, subsidies and credits granted as part of the programme, the Government had to write off – as usual.

After the programme "Aul" even special state-owned enterprises were founded, whose future activities involved the development of high-quality agricultural goods, following a worldwide standard. Still, the efficiency of agricultural production sank from year to year, and expenses rose despite the increasing amount of state investments.

Having spent billions of dollars for the development of the agricultural sector, the basic range of foodstuff still has to be imported, although a key part could be produced in Kazakhstan. In accordance with the criteria of economic safety the share of the agricultural sector in Kazakhstan may not make up less than 15 to 20%. However, despite constantly taken Government measures, the share of agricultural economy in the country's GDP did not only not increase, but shrank more than a six-fold (from 34% in 1990 to 6.3% in 2009).

The guarantee for food security is the most ailing issue of the country. Generally speaking, with regard to that issue only one matter was successfully dealt with in the last 20 years, that is the supply with grain. In doing so, however, the prices for bread have to be kept down not by means of market instruments but by administrative instruments. During that time not a single large depot complex for storing agricultural products was built around big cities in Kazakhstan.

The wage level in agriculture is 4 to 5 times lower than the wage level in the manufacturing industry.

Despite the increasing amount of state investments, the efficiency of agricultural production is shrinking from year to year. During times of the country's sovereignty a fair number of targeted programmes were implemented in this field. However, neither the programmes' results in lifestock farming, nor in the cultivation of crops facilitated the achievement of the main objective, that is to create an efficient and globally competitive agricultural production and to guarantee the people of Kazakhstan accessible and healthy foods.

With respect to **economic management** the realization of programmes, involving strategical development, has been impeded by persistent **corruption** which is connected with the following factors:

- An ineffective legislative basis and a serious shortcoming of applicable laws;
- A lack of parliamentary control over the Government;
- The stealth of economic decisions that bodies of state administration take on a republic-wide and regional level.

All this led to an uncontrollable growth in underground economy. If, according to official statistics, the latter makes up more than 20% of the GDP, in absolute figures 20 to 25 billion dollars, and is hence equivalent to the whole budget of Kazakhstan, then in the judgement of experts the underground economy equals 50 to 60% of the GDP, which would account for a sum of approximately 20 to 25 billion dollars. The two conducted legalisations of black market capital were not able to radically change the situation in the country. Until now a high level of underground economy and corruption remains, and the world crisis only contributed to a deterioration of the situation in this field. Functionaries began to wildly spend money, taken from the National Oil Fund. Audit findings of the Accounts Committee repeatedly bear evidence of that inclination of functionaries. The ever increasing number of law suits against officials of different state structures is only the tip of the iceberg. Therefore the total debt amounts to 110 billion dollars, which equals nearly 7 thousand dollars for every single inhabitant of the country, and the Government, on its own security, borrowed another 15 billion dollars from China within the last 2 years. All that endangers the economic and political safety of the country.

Conclusion

Analysing the subject of the structural transformations, we can identify the following logic behind the programmes applied:

1) The macroeconomic stabilization by means of social cutbacks;

2) The capitalisation and revitalisation of economy by means of selling national resources;

3) The economic growth by means of foreign loans and investors;

4) The anti-crisis programme by means of social cutbacks.

Evaluating the social outcome of these economic reforms, the given scheme reflects a return to the starting point, when all economic achievements were made through and at the expense of the social well-being of the population. In the qualitative judgement of a 20-year cycle we reverted to the initial situation. The dynamics of economic reforms did practically not reverberate in the processes and quality of social transformations.

The realization of reforms and their modernization, aimed at the economic, social and political ensuring of sovereignty, the successful development of Kazakhstan and more led to the paradoxical substitution of the objectives that were set for the conducted transformations. Instead of a market economy and a socially-oriented state a monopolistic clan economy and a social domain, that is ruled by the laws of the market, were established. The state assigned the function of social security (pensions, social services, facilities of social infrastructure and other) almost completely to the population. At this point, the very economy, where market relations were so actively implanted owing to social minimization, transformed into a system of rigid monopolistic administration and regulation. As 20 years ago, the country's economy is characterised by non-competitive conditions, economic activity that is constrained to small businesses, and by the state's maximum power to freely interfere with the market environment.

Solving the problem of initiating economic growth with foreign investments and loans bears witness to the sectoral approach to economic management. This path leads to the erosion of national security or even the loss of sovereignty. In developed countries the competitiveness of the economy and its high development are, first and foremost, based on domestic investments that secure economic strength and efficacy of the state. Domestic investors are the solid backbone of state development and the "foundation" of economy.

While in early stages of the state formation, along with market reforms, the economic concept of a socially-oriented state was actively advocated, it later on was not only an all-around failure but more or less disabled. Moreover, market economy itself was not established since the share, control and distribution of economic resources and means followed monopolistic laws. During that time an oligarchic-monopolised clannish system had formed that excluded any possibilities to create a socially-oriented economy. In such an environment vitally important economic decisions were made by a small circle of a few financial and industrial groups, who lobby for the pragmatic interests of transnational cooperations and of some individuals.

Control over national resources (raw materials) is lost in Kazakhstan since the main export-oriented sectors of economy (oil and mining and melting), that "hold together" the entire domestic economy, belong to foreign investors.

For the last five years the country stands still both with regard to development and to modernization. According to statistical indicators we achieved a certain favourable development, but we still haven't obtained a pertinent advancement of the social sector. Not experiencing any deprivation of financial resources, the Government is disbursing gigantic sums for financing the maintenance of the state apparatus or for consumption, while usually effectivity of administration is determined by the possibility to accumulate savings, to make domestic investments as well as to significantly improve the conditions in the social sphere. Every government holds the same view: problems are to be solved with financial injections were needed, notwithstanding the future impact of macroeconomic mechanisms.

Vasily Astrov, A Note on Kazakhstan's Oil Fund

Introductory Remarks

The economy of Kazakhstan has been growing dynamically over the past decade, largely thanks to the expansion of oil and gas production and exports. In 2004, Kazakhstan's real GDP exceeded for the first time the level of 1992, the first year of independence – much earlier than e.g. in Russia. Since 2004, the size of the Kazakhstani economy has more than doubled. With the official per capita GDP at purchasing power parities of 9 300 EUR in 2010, Kazakhstan is now ranking third in the CIS (behind Russia and Belarus) and has a comparable level to that of the poorest EU members Bulgaria and Romania. The actual incomes are probably higher given the large scope of the shadow economy, although there are also pronounced income inequalities, particularly between cities and the countryside. Thanks to a massive anti-crisis fiscal package, Kazakhstan's economy has also demonstrated remarkable resilience to the global crisis: in 2009, it posted a positive growth of 1.2%, whereas the economies of nearly all transition countries – with the exceptions of Albania, Azerbaijan, Belarus and Poland – were in decline.

The rapid growth in oil production has been made possible primarily thanks to massive inflows of FDI from multinational companies, typically within the framework of production-sharing agreements (PSAs). In some years, FDI accounted for over a half of the country's fixed capital formation, with nearly two-thirds of FDI inflows targeting the energy sector. FDI was facilitated not least by the liberal and reform-oriented image of the country. Among the CIS countries, Kazakhstan has arguably advanced the most in terms of structural reforms. Privatization and – unlike e.g. in Russia – openness to foreign investors have been consistently ranking high on the government agenda, including in the banking sector where International Accounting Standards and a deposit insurance scheme were introduced early. Other, and more controversial, reforms included the introduction of a funded pension system in 1998, the break-up of 'natural monopolies' (electricity and railways) into competing operating units, and the privatization of housing and communal services. Also, in 2001 the authorities implemented capital flight amnesty.

Despite these achievements, the authorities are (rightly) concerned over the country's excessive reliance on energy, and have declared economic diversification as their policy goal. Economic diversification has been impeded not least by institutional shortcomings such as corruption, weak law enforcement and often contradictory legislation. This has had an adverse impact on the security of property rights and has resulted in the prevalence of investment projects with a short pay-off period. Although the regime of President Nazarbaev has ensured remarkable political stability, the latter did not fully translate into stability of the investment climate, particularly outside the energy sector. Another factor which has arguably undermined economic diversification has been the deterioration in human capital as a result of outward migration of the generally well-educated Russian minority, albeit on a smaller scale than in many other CIS countries. The stated goal of economic diversification could be partly addressed using the assets of the National Fund (NF) – the Kazakhstani government's fiscal reserves which have been accumulated over the past years thanks to the booming oil exports. In the present note, we briefly outline the underlying principles of its operation and discuss some policy issues such as the relationship between the NF assets and the public debt, the wisdom of conservative management of NF funds, and issues related to "Dutch disease".

The National Fund: Principles of Operation

Similarly to many other commodity-exporting countries, Kazakhstan is managing a government off-budget fund aimed at collecting "windfall" revenues from commodity exports and investing them abroad. The NF has been operating since May 2001 and has essentially two functions:

1. To accumulate oil wealth for the benefit of future generations (the saving function), and

2. To reduce the vulnerability of economy to external shocks arising from falling oil prices (the stabilization function).

Sources of Funds

The NF accumulates the bulk of oil-related revenues stemming in particular from three taxes: the 20% corporate income tax on oil companies, the volume-based royalties, and the export tax which is applied if the oil price exceeds 40 USD per barrel. Other sources such as the tax on super-profits, bonuses, and the Kazakhstani government share in PSAs play secondary role. In the first few years of NF operation, the still modest oil production volumes, the low level of taxation of the oil sector and the initially generous (for foreign investors) terms of PSAs enabled only a slow accumulation of funds. However, as the oil production expanded, taxes were hiked in response to the rising oil prices, and PSAs were revised in Kazakhstan's favour (reflecting the stronger negotiating position of the government), the NF assets started growing more rapidly and reached by the end of 2011 53,5 billion USD, corresponding to nearly 30% of Kazakhstan's GDP – see Figure 1.

Figure 1 National Fund and Public Debt in 2001-2011. Without debt of the National Bank (% GDP)

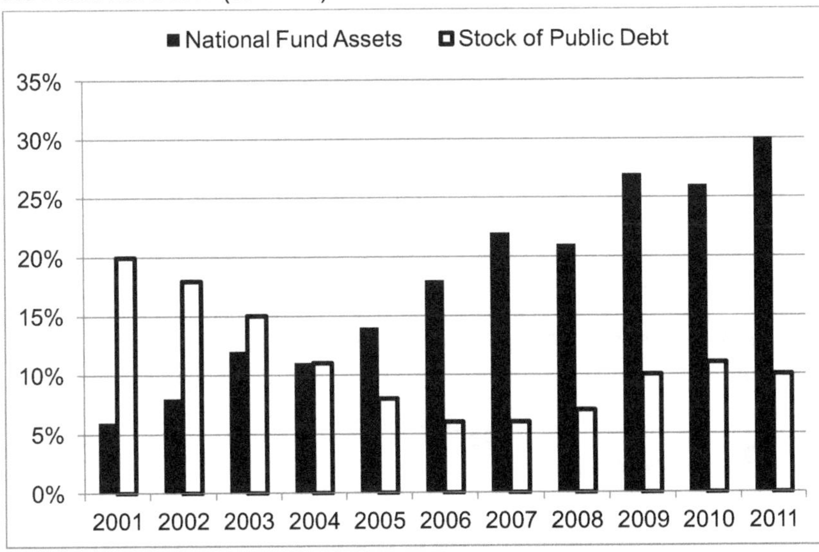

Source: own calculations based on data from the Ministry of Finance.

Investment Allocation

The NF is managed by the National Bank on behalf of the government. Although it receives revenues in both Kazakhstani tenge (KZT) and foreign exchange, its funds are invested entirely abroad, mostly in securities of developed (particularly G-3) countries. This allocation principle is a direct reflection of the saving and the stabilization functions assigned to the Fund. On the one hand, securities of developed countries are believed to be generally low-risk, making them suitable as a safe saving vehicle for future generations. On the other hand, investing the NF in securities issued by countries which would benefit from falling oil prices (which developed countries generally are) provides, to some extent, a hedge against excessive reliance on the oil revenues and thus ensures the stabilization function of the Fund. Two thirds of the NF assets are held as 'saving portfolio', while the remaining third as 'stabilization portfolio'. The saving portfolio is composed mostly of bonds (80% of the total) and equities (17%). Investing into equities – which might have the advantage of higher returns in the long run, as demonstrated by past performance (at least prior to the global crisis), – is in line with e.g. Norway's experience and corresponds to the long-term planning horizon of the saving portfolio. However, particularly in the short and medium term, equities (and even bonds) may be risky and could therefore create a problem for stabilization purposes. Therefore, the stabilization portfolio is held almost entirely (95% of the total) in cash and money-market instruments (i.e. securities with maturity of less than one year), with the rest invested in bonds.[99]

Figure 2 Government Budget in 2001-2011

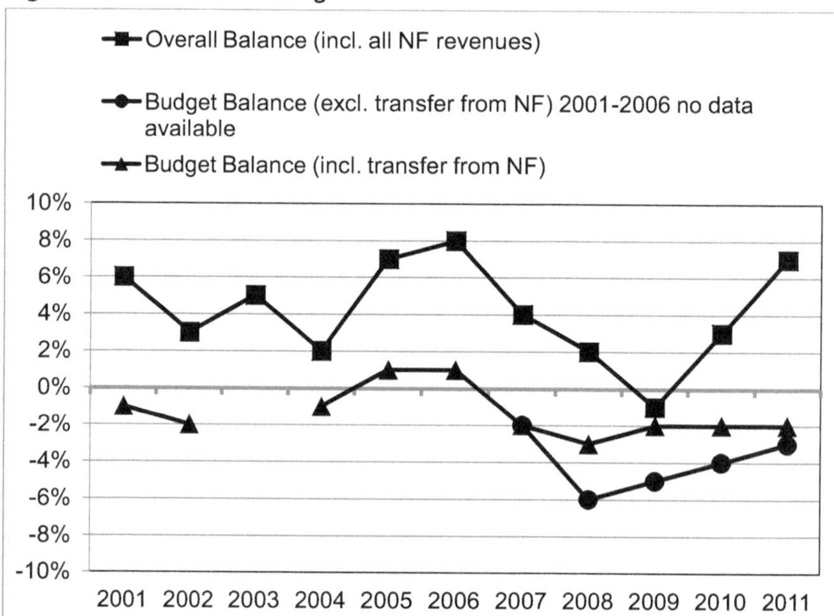

Source: own calculations based on Ministry of Finance data

Use For Fiscal Purpose

The NF assets have been also used to finance the ("non-oil") budget deficits.[100] As can be seen from Figure 2, up until 2006 the Kazakhstani government was running essentially balanced budgets without having to tap the still rather small National Fund. However, the domestic banking crisis in 2007 and the global economic crisis in 2008-2009 translated into a sharp slowdown of Kazakhstan's economic growth and a shortfall in government revenues. Simultaneously, public expenditures shot up as the government implemented a massive stimulus package amounting to 4.5% of GDP.[101] As a result, non-oil budget deficits widened markedly, up to 9% of GDP in 2009, and were increasingly covered by transfers from the NF. The scale of these transfers exceeded 6% of GDP in both 2008 and 2009. Although in subsequent years the pace of real GDP growth picked up impressively, economic activity outside the booming oil sector remained relatively weak, particularly in construction, real estate and the financial sector. Therefore, the non-oil budget deficits declined only moderately and dependence on transfers from the NF remained high. The current legislation adopted at the beginning of 2010 stipulates an annual fixed transfer of 1 200 billion KZT (some 8 billion USD) from the NF into the government budget, provided the NF has accumulated on its balances at least 20% of GDP. The size of this transfer corresponded to 5.5% of GDP in 2010 and 4.5% in 2011.

Finally, Figure 2 also demonstrates that the *overall* fiscal balance – i.e. including all oil revenues accumulated in the NF – has been over the past decade almost invariably in surplus, with the exception of 2009 when it briefly turned negative due to very low oil prices that year.

Policy Issues

Asset Accumulation at the Expense of Borrowing

The annual transfers allocated from the NF starting from 2007 have been covering the non-oil budget deficits only partly, and the rest (typically 2-3% GDP) needed to be financed otherwise – largely by borrowing. As a result, the declining trend of the public debt to GDP ratio, which had been observed in previous years, came to a halt and subsequently reversed. By 2009, the stock of Kazakhstani public debt (excluding debt of the National Bank) exceeded 10% of GDP, and has since stayed at about this level – see Figure 1. Thus, the overall fiscal surpluses and the accumulation of funds in the NF over the past few years have been accompanied by the rising indebtedness of the government. While the stock of public debt is very low by international standards, one may still question the wisdom of this strategy given the existing gap between the low NF profitability and the relatively high cost of servicing the public debt. Table 1 demonstrates that the dynamics of these two latter indicators since 2002 and their relative standing vis-à-vis each other have been widely fluctuating. At the beginning, the cost of servicing the public debt typically exceeded the return on NF assets. However, this reversed in the pre-crisis years, probably reflecting the equity markets boom (and thus higher returns on the NF assets) and the low estimated sovereign risks in Kazakhstan which allowed the government to borrow cheaper than before.[102] With the global crisis of 2008-2009, the pattern switched again – disregarding the one-time strong devaluation of tenge (by 18% against the US dollar), which allowed the government to capitalize on its NF foreign-denominated assets and explains the record-high 28% profitability in tenge terms recorded that year. Apart from that, the return on the NF assets over the past two years has stayed below the cost of public debt service. This should not be much of a surprise, since interest rates and yields on government bonds in developed countries (where the NF funds are invested) plummeted in the aftermath of the global crisis, while the increased risk aversion in the financial markets kept the cost of borrowing for emerging markets – even the "low-risk" ones such as Kazakhstan at a relatively high level.

Table 1.1 Return on National Fund Assets and Cost of Public Debt Service in 2002-2011, in %

	Return on NF assets [1)]	Cost of public debt service [2)]
2002	4.2	6.1
2003	1.3	5.9
2004	2.5	5.1
2005	6.7	4.5
2006	6.9	4.7
2007	5.2	5.0
2008	-2.4	7.6
2009	27.8	6.4

	Return on NF assets [1]	Cost of public debt service [2]
2010	3.0	5.3
2011	1.0[3]	4.9

Notes:

1) In tenge terms. Nominal return divided by National Fund assets at the beginning of the year.

2) Cost of debt service divided by the stock of public debt at the beginning of the year.

3) Based on return in January-September 2011.

Source: own calculations based on data from the Ministry of Finance.

Our calculations suggest that if the government had fully financed the budget deficits by tapping the NF rather than by borrowing, it would have saved on the interest rate differential some 10 billion KZT in 2010 and 20 billion KZT in 2011.[103] More generally the Kazakhstani government could easily pay back *all* public debt using the NF assets and save some 100 billion KZT (700 million USD) on annual basis.[104] This money could be used e.g. for upgrading public infrastructure or the social safety network. Note that paying back all public debt using the NF funds would bring the National Fund only marginally below 20% of GDP – the officially set "floor", below which the NF is not allowed to fall out of precautionary considerations.

Savings Versus Development

The saving function of the NF is based on the idea of intergenerational equity. It is argued that Kazakhstan's oil deposits will be at some point depleted. Therefore, in order to maintain the living standards, future generations should be able to resort to income accrued on assets which need to be accumulated during the period of the oil boom. A similar idea is underlying e.g. Norway's Government Pension Fund. However, it can be argued that concerns about intergenerational solidarity in Kazakhstan should be less relevant than in Norway. Given that the Kazakhstani economy is likely to grow much faster than the Norwegian one (in line with the hypothesis of beta convergence),[105] future generations of Kazakhs will presumably be much wealthier than the present generation even without having to resort to interest accrued on the NF assets.

Some estimates suggest that the current consumption levels in Kazakhstan may be indeed sub-optimal. In other words, the government could increase the use of NF assets for consumption purposes on a current basis without necessarily depriving the future generations of the living standards at least as high as those enjoyed by the "oil boom" generation. For instance, according to the IMF (2010) calculations based on the official long-term projections of oil production[106] and various scenarios with respect to the level of oil prices, the Kazakhstani government could safely spend around 10-11 billion USD annually out of its oil revenues without jeopardizing the NF as a saving vehicle. This is somewhat above the annual fixed transfer of 8 billion USD from the NF to the budget stipulated by the current legislation.

The case for spending more becomes even stronger if we allow for the possibility that the money is not just used for consumption, but also invested. Such investment could, for instance, be directed to upgrading the country's infrastructure, thus encouraging private investment in the non-energy branches of economy. In this way, if the government decided to use the NF funds domestically, it would contribute substantially to the diversification of the economy – its declared goal. This diversification could, in turn, contribute to the stability of public finances. The government could also target e.g. education and health care with these investments, laying the foundation for long-term sustainable economic growth thanks to human capital accumulation. Even the IMF (2011) – which usually advocates conservative fiscal policy and often disregards the social impact of policy measures – acknowledges that in terms of the level of education and the quality of health care, Kazakhstan is lagging behind countries at a similar level of economic development and behind what it could afford.

More generally, Kazakhstan's government expenditures as a share of GDP (just above 20%) are also low for the country's development level. They are much lower than e.g. in Russia or Ukraine (let alone European countries), and more in line with levels observed e.g. in the countries of the Caucasus, all of which are much poorer than Kazakhstan. In January 2012, President Nazarbaev announced a number of investment projects which are to be financed from the National Fund: the construction of roads and railroads, of a fertilizers plant (2 billion USD), of a heat and power plant (2,3 billion USD), of an oil refinery (1,7 billion USD), of a gas processing plant (5 billion USD), and some others – see Pindyuk (2012). Against the background of above arguments, this move appears to be ambiguous. On the one hand, the decision to tap NF funds for development purposes and to invest into public infrastructure is appropriate and arguably overdue. On the other hand, the announced investments into energy and chemicals will hardly contribute to the diversification of the Kazakhstani economy. Private investments into the energy sector, including FDI, have been booming over the past decade. Similarly, chemicals – which according to the IMF (2011) are a "natural" area of comparative advantage for oil-producing countries – should be able to attract private investment. In both cases, there is generally no need for the state to step in. At the same time, neither more technologically advanced branches (such as machinery and equipment) nor social spending – areas where private investment is less likely to come and where the need for the state involvement is arguably more pressing – are targets of the announced programmes.

The National Fund and "Dutch Disease"

Similarly to stabilization funds in many other countries, the NF of Kazakhstan has proved to be an effective instrument of monetary sterilization. That is, by accumulating oil-related foreign exchange inflows on the government account at the National Bank (i.e. off-market) and investing them in foreign assets, the NF has prevented the emergence of excessive appreciation pressures and of the so-called "Dutch disease" (whereby the profitability of non-oil tradable sector is undermined by an overvalued exchange rate). According to IMF estimates, foreign investments of the NF have accounted recently for about 30% of the country's overall capital outflows.

The reverse side of the successful sterilization policy has been however the apparent shortage of funds available for investment into the non-energy sector. The growing domination of oil and gas in the economic structure might be a problem in the long run, as it makes the country even more vulnerable to the volatility of the world oil prices. These structural distortions appear to have little to do with "Dutch disease": had the exchange rate been (even) more competitive, there would probably have been only a modest supply response from the non-oil manufacturing sector due to the limited supply-side capacities. Conversely, one could argue that investing the NF money into non-oil tradable sector (e.g. manufacturing) would result in its higher productivity. The latter could in turn counteract the possible "Dutch disease" effects stemming from higher inflationary pressure and an additional tenge appreciation potentially associated with spending part of the NF reserves. Of course, any sizeable domestic spending of the NF money would pose a challenge to macroeconomic management. It is essential that any major withdrawal of government foreign currency-denominated deposits at the National Bank and their subsequent conversion into tenge be accompanied by corresponding policy coordination with the National Bank. The aim of such an approach would be both to avoid unwelcome appreciation pressure (and the likely speculation on such appreciation) and to leave open the possibility for counteracting any unwarranted depreciation pressure in the future.

At the same time, the appreciation pressure (and the inflationary pressure alike) is likely to be kept within limits as long as additional government spending is import-intensive. One example of import-intensive government spending could be infrastructure development programmes involving large-scale imports of investment goods. Alternatively, subsidizing the education of Kazakhstani students abroad and the foreign treatment of Kazakhstani patients could serve as further examples of import-intensive government expenditures out of the Fund, which could prevent the emergence of excessive appreciation and/or inflationary pressures

Bibliography

International Monetary Fund: "Republic of Kazakhstan: selected issues", 2010, IMF Country Report Nr. 10/237.

International Monetary Fund: "Republic of Kazakhstan: selected issues", 2011, IMF Country Report Nr. 11/151.

Libman, A.: "Structural changes in the economy and industry of Kazakhstan", 2006, paper prepared in the framework of the INDEUNIS Project (Work Package 5), http://indeunis.wiiw.ac.at/, 12.05.2012.

Pindyuk, O.: „Kazakhstan: Strong growth despite banking system vulnerabilities", 2012, in: Gligorov, V.; et al.: „New divide(s) in Europe?", wiiw Current Analyses and Forecasts. Economic Prospects for Central, East and Southeast Europe Nr. 9. pp. 124-127.

Stephan Barisitz[107], The Kazakhstani Banking System: Highly Leveraged Boom, Painful Bust, Costly Recovery

Abstract

Pushed by expanding income (on the back of rising oil prices) and by rapid external debt accumulation, the Kazakhstani banking sector featured one of the most dynamic credit booms in CESEE until 2007. Following the US sub-prime crisis, banks' access to external funding plummeted and credit expansion ground to zero. The global economic crisis that broke out in late 2008 forced credit institutions to drive down their external indebtedness. Moreover, the (temporary) collapse of the oil price and the devaluation of the tenge cut domestic demand, liquidity and solvency. The share of non-performing loans (NPLs) skyrocketed from 5% at end-2008 to 21% a year later, and further to 26% in mid-2011. Large losses stemming from real estate exposure (burst of housing bubble), related-party lending, and fraud, likely played a role. Loan-loss provisions were sharply ramped up, profitability was all but wiped out in 2008 and hefty losses incurred in 2009 (ROA end-2009: -24%), when sector capital even turned negative. The authorities' crisis-response measures included the nationalization of two of the four largest banks and the recapitalization (via the acquisition of minority stakes) of the two others in early 2009 (all four banks together accounting for two thirds of sector assets). The two nationalized banks then defaulted on their high foreign liabilities and initiated debt-restructuring negotiations that produced steep haircuts (53% resp. 76%) for creditors in 2010. The sector's debt burden was thus substantially eased, capital turned positive again and banks witnessed a fragile return to profitability in 2010-2011. However, stubbornly high and even rising credit risk and declining coverage ratios coupled with a weak institutional environment suggest the need for a new government programme to clean up NPLs. Important shock-absorbing factors include: the strong (oil-driven) recovery of the real economy, depositor confidence (underpinned by state-owned firms' deposits), record-level official currency assets, and a modest public debt.

Macroeconomic Background: Resource-Driven Strong, if Volatile, Growth

Following buoyant economic expansion (by over 10% p.a.) in 2000-2007, annual GDP increases decelerated to 3.3% in 2008 and further to 1.2%

in 2009, before re-accelerating to 7,0% in 2010 and remaining at 7,0% in the first half of 2011 (year on year). The impressively strong growth until 2007 benefited from economic recovery after a particularly deep transition depression in the 1990s, from substantial energy price rises and therefore terms-of-trade improvements, from large inflows of capital – FDI as well as debt creating inflows, and from a credit boom. At the same time, the deterioration of the current account balance despite high oil prices signalled economic overheating. Gross external debt swelled to levels of above 90% of GDP in 2006 and 2007, with banks' external debt growing fastest (Table 1). In the period of high oil prices (pre-crisis), gross official reserves also increased and the authorities accumulated substantial financial resources in the National Fund of the Republic of Kazakhstan (NFRK, the country's oil stabilization fund).

Kazakhstan's dependence on external financing made itself painfully felt in the second half of 2007, when the US sub-prime crisis drastically reduced commercial banks' access to external funding. This caused a credit crunch, and substantially cut back economic expansion.[108] The freezing of global financial markets and the dramatic worsening of the economic crisis in the wake of the Lehman default (September 2008) further tightened access to foreign finance and contributed to the sharp slump of oil and raw material prices, thus wiping out previous terms-of-trade gains. The Kazakhstani economy entered a bout of stagnation.

To cope with the renewed – and more serious – destabilization, the state intervened in the banking sector in early 2009, in particular by acquiring ownership stakes in the country's four largest credit institutions. The authorities' entire anti-crisis package[109] provided for the allocation of about 10 billion Euros (about 12% of GDP) over 2009-2010 to support the banking sector, residential construction, SMEs, agriculture and infrastructure development. Worsening external balances, the strong depreciation of the Russian rouble in late 2008 and early 2009 and mounting losses of currency reserves in defending the tenge exchange rate against the US dollar eventually prompted the National Bank of the Republic of Kazakhstan (NBK) to devalue the tenge by 20% in one stroke in early February 2009.

Whereas the country's already high external debt remained at around 77-78 billion EUR during the year 2009, its ratio to GDP sharply increased – to almost 100% – largely as a result of the tenge devaluation. Kazakhstani external debt then declined again to (still high) 77% of GDP in mid-2011, mostly on account of the write-off of ailing banks' external liabilities (see below) as well as of brisk economic recovery.[110] The latter was buoyed by the surprisingly strong recovery of world economic activity and therefore of oil prices in the second half of 2009 through mid-2011, bringing back current account surpluses. Meanwhile, as appreciation pressures re-emerged amidst rising commodity prices, the central bank repeatedly intervened on the foreign exchange market to prevent the tenge from strengthening too fast. Foreign currency reserves were replenished and reached new record levels in the summer of 2011 (Table 1). The weakening of the global economy in the last quarter of 2011 may however soon put pressure on oil prices and Kazakhstani growth. While banking activity and a credit boom had contributed to the overheating until 2007, it did not contribute to the recovery: After turning negative in 2008, annual real credit growth remained negative or very weak to date.

Table 2 Kazakhstan: Selected Macroeconomic Indicators (2005-2011)

	2005	**2006**	**2007**	**2008**	**2009**	**2010**	**2011 (latest data)**
Real GDP growth (annual change, %)	9.7	10.7	8.9	3.3	1.2	7.0	7.0 (Jan-Jun)
Inflation (end-of period, CPI, annual Change, %)	7.5	8.4	18.8	9.5	6.2	7.8	9.7 (Sep)
Budget balance (general gov. % of GDP)	5.8	7.5	-1.7	-2.1	-2.9	-2.4	
Current account balance (% of GDP)	-1.9	-2.5	-7.8	4.7	-3.8	2.9	13.2 (Jan-Jun)
Net FDI inflows (% of GDP)	3.7	8.3	7.5	9.7	8,7	2.0	6.0 (Jan-Jun)
Total gross external debt (% of 4q-rolling) GDP)	76.0	91.4	92.4	80.9	97.8	81.0	77.0 (mid-year)

	2005	2006	2007	2008	2009	2010	2011 (latest data)
-therof banking sector gross external debt (% of (4q-rolling) GDP)	26.8	41.1	43.5	29.4	26.2	13.6	11.5 (mid-year)
Gross international reserves (% of (4q-rolling) GDP)	12.4	23.6	16.8	14.8	19.5	18.6	21.2 (mid-year)
NFRK[1)] assets (% of (4q-rolling) GDP)	14.2	17.4	20.0	20.6	21.2	21.2	24.8 (mid-year)

Source: National Bank of Kazakhstan, wiiw, OeNB calculations

Structural Background: A Dual Economy: Oil, FDI-Driven Versus Non-Oil, Credit-Driven

The Kazakhstani economy appears to consist of two sectors/ circuits that are not very closely connected to each other: the oil or resource sector versus the non-oil or non-resource sector. Oil is pivotal and accounts for nearly 60% of exports, around 40% of budget revenues, and almost 30% of GDP. In 2010 oil contributed roughly half to GDP growth. With recent discoveries in the northern part of the Caspian Sea (Kashagan field), oil will continue to attract major investments and act as a main driver of the country's growth for years to come. Oil exploration, extraction and production is, however, also very import-intensive. The Kazakhstani resource sector is often also understood to include minerals, chemical industry, metallurgy and closely related branches, like transport and communications.

The non-oil sector comprises the rest of the economy and is geared to domestic consumption. It includes farming, parts of manufacturing, construction, real estate, banking and some other services. Whereas the oil sector is largely financed by foreign direct investment (FDI)[111] and international capital markets, the non-oil sector has to rely on domestic credit (and retained earnings) (Al-Eyd and Saker 2010, 29). There are only few links that overcome this segmentation of the Kazakhstani economy: Domestic demand (including credit demand and deposit supply) effects from rising earnings and incomes in the resource sector constitute one such link (although oil company profit transfers and the repayment of loans extended by parent firms abroad can be substantial), spillovers to oil-related services and budgetary re-distribution of oil revenue are two others.[112]

Banking Developments and Reforms

Accelerating Credit Boom and Bubble (up to Mid-2007)

Up to 2007, Kazakhstan had witnessed one of the most rapid credit booms of transition history. In 2005 and 2006, annual growth rates of domestic bank loans to the private sector exceeded 60% in real terms (Table 2); credit focussed, as mentioned above, on the non-resource sector. Banks were mostly owned by domestic private businessmen and financial-industrial groups (conglomerates). This applied also to the four largest banks (in terms of assets). Foreign – incl. Austrian – participation increased to 16% of total banking assets by end-2007. Important acquisitions by foreign strategic investors include UniCredit BankAustria's purchase in June 2007 of a 92% stake in ATF Bank, the fifth-largest (in terms of assets) domestic credit institution at the time, for 1,6 billion EUR, and South Korean Kookmin Bank's purchase in March 2008 of a 30% share (later increased to 42%) in Bank CenterCredit (BCC), the sixth-largest, for 0,4 billion EUR.

The credit boom was fuelled by expanding deposits and particularly by swelling foreign debt (leverage-led growth model). Relatively cheap syndicated bank loans and eurobond issues contributed to raising the share of non-residents in banks' liabilities from about a quarter early in the decade to over half in 2005 to 2007, which even surpassed the share of deposits. Banks' growing external debt (mostly medium- and long-term) was the major force pushing up the country's total foreign debt, and in 2006 and 2007 accounted for almost half of the latter. Mortgage, car, other consumer loans, trade and construction loans grew especially swiftly. Total consumer loans multiplied to reach more than one third of the credit portfolio. In partly speculative investments, banks also increased their own holdings of real estate, financial assets, and investments outside Kazakhstan. Property prices skyrocketed.[113] The share of foreign currency loans in total loans to the private sector remained high, at 48% at end-2006 (Table 2), while in total loans to households it increased markedly to 67% at end-2006. While largely externally financed banking activity became one of the key drivers of economic growth and, in fact, macroeconomic overheating, sizable financial stability risks accumulated: The sheer speed of credit expansion was liable to bear problems for risk management. The substantial share of foreign currency-denominated lending to often unhedged households and firms gave rise to sizable indirect credit risk. And the degree of dependence attained on cross-border capital inflows exposed banks to considerable refinancing and rollover risks. Moreover, off-balance sheet items[114] had grown to over three quarters of the size of balance sheet assets by end-2006. These problems have to be seen against the backdrop of weak corporate governance and banking supervision (see below).

Strong Impact of US Subprime Crisis: Credit Growth Grinds to a Halt, Housing Bubble Bursts

The US subprime crisis of August 2007 immediately heightened international investors' risk aversion and induced large-scale deleveraging, which implied withdrawals from placements in emerging markets. Market perceptions of risk on Kazakhstani assets rose sharply in August and September 2007, as the high degree of dependence on external funding raised analysts' awareness of the built-up debt burden of the Kazakhstani banking sector. After banks' access to external funding had plummeted, rating agencies downgraded some credit institutions and the sovereign in the fall of 2007. Confidence in the banking sector declined and household deposits contracted about 5% in September-October of the year. Thereupon, credit institutions effectively stopped providing new loans[115], which reined in growth of the non-oil economy and drastically affected mortgage and consumer finance. Property price development reversed and prices declined substantially. The Kazakhstani housing bubble burst, residential construction virtually stopped (IMF Staff Report 2009, 3). Over the year 2007, the credit-to-deposit ratio rose by over 30 percentage points to 187% - among the highest relative to peer countries (Table 4).

In response to the liquidity squeeze, the NBK provided large-scale liquidity support to banks through repo agreements, foreign exchange swaps, early redemption of NBK notes and the reduction of reserve requirements. The government established a 800 million EUR (1.1% of GDP) financing facility in the form of earmarked government deposits with banks – to be on-lent to assist construction companies and support SMEs. The central bank also intervened heavily and successfully in the foreign currency market to support the tenge. After declining about 15% in the fall of 2007, official foreign currency assets (comprising NBK reserves and NFRK funds) recovered again and came to 2,84 billion EUR in mid-2008. The (temporary) stabilization of the situation was supported by high and spiking oil prices, until the summer of 2008. Meanwhile, banks' external debt climaxed at 31 billion EUR (44% of GDP) at end-2007, and off-balance sheet items reached 94% of the size of the sector's total assets. Notwithstanding some progress in strengthening the prudential framework, incl. introduction of consolidated supervision, the Financial Supervision Agency (Agency of the Republic of Kazakhstan on Regulation and Supervision of the Financial Market and Financial Organizations (FSA), established in 2004) remained attached to formalistic compliance-oriented schemes instead of moving toward forward-looking risk-based supervision.

Repercussions of Worsening of Global Crisis (2008-2009): Forced Deleveraging, Collapse of Credit Quality, Bank Insolvencies and Nationalizations

The second wave of the US and world financial crisis aggravated the Kazakhstani banking sector's difficulties. Global deleveraging intensified and forced credit institutions to drive down their external indebtedness. The (temporary) collapse of oil and commodity prices and the sharp slowdown of growth struck the banking sector by cutting domestic income, demand, liquidity and solvency. Moreover, the tenge devaluation in early 2009 added to pressures by sharply adjusting debt servicing burdens of unhedged borrowers. After annual loan growth had more than halved to 30% in 2007 (in real terms), the credit volume shrank by 6% in 2008, and by another 4% in 2009. However, in exchange rate-adjusted terms, shrinkage accelerated in 2009 (-12%). Mainly due to the devaluation in early 2009, the share of foreign currency loans reverted back to 52% in the first half of 2009, before receding to a still high 48% at the end of the year (Table 2).

The share of non-performing loans (defined as loans overdue past 90 days) in total loans (as published by the IMF only) approximately doubled to 5% in 2008, from there quadrupled to a disquieting 21% in 2009, and subsequently further swelled (see below).[116] The tenge devaluation in early 2009 certainly contributed to the deterioration. Large losses stemming from real estate exposures, related-party lending, high single-name concentrations, inadequate collateral, intransparent operations, and fraud may also have played a role (Moody's Investor Service 2010, 4-5; Standard & Poor's 2010, 3; Alexander 2010). A considerable share of banks' external holdings turned out to be of questionable quality. This goes particularly for Bank Turan Alem (BTA), the largest credit institution at end-2008, which had invested about half of its assets in Russia, Ukraine and other CIS countries. Many banks became risk-averse and preferred to keep surplus liquidity on accounts with the NBK or purchase low-return government securities.

In reaction to the renewed crisis situation, the authorities' anti-crisis plan (see Chapter 1) focused its intervention and the largest amount of its assistance on supporting the banking sector. Kazakhstan's legislation was adjusted to enable the state to buy stakes in the country's largest credit institutions. Up to mid-2009, about half of the amount provided for by the anti-crisis plan was disbursed: In February 2009 the state holding company Samruk-Kazyna[117] acquired a dominating equity stake (75%) in Bank Turan Alem (BTA, the largest bank), and minority stakes in Halyk bank (the former state savings bank, second-largest, 28%) and Kazkommertsbank (third-largest, 18%) for a total of 1,7 billion EUR. Another 150 million EUR were set aside for a majority stake in Alliance bank (fourth-largest). These four banks together accounted for about two-thirds of the book value of sector assets at end-2008, none of the four was foreign owned.

Samruk Kazyna further placed deposits of 1,3 billion EUR (1.6% of GDP) in the banking sector. Additionally, 1,5 billion EUR were channelled thru the sector to support construction projects, mortgage, SME and farm lending. Support also came from budgetary tax cuts in the non-resource sector. The NBK, in turn, loosened monetary conditions by repeatedly cutting the refinancing rate and by further easing reserve requirements.[118]

The deposit insurance fund (KDIF, established 1999) was strengthened: The KDIF's capital base was increased fourfold to 100 billion KZT (about 0.6% of GDP) and the deposit ceiling for individuals was raised from 700 thousand KZT per depositor per bank to 5 million KZT (around 22 500 EUR).[119] This may have contributed to staving off possible bank runs.

The lion's share of funding for the anti-crisis plan came from the NFRK. An additional safety cushion was put in place by borrowing 7,2 billion EUR as an assistance package from China. In return, the China National Petroleum Corporation was authorized to purchase a major stake in the MangistauMunaiGaz energy concern. Half of the loan was earmarked for bolstering the country's energy sector while the other half was to be transferred to the state-owned Development Bank of Kazakhstan (Pindyuk 2009, p. 122). After having slowed down sharply in 2007, private sector (i.e. non-general government) deposits expanded again in real terms by over a quarter in 2008 and by 14% in 2009. This was partly due to inflows from state-owned entities (Samruk-Kazyna), and (in 2009) partly due to valuation effects from the devaluation. In exchange rate-adjusted terms, real deposit expansion in 2009 came to 5%. Also thanks to NBK liquidity stimulation measures initiated as a reaction to the 2007 crisis and maintained or further reinforced during the 2008-2009 crisis, the ratio of liquid assets to short-term liabilities almost doubled from end-2007 to end-2009. The loan-to-deposit ratio descended again to 116% in 2009 – a level not seen since 2004 – and continued to descend. While NPLs had been rising precipitously over 2008-2009, credit institutions reacted by ramping up loan-loss provisions (and thus complied with NBK instructions). At end-2009, provisions came to 38% of total loans to the private sector and thus fully covered at least one measure of problem loans, namely NPLs (defined as loans overdue past 90 days, as published by the IMF). Banks have also shown flexibility by restructuring part of their loan portfolio with the aim of facilitating customers' debt service.

However, as a consequence of these measures, profitability was all but wiped out in 2008 and hefty losses were incurred in 2009 (ROE end-2009: -1 193%, ROA: -24% Table 2).[120]

Sector capital adequacy collapsed in the course of 2009 (end-2009: -8%). The sector's total debt surpassed its total assets in the second quarter of 2009. Kazakhstani banking capital thus turned negative.[121] At end-2009, the gap between banks' assets and liabilities had widened to more than 5% of GDP. An evaluation of banking sector stability carried out by the FSA at the end of the third quarter of 2009 confirmed a substantial deterioration of stability compared to the situation at the beginning of the year. This deterioration was largely triggered by the erosion of banks' credit portfolio quality and by the increase of provisions.

Thus, the FSA assessed the sector as "unstable" at the end of September 2009; at the same time, if BTA's and Alliance's data were excluded, the sector would still be regarded as "stable, with extremely high risk levels".[122] All in all, the above-mentioned "surprises" and deficiencies related to the two defaulted banks (BTA and Alliance, see Box) point to persisting serious weaknesses of corporate governance, risk management, prudential regulation and supervision. Kazakhstani accounting practices do not yet correspond to IFRS. Due to the frozen international debt market, deleveraging and public assistance, Kazakhstani banks reduced their external liabilities in 2008-2009 by about one third to 21 billion EUR, which came to 34% of their total liabilities at end-2009.[123] Yet banks' total liabilities declined from 91% to 68% of GDP in 2008-2009, despite the above referred-to anti-crisis measures. Without these measures and the resulting partial replacement of banks' declining foreign debt with domestic (state) debt and capital, the impact on banking activity and the functioning of parts of the economy would have certainly been even more severe. Meanwhile, two new foreign players entered the market in 2009: JSC "Shinkhan Bank" (of South Korea) and Vneshtorgbank (VTB, Russia) opened subsidiaries. Foreign-owned banks' share in total sector assets rose to almost a quarter by end-2009; foreign-owned banks' share in total deposits also increased. While this partly reflects weaknesses of domestically owned banks, it is certainly not a sign of eroding confidence.

Box

BTA, Alliance Bank and Temirbank: Default and Balance Sheet Restructuring

Soon after BTA and Alliance Bank were nationalized, it turned out that their financial needs were higher than originally assessed: In mid-2009, the two banks' foreign liabilities were estimated to add up to more than 12 billion EUR (comprising over 40% of credit institutions' total external debt or up to 15% of the country's external debt), of which BTA owed almost three quarters. In April 2009, both banks defaulted on their foreign obligations, which triggered payments on credit default swap (CDS) contracts written on the banks. The authorities declared that they did not intend to guarantee the loans of (nationalized) Bank Turan-Alem, Alliance Bank or of any other credit institution. After extensive and difficult processes, in the summer of 2009 the two insolvent banks signed memoranda of understanding with their foreign creditors in which the latter principally approved to restructure the credit institutions' foreign debt. In November, Temirbank (the eighth-largest), where BTA – and therefore, the state – is a major shareholder, also declared default on its obligations and launched restructuring negotiations.

In December 2009, BTA and Alliance reached preliminary agreements with their creditors in which the latter accepted major haircuts. Subsequently, Samruk-Kazyna took over Alliance entirely.

In March 2010, Alliance signed its final agreement, which i.a. provided for the bank's creditors to take a 33% stake in Alliance (besides

Samruk Kazyna's remaining 67% stake) and for the bank's external debt to be cut from 3,3 billion EUR to 750 million EUR (which corresponds to a 76% haircut). Thanks to this operation, Alliance's capital position reverted from a negative 2,2 billion EUR into positive territory (150 million EUR). Temirbank's final agreement produced a halving of its external debt of 1,1 billion EUR and the acquisition by Samruk-Kazyna of 80% of its capital. Bank Turan-Alem's final arrangement was wrapped up in September 2010. The bank's external liabilities of 9,3 billion EUR were reduced by 5,0 billion EUR to 4,3 billion EUR (-53%). Accordingly, BTA improved its capital position from negative to a positive 1 billion EUR. Samruk-Kazyna also raised its equity stake in BTA to 81.5%. The three banks' balance sheet clean-up contributed to the decline of external liabilities of the banking sector by one third to 15,0 billion EUR (14% of GDP) in 2010. The state's ownership in the banking sector rose to about 25%.

Bank Debt Restructuring: the Main Facts

Source: Marchenko 2011

	Bank Turan-Alem	**Alliance**	**Temir**
Date of default on external debt	April 2009	April 2009	November 2009
Date of principal creditor approval to restructuring plan	May 2010	December 2009	March 2010
Liabilities subject to restructuring	EUR 9,3 billion	EUR 3,3 billion	EUR 1,1 billion
Date of final agreement/ implementation of restructuring operation	September 2010	March 2010	April 2010
Value of debt reduction (size of haircut)	EUR 5,0 billion (53%)	EUR 2,55 billion (76%)	EUR 550 million (50%)

	Bank Turan-Alem	Alliance	Temir
Samruk-Kazyna's/ state's share of bank equity (as result of restructuring)	81.5%	67.0%	80.0%

Recently (2010-2011): Despite Regulatory Reform and Some Signs of Stabilization, Credit Quality and Coverage Ratios Deteriorate, Suggesting the Need for a New Programme to Reduce Problem Loans

In a regulatory response to the crisis, the authorities tightened some elements of banking regulation or plan to do so: The FSA raised banks' minimum capital requirements on 1 October 2009 more than three times to 5,0 billion KZT (approx. 24 million EUR), and then on 1 July 2011 further doubled them to 10,0 billion KZT. There are some exceptions for credit institutions that operate outside the two main cities of Almaty and Astana and are not registered there. These banks from 1 October 2009 faced minimum capital requirements of 2,0 billion KZT (10 million EUR), which were adjusted to 4,0 billion KZT on 1 July 2011. This substantial increase may trigger some mergers and acquisitions in the sector. New domestic foreign currency lending is curbed through higher minimum provisioning requirements on loans to borrowers that do not have effective currency hedges (5% from 1 January 2010, 10% from mid-2010, 20% from 1 January 2011). Some of the tax disincentives to writing off bad loans have been removed.

The authorities further decided to (re-)integrate the Financial Supervision Agency (FSA) into the central bank. It is hoped that this will facilitate the implementation of regulatory policies and better safeguard financial stability (EBRD 2011, 133).The FSA/ NBK aim to limit banks' borrowing in foreign markets to a maximum of 30% of total funding, to cap the loan-to-deposit ratio at 150%, and to contain growth of off-balance sheet liabilities potentially thru a ban on certain types of transactions (Standard & Poor's 2010, 18-19). Moreover, minimum capital adequacy is to be raised to 8% (mid-2012), and to 9% (mid-2013).

Meanwhile, as regards the first two goals, things are moving in the right direction: Continued forced deleveraging and the write-down of the three defaulted banks' external debt pushed down the share of liabilities to non-residents in total banking sector liabilities from 34% at end-2009 to

25% at end-2010. The loan-to-deposit ratio also fell further from 116% at end-2009 to 104% at end-2010, and then seems to have stabilized at around 100% in 2011.

While they had dipped in late 2008 and early 2009, combined NFRK funds and NBK reserves subsequently benefited from the brightening external environment and the recovery of commodity prices in the second half of 2009 thru mid-2011. Combined NFRK funds and NBK reserves expanded to 44,3 billion EUR at end-2010, and to 52,5 billion EUR at end-October 2011 (about 46% of GDP, among their highest-ever combined levels, see Table 1).

Credit institutions' overall liquidity situation improved in the last two years. Supported by state-owned entities, deposit growth (in real terms) remained positive in 2010 and slightly accelerated in recent months (8% at end-Oct, year on year). After the devaluation of the tenge in February 2009 had contributed to lifting the share of foreign exchange-denominated deposits to above 40% of total deposits, recovery of confidence in the Kazakhstani currency and some slight re-appreciation drove this share back down to about one third, which corresponds to its pre-crisis level. The loan-to-deposit ratio (referred to above) receded to levels not seen for a decade. The ratio of liquid assets to short-term liabilities further increased as of end-March 2011.[124]

Thanks to the debt write-off of the three defaulted banks (particularly of Bank Turan Alem, see Box), the banking sector's overall capital turned positive again in the third quarter of 2010. Accounting of extra-ordinary revenues related to these debt write-offs might contribute to explaining the extra-ordinarily high profitability ratios from 2010 onwards (Table 2). While capital adequacy had still been negative in mid-2010, it was positive at end-2010 (17.9%) and remained at the attained level (17.7%) at end-October 2011.[125] Despite abundant liquidity and the return of impressive economic growth figures, lending is only recovering very hesitantly and slowly. Largely due to write-offs of loss loans by banks undergoing restructuring, credit to the private sector still contracted in real terms in 2010 (-8% year on year). Following stagnation until mid-2011, as of end-October, lending exhibited fragile growth of around 4% (year on year). State-sponsored loan programs contributed to this growth, though. Many banks continue to invest in low-interest money market instruments and to accumulate government securities. This weakness of credit or reluctance to lend is explained by constrained demand from still highly indebted non-oil corporate borrowers and notably by persisting high and partly even rising levels of impaired loans. In their Financial Stability Report for 2010, the NBK and the FSA i.a. assess that, in a number of cases, the low volume of new lending is also linked to overestimation of risks associated with borrowers (NBK/ FSA 2010, 19).

Nonperforming loans (defined as loans overdue past 90 days, as published by the IMF) in the first half of 2010 rose to 25% of total loans, then slightly declined (24% at end-2010), before increasing again to 26% in mid-2011 (Table 2).[126] NPLs remain heavily concentrated in the real estate, mortgage and construction sectors. While provisioning coverage of overdue loans (coverage ratio) remained high, it declined from end-2009 to end-Sept 2011 (according to whatever definition), as provisions declined while credit risk rose (with both problem loans according to national definition as well as NPLs as published by the IMF increasing further from already high levels).

Moreover, the rise in credit risk as shown by these indicators may still understate its true rise, because recoveries of restructured loans, which have been removed from the NPL classification, remain doubtful, as pointed out by the IMF (IMF Staff Report 2011, 8).

Thus, some restructured loans may not be properly serviced (possible ever-greening activities), and therefore may continue to be de-facto nonperforming. Another factor complicating the resolution of the bad loan problem is that banks seem to be reluctant to proceed with fire sales of real estate assets in a low volume market (Standard & Poor's 2011, 13).

Notwithstanding the duality and segmentation of the Kazakhstani economy, the simultaneousness of robust economic expansion and low and further deteriorating credit quality would suggest that not all banks have been properly valuing (and provisioning) their loans. Therefore, while capital adequacy of 17.7% at end-Oct 2011 seems to constitute a good buffer, concerns that NPLs may still be measured too low raise questions as to whether this buffer is really sufficient. In the case of the already bailed-out Bank Turan-Alem (see Box) recent upward corrections of bad loan provisions contributed to producing a loss of 1 billion EUR in the first nine months of 2011. After breaking even in 2010, BTA's capital turned negative again. A new rescue plan for BTA is being discussed. According to market participants, BTA may await a new capital injection, a new restructuring of its remaining 3,7 billion EUR of liabilities, or outright closure (Dow Jones Business News 2011).[127] Alliance Bank has also witnessed a decline in asset quality which recently caused its capital to dip back into negative territory (IMF Staff Report 2011, 8).

Whereas, back in 2008, BTA and Alliance Bank had occupied ranks 1 and 4 of Kazakhstani credit institutions measured by assets, until March 2011 the two slipped to ranks 3 and 6. As Table 3 shows, the country's two largest banks today are the (still) majority privately-owned Kazkommertsbank and Halyk Savings Bank.

More generally, as referred to above, the NPL problem has attained such a dimension that the authorities have drawn up plans for government intervention to promote/ accelerate bad loan work-outs and to set up a bad bank to deal with (other) impaired loans, in order to get banks to reactivate lending more quickly.

While the authorities have so far been hesitant to carry out the intervention, and have been sanguine that the economic recovery and improved regulatory framework will help restore banks' health, the IMF rather favors going forward with the sector-wide plan (IMF Staff Report 2011, 1,11-13): The plan aims to remove NPLs with an approximate face value of 6 billion USD (around 40% of total NPLs) from credit instititions' balance sheets to facilitate re-acceleration of lending, while limiting costs and checking moral hazard.

Although details are preliminary, the plan features a three-pronged approach: First, banks would establish special purpose vehicles to act as private asset management companies (decentralized work-out). These entities would receive problem assets related to real estate with a face value of about 4 billion USD.

Second, a distressed asset fund (centralized bad bank) would be set up and owned by the NBK. The fund would acquire and dispose of other NPLs worth 2 billion USD (with an assumed average discount of 50%). Under the fund, banks would swap provisioned NPLs for bonds at a value determined by independent assessors.

Third, regulatory standards would be harmonized with best international practice and the Basel III framework, i.e. by strengthening core capital and adjusting systemic risks through dynamic provisioning and enhanced capital buffers. Whatever strategy is adopted, once the balance sheet problems of credit institutions are resolved or overcome, the state plans to divest its stakes in the sector.

Assessment of Current Risks

Kazakhstani credit institutions are definitely not yet driving the recovery of the national economy, they rather remain preoccupied with overcoming their own serious earnings and capitalization problems. Obviously, a large amount of resources was misallocated to real estate during the boom phase. Risks continue to be focussed on credit quality.

Very High and Even Further Rising Credit Risk

Very high NPLs reflect pronounced credit risk and are also largely responsible for the continuing credit crunch. This goes particularly for the still substantial share of foreign currency lending – to an important extent to unhedged households. Mounting loan-loss provisions temporarily wiped out profits, generated losses and pushed capital and capital adequacy into negative territory. Capital positions are recovering only hesitantly and sluggishly. While provisions are even higher than some specific measure of NPLs, it is unclear whether they are high enough, taking into account the risk that these measured NPLs do not fully reflect actual credit quality, as is suggested by other indicators of credit risk, like the nationally defined "problem loans" (see table 2 and subchapter 3.4). Moreover, whatever credit risk measure is taken, the coverage ratio (i.e. coverage of overdue loans by loan-loss provisions) declined from end-2009 to mid-2011, as provisions declined, while both credit risk measures increased. Therefore, further capitalization and/or restructuring measures may appear warranted. Moreover, after various upward corrections of NPLs lately, an accurate valuation of the entirety of problem assets and a full recognition of bank losses may be in need.

High Exposure of Kazakhstani Economy to Volatile Oil Price and Weakening International Business Environment

A lot will depend on the further development of the external environment, especially with regard to global demand and the oil price as well as external financing conditions. While the external environment has so far been supportive of the Kazakhstani recovery, most recently, unfortunately, global activity has become more fragile and confidence has fallen. Furthermore, against the backdrop of the dual structure of the Kazakhstani economy, strong signs of recovery of the resource sector fail to yet translate into tangible signals of recovery of the non-resource sector, incl. banking activity. However, without continuing growth of the resource sector, not only the stability of the currency would be in jeopardy, there would also be no positive linkages to the non-resource and financial sector, and probably no prospects for improving credit quality and achieving sustainable growth of Kazakhstani financial intermediation. On another point: in contrast to banks' foreign debt which has fallen sharply thanks to deleveraging and restructuring, banks remain exposed to a high share of (i.e. domestic and external) foreign currency-denominated liabilities in total sector liabilities.

Uncertainty Triggered by Persisting Feeble Institutional Environment

Given Kazakhstan's traditional reputation of having the best managed banking sector of the CIS, some observers may not have expected the persistence of institutional shortcomings/ flaws with regard to corporate governance, risk management, creditor rights, accounting (incl. substantial and largely intransparent off-balance sheet items), banking regulation and supervision. Problems with respect to oversight are most visibly reflected by the fact that the above-mentioned two large domestically-owned banks were able to surprise the authorities – who had even become their major owners – about their real financial state. And some of the financial problems of these two banks continue. Important regulatory and supervisory reforms recently initiated (see subchapter 3.4) will hopefully bring about a qualitative improvement of governance.

Bibliography

Alexander, P.: "BTA Bank: One bank, two stories – Debt restructuring", 2010, The Banker. pp. 36-40.

Alexander, P.: "Kazakhstan: Toxic legacy opens the door to new players", 2011, The Banker. pp. 56-58.

Al-Eyd, A.; Saker, N.: "Financial Market Development in Kazakhstan", 2010, IMF: Republic of Kazakhstan – Selected Issues. pp. 26-37.

Barisitz, S.: "Macrofinancial Development and Systemic Change in CIS Central Asia", 2009, Focus on European Economic Integration, 3, OeNB. pp. 38-61.

Barisitz, S.; Lahnsteiner, M.: "From Stormy Expansion to Riding out the Storm: Banking Development in Kazakhstan", 2010, OeNB Financial Stability Report, 19.

Dow Jones Business News: "Kazakhstan's BTA to present rescue plan to central bank by year end", 2011.

EBRD: "Transition Report 2011. The People's Perspective", 2011, London.

Euromoney Vienna: "Kazakhstan cleans up after the bubble bursts", 2010. pp. 32-36.

IMF Global Markets Monitor: "Kazakhstan: BTA Bank has officially defaulted on a $2 bn 2018 eurobond according to newswires", 2012.

IMF Staff Report: "Republic of Kazakhstan – Staff Report for the 2008 Article IV Consultation", 2009.

Table 3 Kazakhstan's Top Six Banks (Ranked By Balance Sheet Size, End-March 2011)

Rank	Credit institution	Major shareholders (>10% of equity	Assets (EUR billion)	Share of banking sector´s total assets
1	Kazkommerts-bank	Domestic private investors (N.S. Subkhanberdin et a.) 33%, Alnair Capital Holding (Abu Dhabi) 29%, Samruk-Kazyna (state) 13%	13,73	19.5
2	Halyk Savings Bank	Almex (domestic financial-industria group) 51%, Samruk-Kazyna (state) 13%	12,32	17.5
3	Bank Turan-Alem	Samruk-Kazyna (state 82%, JSC "Central Securities Depository" (mostly state) 16%	11,34	16.1
4	Bank Center Credit	Kookmin Bank Co. Ltd (South Korea) 42%B.R. Beiseitov (domestic businessman) 25%, IFC 10%	6,69	9.5
5	ATF Bank	Uni Credit Bank Austria 92%	5,7	8.1
6	Alliance Bank	Samruk-Kazyna (state) 67% foreign creditors 33%	2,89	4.1

Table 4 Kazakhstan: Selected Banking Sector Stability Indicators (2005-2011)

	2005	2006	2007	2008	2009	2010	End-Sep 2011*
Credit risk							
Balance sheet assets (ratio to GDP, %)	59.5	86.9	90.9	74.1	68.0	62.3	64.0 (end-Mar)
Loans to the private sector (bank credits, ratio to GDP, %)	34.1	45.9	56.5	46.5	44.9	35.3	33.5 (mid-year)
-annual real growth (%)	62.4	67.0	30.2	-6.1	-3.7	-8.0	3.4
-annual real growth (exchange-rate readjusted, %)[1)2)]	63.7	71.6	33.7	-6.3	-12.4	-6.6	4.9
Loans to households (% of total loans)	25.8	32.7	35.3	31.3	29.1	27.9	26.9
Loan loss (loans classified as loss, % of total loans)	2.2	1.6	1.5	4.4	30.6	20.1	22.2
Problems loans (classified as doubtful category 5 and loss, % of total loans)	5.0	3.4	3.5	8.6	47.0	45.7	51.5

	2005	2006	2007	2008	2009	2010	End-Sep 2011*
Non-performing loans (overdue past 90 days, % of total loans)[2a]			3.5	5.2	21.2	23.8	26.3 (end-year)
Exchange rate-related and interest-related risk (%)							
Share of liabilities to non-residents in total sector liabilities	50.7	51.6	53.3	45.0	34.0	25.0	
Share of forex-denominated liabilities in total sector liabilities	67.9	62.3	62.2	59,7	53.8	44.3	53.8 (end-Mar)
Foreign currency deposits (share in total deposits)	41.9	35.2	32.0	35.4	43.7	34.9	32.9
Foreign currency loans (share in total loans)	51.5	48.4	42.7	44.2	48.4	42.3	36.8
Share of foreign currency loans in total loans to households	55.6	44.5	36.7	36.0	39.4	36.1	30.3
Deposit rate[4)]	9.1	9.1	11.5	11.3	10.0	8.8	8.6
Lending rate[5)]	13.0	12.2	14.8	16.1	14.3	12.9	11.3

	2005	2006	2007	2008	2009	2010	End-Sep 2011*
Liquidity risk							
Private sector deposits (clients´ deposits, ratio to GDP, %)	21.8	30.1	30.3	33.7	38.7	34.1	34.5 (mid-year)
-annual real growth (%)[1)]	21.1	71.7	6.4	27.0	14.2	3.3	7.5
-annual real growth (exchange rate-adjusted, %)[1)2)]	22.1	75.9	8.4	26.8	4.9	5.4	8.1
Household deposits (% of total deposits)	33.5	33.1	36.8	27.2	28.8	29.9	30.0
Credit to deposit ration (%)	157	152	187	138	116	104	98
Liquid assets to short-term liabilities (%)	95	118	97	158	212	248	289 (end-Mar)
Off-balance sheet items (% of total assets)	63.8	76.4	94.4	82.1	69.3[6)]		
Profitability							
Return on assets (ROA, %)	1.6	1.4	2.3	0.2	-24.1	12.1	9.7 (end-Mar)

	2005	2006	2007	2008	2009	2010	End-Sep 2011*
Return on equity (ROA, %)	16.6	14.6	18.4	1.9	-1192.6	2920.8	201.1 (end-Mar)
Shock-absorbing factors							
Loan-loss provisions (%of total loans)	5.6	5.0	5.9	11.1	37.7	30.9	32.9
Capital adequacy (capital to risk-weighed assets, %)	14.9	14.5	14.2	14.9	-8.0	17.9	13.4[7a)]
Memorandum items							
Number of operating banks (of which foreign-owned)	34 (14)	33 (14)	35 (18)	37 (13)	38 (14)	39 (…)	39 (…)
Share of banks´ debt in Kazakhstan´s gross external liabilities (%)	35.5	45.0	47.1	36.3	26.8	16.8	14.9 (mid-year)
Share of majority—foreign-owned banks in total sector assets (%)	7.3	5.9	15.8	15.8	22.7	22.9[8]	25.0
EBRD index of banking sector reform[8)]	3	3	3	3	2.7	2.7	2.7

Notes:

* unless mentioned otherwise

1) deflated by CPI

2) unchanged exchange rate of end-2007: 120.30 KZT/USD used throughout the observation period

2a) As published only by the IMF, without corresponding confirmation by national sources

3) mid-2008

4) refers to weighted average of interest rates on time deposits of individuals, in tenge by maturity

5) refers to weighted average of interest rates on credits extended to legal entities, excluding banks in tenge by maturity

6) Apr 2009

7) includes contingent claims, contingent liabilities, transactions in forex and precious metals, and derivatives

7a) the figure for end-Oct 2011 was 17.7

8) end-Sep 2010

9) indicators run on scale from 1 (few reforms) to 4+ (standard of advanced market economy)

Hans-Georg Heinrich, Ludmilla Lobova, Summary and Conclusions

The record of post-Soviet Kazakhstan is a mixed bag of rich opportunities, dashed hopes and drab realities. Kazakhstan won early rounds of applause for its handling of regional policy and has a catastrophic image in the West for its human rights conduct. This, however, eclipses cautious but real advances in bottom-up democratization. There are certainly unwritten rules which set limits for political opposition and criticism. Nevertheless – and this volume is a case in point – open criticism is a feature of Kazakhstan's authoritarian system.

Unsurprisingly, the Achilles heel of the grand schemes projected by an up-to-date legislative framework is implementation on the ground. The shortcomings of evolving or continuing practices prompt demands for the revision of the legislative basis in their turn. The country can boast a vibrant civil society which is definitely no fig leaf put up by the government in order to improve its international image. It is, among other things, a provider of important social services, it fills a gap in the activities of governmental and budget-financed institutions; and last not least, it is a provider of jobs. Civil society regards itself as a champion of modernization.

Modernization and Europeanization implies looking for and adopting European and, where appropriate, post-Soviet best practices. The European Union recognizes the importance of Kazakhstan as a regional front runner, a fuel provider and security partner, particularly as a backstop for the ISAF and other missions to Afghanistan. The various strategies and dialogues, however, are poorly coordinated and give little hope for an implementation of the plans to introduce European standards ("The Path to Europe") any time soon.

Kazakhstan's adroit conduct in regional and global affairs is undoubtedly a highlight in its post-Soviet development. Its apt maneuvering between Russia and China, its positive involvement in regional conflicts as a respected go-between, and overall, as a champion of peaceful co-existence and nuclear disarmament have placed Kazakhstan into the position of a regional lead nation.

Many of Kazakhstan's security priorities, such as the fight against drug trafficking and religious extremism track with the security agenda of major world powers and international organizations. In recognition of its role in international politics, Kazakhstan was entrusted with the OSCE chair during 2011. Kazakhstan's prestige in the Islamic world is indicated by its chairmanship of the OIC (June 2011 to June 2012.)

Kazakhstan's economic development shows the typical pattern of a raw material based post-Soviet system. As in the case of Russia, rising raw material prices provided the means for economic growth and investments, but also stimulated corruption, an uncontrollable and highly politicized growth of budget expenditure, overheated financial markets and soaring foreign debts. Kazakhstan's financial sector experienced a devastating meltdown during the financial crisis. The two largest banks actually defaulted on their foreign liabilities and had to be bailed out by the state. Nevertheless, an oil-driven recovery is under way. On the other hand, the priority for prestige projects and the buildup of a clientelist administration actually prevented economic modernization. Depending on different calculations, between 40 and 70% of budget revenues come from raw material exports. Diversification strategies have failed ("Dutch disease"). Due to the demand for fuels and raw materials in the world markets, foreign loans and investment are available for the extractive industries. In contrast, the industries and service branches outside the extractive sector have to rely on domestic credit. Consequently, the state of agriculture and living standards of the population employed in this sector are deplorable.

Besides its economic woes, modern Kazakhstan faces a problem of managing diversity. Soviet-style forced migration has left sustainable traces in Kazakh society. The Kazakh state which mirrors the struggle to shape a modern Kazakh identity is not recognized as a shared entity by all ethnic groups. New cleavages are opening up as migrants and guest workers from the neighbouring regions enter the fray and exacerbate ethnic and religious tensions. Nevertheless, Kazakh society has managed to avoid the pernicious inter-ethnic wars which ravaged other Central Asian states. The country is more stable than its Central Asian neighbours, but cannot remain aloof of global trends. Strikes and protests occurring in the wake of the Arab revolutions should be taken as an indicator of primarily social problems which have to be remedied and addressed, even if they imply action against established interest groups.

The authors of this volume

Akhmetzhanova Gulnara Kairbaevna - Kazakh Institute for Development

Amrebaev Aidar – Deputy Director, Institute of World Economics and Politics, Foundation of the First President of the Republic of Kazakhstan, Almaty

Astrov Vasily - The Vienna Institute for International Economic Studies

Baynazarova Elnara - Department Head of Department for Europe-Asia Research, Institute of World Economics and Politics, Foundation of the First President of the Republic of Kazakhstan, Almaty

Barisitz Stefan – Senior Economist, Austrian National Bank

Busek Erhard – Former Vice Chancellor of Austria

Heinrich Hans-Georg – Vice President, ICEUR-Vienna

Kunserkin Zhangazy Karimovich - Alma-Ata Bar Association Almaty

Legeland Gregor - Department of Political Science, Vienna University

Lobova Ludmilla – Scientific Director, ICEUR-Vienna

Solov´eva Aigul´ - President, Civil Alliance of Kazakhstan

Spanov Magbat Uarysbekovich - President, Kazakh Institute for Development; Almaty

Tuleshov Valikhan - Institute for World Economy and Politics, Almaty

Aydar Amrebaev: The Cultural and Civilisational Basis for the Development of Kazakhstan

1 Gumilev, L.N.: "Ethnogenesis and the biosphere of earth", 2005, Moscow, AST Astrel. p. 512.
2 Gachev, G.: "National images of the world", 1988, Moscow, Soviet writer. p. 448.
3 Gurevich, A.Ya: "Categories of medieval culture", 1984, Moscow, Art. p. 350.
4 See book: Baizhumin, Zh.: "The story of the birth, life and death of the shepherd Abel", 2009, Almaty, Aryan lexicon, Book 2.
5 Jaspers, K.: "The origin and goal of history", 1991, Moscow, Publ. Political literature.
6 Mackinder, H.J.: "The Geographical Pivot of History", 1995, POLIS, 4.
7 Suleimenov, O.O.: "Az i Ya", 1990, Alma-Ata, Publ. Zhalyn.
8 Tuleshov V. U.: "The Asian way: the history of the 21st century", 2010, Almaty, Almatykitap baspasy. p.192.
9 Fukuyama, F.: "Trust", 2008, Moscow, AST. p.736.
10 See book of Sarsenbaeva, Z.N.: "Ethnicity and values", 2009, Almaty.
11 See book: Nazarbaev, N.A.: "In the stream of history", 1999, Almaty, Atamura.
12 Ibid.
13 Ibid.
14 Ibid.
15 Ibid.
16 Ibid.
17 Umbetalieva, T.: "Tribalism in Kazakhstan. Tribal differentiation - the basis of the political system", 2003, http://www.centrasia.ru/newsA.php?st=1041591120, 25.04.2012.
18 Masonov, N.E.: "The nomadic civilisation of the Kazakhs", 1995, Almaty, Gorizont.
19 Ibid.
20 Sultangalieva, A.K.: "The city and the people: socio-cultural transformation in Kazakhstan", 2010, Almaty.
21 Sultangalieva, A.K.: "The city and the people: socio-cultural transformation in Kazakhstan", 2010, Almaty. p.179.

V. Tuleshov: Characteristics of the Political Modernization in Present Kazakhstan

22 Nazarbaev, N.A.: "In the stream of history", 1999, Almaty, Atamura. p.34.
23 Sarsenbaeva, Z.N.: "Ethnicity and values", 2009, Almaty. p.157-158.
24 Ibid. p.35.
25 Ibid. p.35-36.
26 Ibid. p. 39-40.
27 Ibid. p. 40-41.
28 Ibid.

29 Umbetalieva, T.: "Tribalism in Kazakhstan. Tribal differentiation - the basis of the political system", 2003, http://www.centrasia.ru/newsA.php?st=1041591120, 25.04.2012.

30 Sultangalieva, A.K.: "The city and the people: socio-cultural transformation in Kazakhstan", 2010, Almaty.

31 Address of the President of the Republic of Kazakhstan N. Nazarbaev at the 14th session of the APK, 2008, http://www.zakon.kz/124086-vystuplenie-prezidenta-rk-n.a.html, 25.04.2012.

32 Tuleshov, V.U.: "How the Kazakh consciousness changes us?", 2006, Central Asia Monitor, 4 (69).

33 Address of the President of the Republic of Kazakhstan N. Nazarbaev at the 14th session of the APK. http://www.zakon.kz/124086-vystuplenie-prezidenta-rk-n.a.html

34 Novosti Kazakhstan: "Kazakhstan opredelil strany SNG po pokazatelyam snizheniya urovnya korrupcii, 2010, http://www.newskaz.ru/society/20101027/871260.html, 25.04.2012.

35 Vesti: "Amerikancy ocenili uroven korrupcii v Kazakhstane na troyku", 2009, http://vesti.kz/economy/6291/, 25.04.2012.

36 In this regard, for example, the awarding of the Nobel Peace Prize to the Chinese dissident Liu Xiaobo for "disturbing the social order" and "calls for changes in the social system of China" after a visit of M.S.Gorbachev to China, from the point of view of the eastern universalism could be classified as an assault on the hierarchy of the Chinese nation's foundations which the Chinese authorities inherently could not allow. They could not allow that the requirements of an expansion of personal rights and freedoms "destroy the common and collective" which formed the body and the soul of the nation throughout all previous stages, "demolish the country" (as, for example, it became possible in the Soviet Union), violating "the prevailing balance" and creating an unmanageable chaos with its collapse. Therefore, from the point of view of the eastern universalism, the reaction of the Chinese authorities was more than natural and predictable. It was logical, because the way of evolution of the system which was put forward by Deng Xiaoping, (even from the point of view of Western rationalism) seemed, if it is not approached with prejudices (as did western politicians in their lack of understanding), objective and true.

Zhangazy Karimovich Kunserkin: The Judicial and Legal System in Kazakhstan: Modern Requirements and the Approach to International

37 Almanakh "Nevolya" (Prilozhenie k zhurnalu "Indeks/Dose na cenzuru": "Tyuremnoe naselenie v stranakh mira", 2008, http://www.index.org.ru/nevol/2008-15/statmir_n15.html, 02.05.2012.

38 Note of the translator: compare the data available for 2011: http://globalization.kof.ethz.ch/static/pdf/rankings_2011b.pdf, 14.04.2012.
39 Nazarbaev, N.A.: "Strategiya radikalnogo obnovleniya globalnogo soobshchestva i partnerstva civilisaciy", 2010, Zhibek zholy. p.30.
40 WTO Database: "Country profiles: Kazakhstan", 2011, http://stat.wto.org/CountryProfile/WSDBCountryPFView.aspx?Language=E&Country=KZ, 15.2.2012.
41 Nazarbaev, N.A.: "Epicenter of Peace", 2001, Puritan Press, http://www.akorda.kz/files/f0000000000000000001/epicenter_1270567160503.pdf, 15.2.2012. p.13.
42 Asanov, Zh.A.: "Centralnoaziatsko-Kaspiyskiy region v sisteme aziatskoy i globalnoy bezopasnosti", Pervyy Forum po problemam bezopasnosti i sotrudnichestva v Centralnoaziatsko-Kaspiyskom regione: Materialy Foruma, Pod redakcii M.E. Shaykhutdinova, 2008, http://iwep.kz/stariysite/images/document/books%20of%20IWEP/Pervyi%20forum.pdf, 24.02.2012. p.83.
43 Ibid.
44 Galtung, J.: "Desyat tendenciy, menyayushchikh mir", 2011, Rossiya v globalnoy politike 4, http://www.globalaffairs.ru/number/Desyat-tendentcii-menyayuschikh-mir-15276, 16.2.2012.
45 Bogaturov, A.D.: "Sovremennyy mir: sistema ili konglomerat? Ocherki teorii i politicheskogo analiza mezhdunarodnykh otnosheniy", 2002, Otv.red. A.D. Bogaturov, N.A. Kosolapov, M.A. Khrustalev, NOFMO. pp.129-144.
46 Hettne, B.: "Globalization. New Regionalism and East Asia", Septembre 2nd 6th 1996, Selected papers delivered at the United Nations University Global Seminar '96 Shonan Session. p.6.
47 Sevastyanov, S.V.: "Mezhpravitelstvennye organizacii Vostochnoy Azii: evolyuciya, effektivnost, rossiyskoe uchastie", 2008, Dalnauka. p.56.
48 Gadzhiev, Amur G.: K itogam 3-ogo stambulskogo sammita. Sobeshchaniya po vzaimodeystviyu i meram doveriya v Azii, http://www.iimes.ru/rus/stat/2010/10-06-10a.htm, 24.02.2012.
49 Vystuplenie Prezidenta RK N.A. Nazarbaev na tretem sammite SVMDA, 08.06.2010, http://www.akorda.kz/ru/-speeches/external_forums/memleket_basshysy_nnazarbaevty_aziya_keesn_3sh_sammitnde, 24.02.2012.
50 Pervyy Forum po problemam bezopasnosti i sotrudnichestva v Centralnoaziatsko-Kaspiyskom regione: Materialy Foruma, pod redakcii M.E. Shaykhutinova, 25 avgusta 2008, http://iwep.kz/stariysite/images/document/-books%20of%20IWEP/Pervyi%20forum.pdf, 24.02.2012. p.114.

Legeland: Kazakhstan and the European Union – Challenges and Prospects for a Close Collaboration

51 Kazakh State Programme: "The Path to Europe" 2009-2011, 2008, http://www.eucentralasia.eu/fileadmin/user_upload/PDF/other_related_publications/path_to_Europe.pdf, 20.02.2012.

52 European Commission, Directorate General for Trade: „Kazakhstan EU Bilateral Trade and Trade with the World", 8 June 2011, http://trade.ec.europa.eu/doclib/docs/2006/september/tradoc_113406.pdf, 20.02.2012.

53 Lillis, J.: "Kazakhstan: Astana Confronts Extremist Threat", September 6th 2011, eurasianet.org, http://www.eurasianet.org/node/64133, 20.02.2012.

54 Human Rights Watch: "World Report 2011: Kazakhstan", http://www.hrw.org/world-report-2011/kazakhstan, 20.02.2012.

55 Amnesty International: "Annual Report 2011: Kazakhstan", http://www.amnesty.org/en/region/kazakstan/report-2011, 20.02.2012.
Freedom House: "Freedom in the World 2011 – Kazakhstan", http://expression.freedomhouse.org/reports/freedom_in_the_world/2011/kazakhstan, 20.02.2012.

57 Transparency International: "Corruption Perceptions Index 2010 Results", http://www.transparency.org/policy_research/surveys_indices/cpi/2010/results, 20.02.2012.

58 Reporters Without Borders: "2010 World Press Freedom Index: Europe Area", http://www.reporter-ohne-grenzen.de/fileadmin/rte/docs/2010/101019_Europa_GB.pdf, 20.02.2012.

59 OSCE/ ODIHR: "Republic of Kazakhstan, Early Presidential Election, 3 April 2011, Election Observation Mission Final Report", http://www.osce.org/odihr/elections/78714, 20.02.2012.

60 TACIS, acronym for Technical Aid to the Commonwealth of Independent States. "TACIS in Tables", April 2007, http://tacis.uz/docs/Tacis_tables_EN.pdf, 20.02.2012.

61 Emerson, M.; Boonstra, J.; et al.: "Into EurAsia, Monitoring the EU's Central Asia Strategy", 2010, EUCAM (EU-Central Asia Monitoring) http://www.fride.org/download/EUCAM_Final_Report.pdf, 23.02.2012. p.58.

62 TRACECA, acronym for Transport Corridor Europe Caucasus Central Asia.

63 INOGATE, acronym for Interstate Oil and Gas Transport to Europe.

64 CADAP, acronym for Central Asia Drug Action Programme.

65 BOMCA, acronym for Border Management Programme in Central Asia.

66 Council of the EU: "European Union and Central Asia: Strategy for a New Partnership", October 2007, http://eeas.europa.eu/central_asia/docs/2007_eu_strategy_new_partnership_centralasia_en.pdf, 20.02.2012.

67 Boonstra, J.; Denison, M.: "Is the EU-Central Asia Strategy running out of Stream?", EUCAM (EU-Central Asia Monitoring) Policy Brief 17, May 2011, http://www.eucentralasia.eu/fileadmin/user_upload/PDF/Policy_Briefs/Policy_Brief_17.pdf, 20.02.2012.

68 Ibid.

69 Delegation of the European Union to the Republic of Kazakhstan: "Joint Press-Briefing following 11th Session of European Union – Kazakhstan Cooperation Committee & Negotiations on new enhanced Partnership and Cooperation Agreement between the EU and Kazakhstan", October 12th 2011,http://www.eeas.europa.eu/delegations/-kazakhstan/documents/press_corner/20111012_01_en.pdf, 20.02.2012.

70 Kucera, J.: "Child labour and U.S. Military Cooperation in Uzbekistan", September 23rd, 2011, eurasianet.org, http://www.eurasianet.org/node/6342, 14.04.2012.

71 Laruelle, M.: "Involving Central Asia in Afghanistan's Future – What can Europe do?", EUCAM (EU-Central Asia Monitoring) Policy Brief 20, August 2011, http://www.eucentralasia.eu/fileadmin/user_upload/PDF/Policy_Briefs/EUCAM-Brief.20.pdf, 20.2.2012.

72 Kucera, J.: „Kazakhstan's Islamist Threat?", August 15th 2011, the-diplomat.com, http://the-diplomat.com/2011/08/15/kazakhstan%E2%80%99s-islamist-threat/, 20.02.2012.

73 Lillis, J.: "Kazakhstan: Astana Confronts Extremist Threat", September 6th, 2011, eurasia.org, http://www.eurasianet.org/node/64133, 14.04.2012.

74 Bowyer, A.C.: "Islamic Movements and Democracy in Central Asia: Integration or Isolation?", May 2008, http://www.ifes.org/publication/247475edefe5e2d597c691c7bb0863eb/IslamDemocracyPaperBOWYER.pdf, 20.02.2012. p.4 et seqq.

75 UNODC: "World Drug Report 2011", http://www.unodc.org/documents/data-and-analysis/WDR2011/World_Drug_Report_2011_ebook.pdf, 23.02.2012.

76 UNODC: "World Drug Report 2011", http://www.unodc.org/documents/data-and-analysis/WDR2011/World_Drug_Report_2011_ebook.pdf, 23.02.2012.

77 UNODC: „Addiction, Crime and Insurgency. The transnational threat of Afghan opium", 2009, http://www.unodc.org/documents/data-and-analysis/Afghanistan/Afghan_Opium_Trade_2009_web.pdf, 23.02.2012. p.66.

78 UNODC: "Illicit Drug Trends in Central Asia", April 2008, http://www.unodc.org/documents/regional/central-asia/-Illicit%20Drug%20Trends_Central%20Asia-final.pdf, 23.02.2012. p.32.

79 UNODC: "Addiction, Crime and Insurgency. The transnational threat of Afghan opium", 2009, http://www.unodc.org/documents/data-and-analysis/Afghanistan/Afghan_Opium_Trade_2009_web.pdf, 23.02.2012. p.102 et seqq.

80 Council of the European Union: "2009-2013 Action plan on Drugs between the EU and Central Asian states", May 19th 2009, http://www.cadap.eu/sites/default/files/EU%20-central%20Asia%20Drug%20Action%20Plan%202009%20-%202013.pdf, 23.02.2012.

81 Laruelle, M.: "Involving Central Asia in Afghanistan's Future – What can Europe do?", EUCAM (EU-Central Asia Monitoring) Policy Brief 20, August 2011,

http://www.eucentralasia.eu/fileadmin/user_upload/PDF/Policy_Briefs/EUCAM-Brief.20.pdf, 23.02.2012.

82 BP: "BP Statistical Review of World Energy", June 2011, http://www.bp.com/liveassets/bp_internet/globalbp/globalbp_uk_english/reports_and_publications/statistical_energy_review_2011/STAGING/local_assets/pdf/statistical_review_of_world_energy_full_report_2011.pdf, 23.02.2012.

83 Europe's Energy Portal, 2011, http://www.energy.eu/#saving, 23.02.2012.

84 European Commission: "Green Paper. Towards a European Strategy for the Security of Energy Supply", 2000, http://ec.europa.eu/energy/green-paper-energy-supply/doc/green_paper_energy_supply_en.pdf, 23.02.2012.

85 Denison, M.: "The EU and Central Asia: Commercialising the Energy Relationship", 2009, EUCAM (EU-Central Asia Monitoring) Working Paper 2, http://www.eucentral-asia.eu/fileadmin/user_upload/PDF/Working_Papers/WP2_e-EN.pdf, 23.02.2012.

86 Silk Road Intelligencer: "Kazakhstan not ready to join EU-backed gas pipelines", neweurasia.com, http://neweurasia.info/en/index.php/13-special-projects/698-kazakhstan-not-ready-to-join-eu-backed-gas-pipelines, 23.02.2012.

87 Magomedov, A.; Nikerov, R.: "The South Stream vs. Nabucco: The "Pipeline War Gains Momentum", 2011, Institute of Strategic Studies of the Caucasus: The Caucasus & Globalization 5(1-2), http://www.ca-c.org/c-g/2011/journal_eng/c-g-1-2/c-gE-1-2.2011.pdf, 23.02.2012.

88 Rywkin, M.: "Security and Stability in Central Asia: Differing Interests and Perspectives", 2006, American Foreign Policy Interests 28(3). p. 200.

89 Chow, E.; Hendrix, L.: "Central Asia's Pipelines: Field of Dreams and Reality", 2010, The National Bureau of Asian Research, NBR Special Report 23, http://csis.org/files/publication/1009_EChow_LHendrix_CentralAsia.pdf, 23.02.2012, p.34 et seqq.

90 Emerson, M.; Boonstra, J.; et al.: „Into EurAsia. Monitoring the EU's Central Asia Strategy. Executive Summary and Recommendations", 2010, EUCAM (EU-Central Asia Monitoring) Policy Brief 13, http://www.eucentralasia.eu/fileadmin/user_upload/PDF/Policy_Briefs/PB13.pdf, 23.02.2012.

91 Bissenova, A.: "Striking Kazakh oil workers quit ruling party, August 11th", August 17th 2011, CACI (Central Asia – Caucasus Institute) News Digest, http://www.cacianalyst.org/?q=node/5615, 24.02.2012.

92 Worldbank: "GNI per capita PPP (current international $)", http://data.worldbank.org/indicator/NY.GNP.PCAP.PP.CD/countries, 24.02.2012.

93 Frey, M.; Wieslhuber, C.: "Do Kazakh Regions Converge?", 2011, Osteuropa-Institut Regensburg, Kurzanalysen und Informationen 52, http://www.oei-dokumente.de/publikationen/info/info-52.pdf, 24.02.2012.

94 Abazov, R.; Istybayeva, D.: "Will the 'People's IPO' Help Address Social Polarization in Kazakhstan?", 2011, CACI-Analyst (Central Asia Caucasus Institute), http://www.cacianalyst.org/?q=node/5553, 24.02.2012.

95 Statement of Kazakh President N. Nazarbaev at the Joint Sitting of two Parliament Chambers, September 1st 2011, http://en.tengrinews.kz/kazakhstan_news/4202/, 24.02.2012.

96 Nuttall, C.: „Is Kazakhstan Now an Enemy of the Internet?“, September 12th 2011, silkroadintelligencer.com, http://silkroadintelligencer.com/2011/09/12/is-kazakhstan-now-an-enemy-of-the-internet/, 24.02.2012.

97 Bissenova, A.: "Kazakhstan Approves Restrictive Religion Law“, 2011, CACI-Analyst (Central Asia-Caucasus Institute) News Digest, http://www.cacianalyst.org/?q=node/5642, 24.02.2012.

98 Nicloas, L.: "EU-Arab Relations after Arab Uprisings“, 2011, http://leilanrahbany.wordpress.com/2011/07/26/eu-arab-relations-after-arab-uprisings/, 24.02.2012.

Vasily Astrov: A Note on Kazakhstan's Oil Fund

99 As of end-September 2011.

100 Strictly speaking, these deficits are not entirely "non-oil", since some oil-related government revenues (which are not captured by the National Fund) flow directly into the budget. According to IMF calculations, the "true" non-oil deficits have typically been several percentage points of GDP higher.

101 Taking into account the quasi-fiscal expenditures of Kazakhstan's development agency Samruk Kazyna, the enacted fiscal package reached an estimated 7.5% of GDP.

102 Though the balanced budgets in the pre-crisis years hardly required new government borrowing, the stock of public debt inherited from previous years still had to be refinanced.

103 For simplicity, the calculation assumes that the interest rate paid on newly borrowed funds is the same as the interest rate paid on the entire public debt stock (i.e. that the marginal rate equals the average rate). The same assumption applies to the return on the NF assets.

104 Under the assumption that the interest rate differential stays at the level of 2011.

105 According to the hypothesis of beta convergence, developing countries have the potential to grow faster than developed countries – in part because they can replicate technologies already used in developed countries, and also because they can use their scarce capital stock more efficiently.

106 In line with these projections, oil production in Kazakhstan will peak in 2016-2017 at 2,5 million barrels per day (when the vast Kashagan oil field is put onstream), will stay at this level until 2040, and decline thereafter by 1% per year.

Stephan Barisitz: The Kazakhstani Banking System: Highly Leveraged Boom, Painful Bust, Costly Recovery

107 This study corresponds to a substantial update and further elaboration of the article: Stephan Barisitz and Mathias Lahnsteiner: "From Stormy Expansion to Riding out the Storm: Banking Development in Kazakhstan", OeNB Financial Stability Report 19 – June 2010. The author is grateful to Peter Backé, Mathias Lahnsteiner and Thomas Reininger (all OeNB) for valuable comments.

108 Kazakhstani GDP growth declined from the first half-year of 2007 to the first half-year of 2008 by more than 4 percentage points in year-on-year terms. No other CESEE economy experienced such a growth slump in this period.

109 "Joint Action Plan of the Government, National Bank and Financial Supervision Agency for Stabilization of the Economy and Financial Sector for 2009-2010", adopted in late 2008 and later slightly amended.

110 As to the structure of the external debt, the share of intercompany loans increased (from 37% of total external debt in 2008 to 45% in mid-2011), whereas that of bank external debt substantially declined (from 36% to 15%).

111 About 75% of FDI inflows target the oil and gas sector.

112 On the dualism between the country's resource (as a proxy for: tradable) sector and non-resource (as a proxy for non-tradable) sector see also IMF Survey Online, 2011.

113 For instance, annual price increases for new houses rose from 20% in mid-2006 to above 60% in July 2007 (IMF Staff Report 2008, 4).

114 Off-balance sheet items include contingent claims, contingent liabilities, transactions in foreign currencies and precious metals, and derivatives.

115 Month-on-month credit growth ground to zero.

116 The share of problem loans (loans classified as doubtful category 5 and loss loans) tripled to almost 10% of total loans in 2008, then quintupled to 47% (!) in 2009 (Table 2). NPLs (of whatever definition) do not comprise restructured loans (incl. deferrals of past due repayments, prolongation of total loan term, and adjustment of maturities), which probably account for an additional 20-25% of the total volume.

117 Samruk-Kazyna is a public entity created by the end-2008 merger of the state asset holding company Samruk and the sustainable development fund Kazyna. Samruk-Kazyna manages public assets of about EUR 50 billion and employs more than 260 000 people among 404 subsidiaries spread across key sectors of the economy, including energy, mining, telecoms, transportation, finance and banking. Samruk-Kazyna estimates that total deposits by its entities in the top 10 Kazakhstani banks account for more than one third of the latters' deposit base (IMF Staff Report 2009, 9), while deposits by Samruk Kazyna's entities in the whole banking sector are estimated to come to about one quarter of the entire base (IMF Staff Report 2010, 7).

118 Overall, in the assessment of NBK governor Marchenko, the authorities spent about EUR 13 billion in 2008- 2009 to shore up the banking sector (Euromoney 2010, 32). This figure may include funds channeled via banks to other sectors as well as estimates of indirect support via tax cuts and monetary loosening.

119 However, KDIF reserves are not sufficient to cover deposits at the largest credit institutions. The KDIF has the right to borrow from the NBK (IMF Staff Report 2009, 11).

120 Notwithstanding this dramatic deterioration, many credit institutions have apparently still been reluctant to recognize their losses (NBK-FSA 2009, 51).

121 The negative equity values of the two large players Bank Turan-Alem and Alliance Bank pushed overall sector capital below zero (NBK-FSA 2009, 58).

122 NBK-FSA 2009, 59; stability evaluation is carried out by calculating the Aggregate Financial Stability Index (AFSI), as described in the NBK-FSA 2008.

123 Net external debt of the financial sector was cut much more over this time span: It contracted by three quarters to 4,9 billion EUR at end-2009 (Standard & Poor's 2010, 4).

124 Even the foreign financing channel has – slightly – opened up again: Halyk Bank became the first Kazakhstani credit institution to re-enter the eurobond market since the crisis, with a 500 million USD 10-year issue in January 2011 (Alexander 2011, 57).

125 As indicated in Table 2, capital adequacy had declined to 13.4% at end-September 2011, before increasing again to 17.7% at a month later. Such a strong increase in one month may appear unusual.

126 Problem loans (doubtful category 5 and loss) slightly declined from 47% of total loans at end-2009 to 46% at end-2010, but then expanded to 52% at end-October 2011. Impaired loans are particularly elevated in the three restructured banks BTA, Alliance and Temir.

127 Meanwhile, BTA is reported to have defaulted on a 2 billion USD eurobond in mid-January 2012 (IMF Global Markets Monitor 2012).

ICEUR Insight Studies

Edited by Hans-Georg Heinrich and Ludmilla Lobova

Vol. 1 Aydar Amrebaev / Hans-Georg Heinrich / Ludmilla Lobova / Valikhan Tuleshov (eds.): Modern Kazakhstan. Image and Realities. 2013.

www.peterlang.de

Balihar Sanghera / Sarah Amsler / Tatiana Yarkova (eds)

Theorising Social Change in Post-Soviet Countries

Critical Approaches

Oxford, Bern, Berlin, Bruxelles, Frankfurt am Main, New York, Wien, 2007. 367 pp.
ISBN 978-3-03910-329-4 · pb. € 69,60*

The book traces three main approaches to the sociology of post-Soviet societies: studies guided by neoliberal theory and/or practice; work which may be termed neoconservative in orientation, and which is often a response to the first; and a third type of work that is considered both critical and reflexive, and which seeks to transcend the limitations of the other approaches. The book is divided into three parts, addressing polity, culture and economy. In each section, authors endeavour to transcend both neoliberalism and neoconservatism, and reach for a third approach, 'critical social science'. This is a broad movement, and the authors vary in their own explanatory and normative ideas as they carve out frameworks that will enable them to develop a more rigorous and at the same time more comprehensive and critical understanding of social change.

Contents: Sarah Amsler/Balihar Sanghera: Introduction. Post-Soviet Social Science: Reaching Beyond Neoliberalism and Neoconservatism · Boris Kapustin: Violence and Post-Communism · Vanessa Ruget: Social Rights and Citizenship in Kyrgyzstan: A Communitarian Perspective · George Welton/ Adrian Brisku: Contradictory Inclinations? The Role of 'Europe' in Albanian Nationalist Discourse · Donnacha Ó Beacháin: Transformation of Social Status: Ethnic Russians in Post-Soviet Kazakhstan · Zoltán Berényi: Weak Civic Culture in Hungary: An Examination of Some Consequences of Economic Inequality · and more

„[This book] is a valuable resource for policy-makers, scholars, students and anyone interested in the controversies of the first post-socialist decade." (Maria Yelenevskaya, International Sociology Review of Books)

FSC
www.fsc.org
MIX
Papier | Fördert gute Waldnutzung
FSC® C083411

Kolibri 360 GmbH
Ferdinand-Jühlke-Straße 7
99095 Erfurt, Deutschland
produktsicherheit@kolibri360.de